BLOOMSBURY

ESSENTIALGUIDE
FORREADINGGROUPS

SUSAN OSBORNE

A & C Black · London

Second edition 2008
A & C Black Publishers Limited
38 Soho Square
London W1D 3HB
www.acblack.com

First published 2002 by Bloomsbury Publishing plc

© 2008, 2002 Susan Osborne

ISBN 978-0-7136-7598-6

A CIP catalogue record for this book is available from the
British Library

This book is produced using paper that is made from wood
grown in managed, sustainable forests. It is natural, renewable
and recyclable. The logging and manufacturing processes conform
to the environmental regulations of the country of origin.

Typeset in Meta Light 8.5/12pt
Printed in the UK by Cox & Wyman Ltd, Reading, Berkshire

CONTENTS

INTRODUCTION v

SETTINGUPANDRUNNING
AREADINGGROUP 1

THEMES 7

READERS'GUIDES 20

FICTION 21

NON-FICTION 202

RESOURCES 251

SUGGESTEDFURTHERREADING 259

INDEX 262

INTRODUCTION

Six years after introducing the first edition of this book by saying that reading groups had found themselves in the limelight over the past few years, not only is that light still shining brightly but reading groups have gained a good deal of influence. Newspapers continue to devote space to them, perhaps never more so than when the all-male group called The Racketeers won the annual Penguin/Orange reading group prize in 2004, followed by a group based in High Down Prison the next year. Not only has Oprah Winfrey returned as a champion of reading groups in America but she has been joined in the UK by Richard and Judy whose choices frequently dominate the bestseller charts. The monthly Radio 4 Bookclub continues to discuss interesting choices overseen by Jim Naughtie, often attended by the author, and publishers have begun to court reading groups, occasionally offering them advance copies of books and seeking their opinions before publication. Such a growth in popular influence is surely to be celebrated and can only serve to encourage more people to join in.

All sorts of people join reading groups, sharing their enjoyment of books in discussions which can add both insight and pleasure to the experience of reading while developing friendships that can last a lifetime. A prospect to fill any avid but sociable reader with enthusiasm. But if you can't find an existing group to join, how do you set about creating your own group and, once established, how do you keep discussions lively and focused? This book is designed to help you achieve both. It offers advice on setting up a new group, resource listings to help you find information on books and reading groups plus readers' guides for seventy-five of the best books I have read over the last ten years, all of which have provoked spirited discussion with friends and family.

The book is divided into six sections.

Setting up and running a reading group, page 1
This section offers advice on starting your own group, from laying the foundations at the first meeting to leading a discussion.

Themes, page 7

In this section, the seventy-five books are listed thematically, with a brief introduction to each theme, so that your group can match interests to book choice.

Readers' guides, page 20

Central to the book is a set of Readers' Guides to seventy-five books (sixty novels and fifteen non-fiction), expanded from the original fifty from the first edition, all of which come heartily recommended and all of which provide more than enough ideas to stimulate a lively discussion. The format of the guides has been amended since the previous edition: each guide now includes a summary of the book, a brief author biography, discussion points to spark debate and a set of titles for further reading that pick up on the book's general themes together with a background section the contents of which vary from a profile of the author, historical background to the book or what made the writer decide to write it. The fifty guides included in the original edition have all been updated to this format which also includes references to useful websites.

Resources, page 251

This section lists details of books, magazines, websites and other resources which should help you choose books for discussion, track down background information and find out about literary events. Online reading groups are also included in this section.

Suggested Further Reading, page 259

In addition to the suggestions included in the Readers' Guides, this section includes a further seventy-five books which I've thoroughly enjoyed and would highly recommend for discussion.

SETTINGUPANDRUNNING AREADINGGROUP

WHAT IS A READING GROUP?

Reading groups range from a few friends who meet regularly to talk about particular books that they have all read, often sharing a few bottles of wine to ease the discussion along, to more formal meetings, perhaps led by an academic, which explore literature in a more structured manner, rather like a seminar. Over the past few years reading groups have increased in popularity as people meet to share their enjoyment, turning a solitary pleasure into a stimulating social experience. Many reading group members find their reading becomes more rewarding, more focused, and that an exchange of ideas with others can provide a whole new slant on a book. Readers in a rut will be introduced to books they would never have thought of reading, thanks to the recommendations of other group members, while new readers can find a route into what can seem to the uninitiated to be a bewilderingly vast array of books.

I'D LIKE TO JOIN A READING GROUP. HOW DO I GO ABOUT FINDING ONE?

If you're interested in a formal discussion group with a strong element of guidance, you could try your local university. Most universities run extramural studies programmes and they will either send you a prospectus or you should be able to pick one up from your local library.

If you want a more informal approach it's worth putting the word out among friends and colleagues. Reading groups are very much word-of-mouth outfits and you may find that you already know someone involved in a group which would welcome a new member with a fresh point of view. There may even be a reading group where you work. Some companies such as Orange, which sponsors the Orange Broadband Prize for Fiction, are particularly sympathetic to workplace reading groups. Many libraries have also begun to set up their own reading groups or keep contact details of local groups. Some bookshops keep information on local groups and an increasing number play host to reading groups on their premises. If you have access to the internet, try posting a message on a reading group notice board. The publishers Bloomsbury and Penguin both have notice boards in the reading group sections of their websites which are designed to put groups in touch with each other. You could also consider joining an online group. Although many of these are US-based, there are several UK websites, including *The Guardian*, which host reading groups (see page 253 in the Resources section for website details).

If you can't find a group to join, why not set up one of your own? You may find that your enquiries have sparked some interest and you already have the makings of a group.

HOW DO I START MY OWN GROUP?

The easiest way to start a reading group is to begin with friends and acquaintances, but there are advantages to setting up from scratch with people you don't know. Discussions can be a little predictable among close friends and you are more likely to be introduced to new books by someone from outside your circle. If you do decide to form a new group, community notice boards, particularly in libraries and bookshops, are good places to advertise for members. If you have a staff room at work, perhaps you could put up a notice there. You may be able to negotiate the use of a meeting room. Lunch hours could become much more stimulating than just a sandwich and a rehash of last night's soaps.

Depending on the response, you'll need to decide how many members you want. Around six to ten seems to work well. Too many people and not everyone gets a say, particularly bashful types; too few, and it's hard to get a range of views on which to base an interesting discussion.

THE FIRST MEETING – LAYING THE FOUNDATIONS
Planning the meeting

As you're the one taking the initiative, you'll also be the one who organizes the group's first meeting. If you don't know each other, you may feel more comfortable holding the meeting in a public place rather than your own home. Wherever you choose will need to be reasonably quiet so that you can have a relaxed discussion without shouting to make yourself heard. Ask people to bring their diaries so you can get some idea of what sort of schedule to set up. You'll need to plan what needs to be discussed, allowing enough time so you can cover everything and give everyone a chance to speak.

What do you all want to get out of the group?

This is a good starting point for the first meeting and a quick canvassing of opinion around the table should get everyone talking. Do you want an in-depth analysis of the text or do you just want to exchange opinions about the story? Is everyone happy for members to attend if they have not had time to read the book? You may want to stress that this should only happen occasionally, otherwise you could find you have lots of spectators and not much discussion. Many of us read hurriedly when we can find the time, but a book to be discussed needs more attention and you might want to agree some guidelines for preparation. Members might find it helpful to make a few notes as they read, for instance, jotting down themes that they want to discuss or particular passages in the book that catch their imagination. You may also want to back up your discussions with a bit of research. Some groups use the internet or the library to find out about the author or the context of the book before they discuss it.

Who should lead discussions?

Most reading groups appoint a member to lead meetings to give the discussion a structure and to make sure that everyone who wants to speak gets the opportunity. You may want to avoid one person bearing sole responsibility for running the group. One solution, if you're meeting in each other's homes, is for the host to run the session. Another might be for the member who chose the book to lead the discussion. Whatever you decide, the leader will need to know well in advance of the meeting so that they can prepare.

Where will you meet?

Lots of groups take it in turns to meet in each other's homes, or you could hire a room at your local university, village hall or even a pub. Some groups like the idea of meeting on neutral ground, which gets around any pressure that hosts might feel in their own homes.

How often should you meet?

You will want to make sure that everyone's schedule is catered for as far as possible. Monthly meetings will probably suit most people's available free time and will also mean they have time to prepare. It's a good idea to make sure that there's a list of everyone's names and phone numbers so that members can be informed of any changes to arrangements. Make sure that people are aware that they should let the discussion leader know if they can't make it; if you have a small group, two missing members might mean you want to reschedule.

How long should meetings last?

Two hours should probably be enough for a lively discussion but if you all know each other well, you might think about setting aside some time for socializing. Gossip is deliciously seductive, so much so that if you don't set a time limit, you may never get around to discussing the book.

Refreshments

Do you want to have food and drink and, if so, how will this be organized? You may want a simple bring-a-bottle-and-a-little-something-to-eat policy, or arrange a kitty. For some groups, food and drink are essential elements, almost as important as discussing the book – sometimes more so. Many American reading group websites even include a monthly recipe. Some members, however, may feel pressured by having to provide an enticing spread when it's their turn to host the group. Deciding a policy from the outset will avoid any embarrassment and establish the group's priorities.

CHOOSING BOOKS

Perhaps the easiest way to decide which book to discuss next is for each member to take a turn in nominating a title. Some people will already have favourites in mind. Other sources of information include paperback sections of the weekend papers; booksellers and librarians, who are usually happy to recommend books; Radio 4's excellent book coverage which includes its own book club; and the legions of book-related sites on the internet. Listed in the Resources section, you'll find details of magazines, websites and books that offer lots of information and recommendations for books to discuss.

It's worth making your choice some time in advance of the discussion. Books can go out of print which means bookshops will not be able to order them, or it may simply be that your local bookshop doesn't usually keep more than one or two copies of the book you've chosen and will need to order extra copies for you.

As a starting point, this book contains seventy-five Readers' Guides for books which contain lots of possibilities for a lively discussion. Each guide includes a detailed In Brief section together with a list of suggested further reading on a similar theme. All the books are available in paperback and should be reasonably easy to obtain; you'll find a thematic listing of the books beginning on page 7. A further set of seventy-five highly recommended books can be found in the Suggested Further Reading section at the back of the book.

LEADING A DISCUSSION

This may seem a bit daunting but it's really a case of getting the discussion going and making sure that everyone gets a chance to have their say if they want to. You may feel more comfortable leading the discussion if you have prepared a list of points as you read the book, noting its main themes, points at which particular characters change or significant passages. Each of the seventy-five Readers' Guides in this book lists a set of questions designed to get a discussion off the ground. This should help in the group's early days when members may be a little shy of each other.

You could start the ball rolling by asking the person who nominated the book to summarize it briefly and state its main themes, then ask each of the other members what they thought. Try to make sure that any questions you ask the group are open-ended. 'Did you like the book?' could result in 'Yes' or 'No' followed by silence, but 'What did you think of the book?' is an opening for discussion. Try to get people to explain their reactions. If they didn't like the book, what was it that didn't work for them? Was it a particular character? The writer's style? Equally, if they liked the book, what worked for them? Look out for anyone who seems to be bursting with something to say but having trouble finding a gap in the conversation. Try to avoid pushing more bashful members into the full glare of the spotlight. Round-the-table questions are one way to give quieter members a chance to have a say if they want it.

Opinions may differ radically but there aren't any rights and wrongs in the interpretation of a book. We all bring our own experience to reading. Everyone's opinion is valid, as long as it's expressed tactfully, but you probably want people to explain their conclusions and compare them with other members' ideas. Don't worry if the discussion gets a little heated; it's a good sign that people are thoroughly involved. As long as everyone's opinion is taken seriously, you should all part as friends.

Before you go home, check that everyone knows when and where the next meeting will be and what the next book choice is. If you're rotating the leadership, make sure that the next leader knows it's their turn.

SOME DISCUSSION POINTS

What were your reactions to the book and why?

What are the book's main themes? What message is the author trying to get across?

Does the book tackle any contemporary or universal issues such as racism, war or the environment and, if so, how did it change or clarify your views?

Who are the main characters? How much do they change over the course of the book and why?

Did particular characters engage your sympathy? Were there others that you couldn't stand? What are your reasons?

Did the book have any relevance to your own experience and, if so, in what way?

Are aspects of the author's life reflected in the book and, if so, what are they?

Did the book remind you of anything else you've read?

How important is the author's use of language? Were there particular passages that caught your imagination and, if so, why?

Was there anything unusual about the structure of the book and, if so, was it effective? Perhaps the book was in letter form or composed mainly of flashbacks.

If you nominated the book, have your feelings about it been changed by exchanging views with others?

THEMES

This section has been arranged thematically to help you choose a book which suits your particular interests. Each of the headings identifies a major theme which should provoke an interesting discussion. Books relevant to that theme are then listed, but because each book may have more than one theme, some titles appear under several different headings. The page number beside each title refers to the full Readers' Guide. You'll also find a brief summary of the book in the In Brief section of each book's guide.

CHILDHOOD

Traditionally portrayed as a time of blissful innocence, childhood can often be beset by anxiety and puzzlement at the way in which adults behave. Several of the books listed here explore this theme. Shena Mackay's *The Orchard on Fire*, for example, is told through the voice of an eight-year-old, while Jenny Diski's autobiographical *Skating to Antarctica* explores the effects of a difficult childhood on adult life.

Behind the Scenes at the Museum by Kate Atkinson, page 27
Skating to Antarctica by Jenny Diski, page 208
Talking to the Dead by Helen Dunmore, page 64
Stones From the River by Ursula Hegi, page 92
The Kite Runner by Khaled Hosseini, page 97
The Orchard on Fire by Shena Mackay, page 125
The Icarus Girl by Helen Oyeymi, page 147
Anita and Me by Meera Syal, page 184
The Story of Lucy Gault by William Trevor, page 190

GROWINGUP

For most of us, struggling through adolescence is an uncomfortable experience marked by embarrassment, awkwardness and an excruciating hypersensitivity. Some of the books listed below, such as Eva Hoffman's account of her painful uprooting from one culture to another and Pearl Abraham's tale of a young Hasidic girl's battle for independence, examine what it is to cope with this experience in the most straitening of circumstances. Others, such as Iain Banks's *The Crow Road* and Emma Tennant's *Girlitude*, explore a process of growing up that continues well past adolescence.

The Romance Reader by Pearl Abraham, page 21
The Crow Road by Iain Banks, page 35
Disobedience by Jane Hamilton, page 86
Lost in Translation by Eva Hoffman, page 220
The Buddha of Suburbia by Hanif Kureishi, page 110
So Long, See You Tomorrow by William Maxwell, page 131
The World Below by Sue Miller, page 141
In a Land of Plenty by Tim Pears, page 152
Bad Blood by Lorna Sage, page 238
The Hacienda by Lisa St Aubin de Terán, page 241
Girlitude by Emma Tennant, page 244

GROWINGOLDER

Ageing has become something of a thorny issue in our youth-obsessed society. Angela Carter's feisty septuagenarian twins and Lesley Glaister's eccentric elderly artist are vivid depictions of characters who refuse to lie down and be quiet. In contrast, Oscar Hijuelos offers a tender portrayal of a vibrantly sexual woman gradually accepting fewer turned heads as she walks down the street.

Wise Children by Angela Carter, page 53
Sheer Blue Bliss by Lesley Glaister, page 77
Empress of the Splendid Season by Oscar Hijuelos, page 95
Larry's Party by Carol Shields, page 171
The Last Time They Met by Anita Shreve, page 175

DEATHANDHOWWECOPEWITHIT

In a society where youth is prized and life expectancy seems constantly to be extended, death has become the great unmentionable – and yet we all have to face both our own death and the death of those we love. These books explore the ways in which we cope with death and bereavement, from Isabel Allende's family history written for a much-loved daughter struck down by a rare disease, to Blake Morrison's unflinching account of his father's last weeks.

Paula by Isabel Allende, page 202
Being Dead by Jim Crace, page 58
And When Did You Last See Your Father? by Blake Morrison, page 235
The Boy in the Moon by Kate O'Riordan, page 144
The Magician's Assistant by Ann Patchett, page 150

FAMILYLIFEANDTHETIESTHATBIND

Our families, dysfunctional or otherwise, shape us all to some extent, and this theme is endlessly explored in fiction. The books listed below range from explorations of the effects of war, social upheaval and deception on family life to an attempt to create a family out of a group of friends in Michael Cunningham's *A Home at the End of the World*.

Behind the Scenes at the Museum by Kate Atkinson, page 27
The Crow Road by Iain Banks, page 35
Visible Worlds by Marilyn Bowering, page 50
A Home at the End of the World by Michael Cunningham, page 62
Middlesex by Jeffery Eugenides, page 67
Hidden Lives by Margaret Forster, page 214
Disobedience by Jane Hamilton, page 86
The Buddha of Suburbia by Hanif Kureishi, page 110
The World Below by Sue Miller, page 141
In a Land of Plenty by Tim Pears, page 152
Bad Blood by Lorna Sage, page 238
Anita and Me by Meera Syal, page 184
The Hundred Secret Senses by Amy Tan, page 187
The Story of Lucy Gault by William Trevor, page 190

FRIENDSHIP

From the vivid intensity of childhood friendship, exemplified by the 'us against the rest of the world' alliance between Ruby and April in *The Orchard on Fire*, to the curious, unearthly friendship that grows between man and angel in *The Vintner's Luck*, these novels explore the importance of relationships which can often be as strong as family ties.

The Crow Road by Iain Banks, page 35
The Voyage of the Narwhal by Andrea Barrett, page 41
A Home at the End of the World by Michael Cunningham, page 62
The Kite Runner by Khaled Hosseini, page 97
The Vintner's Luck by Elizabeth Knox, page 107
Charming Billy by Alice McDermott, page 120
Brightness Falls by Jay McInerney, page 122
The Orchard on Fire by Shena Mackay, page 125
So Long, See You Tomorrow by William Maxwell, page 131
Balzac and the Little Chinese Seamstress by Dai Sijie, page 178
Anita and Me by Meera Syal, page 184

LOVE, MARRIAGE AND INFIDELITY

Although Anita Shreve's *The Last Time They Met* is perhaps the only book included here that could be described primarily as a love story, these novels all explore the complexities of love and marriage, while several, in particular Jane Hamilton's *Disobedience*, examine the painful effects of betrayal.

Visible Worlds by Marilyn Bowering, page 50
Being Dead by Jim Crace, page 58
Talking to the Dead by Helen Dunmore, page 64
Birdsong by Sebastian Faulks, page 70
Sheer Blue Bliss by Lesley Glaister, page 77
Disobedience by Jane Hamilton, page 86
The Photograph by Penelope Lively, page 116
Charming Billy by Alice McDermott, page 120

Brightness Falls by Jay McInerney, page 122
The World Below by Sue Miller, page 141
The Magician's Assistant by Ann Patchett, page 150
The Shipping News by Annie Proulx, page 155
Larry's Party by Carol Shields, page 171
The Last Time They Met by Anita Shreve, page 175
The Hundred Secret Senses by Amy Tan, page 187

SECRETS

The revelation of a secret that has haunted a book since the first page makes for an immensely satisfying read, particularly in tightly plotted novels. Clues and hints are strewn through several of the books listed here, including Kate Atkinson's *Behind the Scenes at the Museum* and Jonathan Coe's *The House of Sleep*, so that you want to go back and read the book again, fitting each piece of the puzzle into place. Other books, such as Alice McDermott's *Charming Billy* and Margaret Forster's family history, *Hidden Lives*, explore the effect of long-concealed secrets while Penelope Lively's *The Photograph* shows how a revelation can overturn long-held perceptions.

Behind the Scenes at the Museum by Kate Atkinson, page 27
The Crow Road by Iain Banks, page 35
Visible Worlds by Marilyn Bowering, page 50
Wise Children by Angela Carter, page 53
The House of Sleep by Jonathan Coe, page 56
Talking to the Dead by Helen Dunmore, page 64
Hidden Lives by Margaret Forster, page 214
Disobedience by Jane Hamilton, page 86
The Vintner's Luck by Elizabeth Knox, page 107
The Photograph by Penelope Lively, page 116
Charming Billy by Alice McDermott, page 120
The Boy in the Moon by Kate O'Riordan, page 144
The Magician's Assistant by Ann Patchett, page 150
The Last Time They Met by Anita Shreve, page 175

HISTORICAL

The books listed here are all set at a time far removed from our own, from the eighteenth century *Ingenious Pain*, teetering on the brink of the modern age, to Barry Unsworth's *Morality Play*, performed against the backdrop of a fourteenth-century England battle-scarred from the long wars with France and stricken with plague and famine.

Alias Grace by Margaret Atwood, page 29
The Voyage of the Narwhal by Andrea Barrett, page 41
The Leper's Companions by Julia Blackburn, page 47
Cold Mountain by Charles Frazier, page 74
The Vintner's Luck by Elizabeth Knox, page 107
Remembering Babylon by David Malouf, page 128
Ingenious Pain by Andrew Miller, page 138
Promised Lands by Jane Rogers, page 161
Morality Play by Barry Unsworth, page 193

COLONIALISMANDEXPLORATION

From the nineteenth-century Arctic explorers in *The Voyage of the Narwhal* to the settling of Sydney in *Promised Lands*, these four novels explore the repercussions of colonialism and exploration on both the indigenous peoples and those who set out to colonize their land, even in places as close to home as Ireland as William Trevor's *The Story of Lucy Gault* so poignantly illustrates.

The Voyage of the Narwhal by Andrea Barrett, page 41
Remembering Babylon by David Malouf, page 128
Promised Lands by Jane Rogers, page 161
The Story of Lucy Gault by William Trevor page 190

DIFFERENTCULTURES

Each of these books is set against a different cultural backdrop, ranging from an Indian apartment block in Manil Suri's *The Death of Vishnu* to Barbara Kingsolver's *Animal Dreams*, which includes a depiction of a Native American community in Arizona. Some, such as *Anita and Me* and *The Hundred Secret Senses*, explore the conflict that can arise between different cultures and the feelings of dislocation that can result from being caught between two very different worlds while Abdulrazak's Gurnah's *By the Sea* vividly evokes the alienation and longing of those who have left their homeland behind.

The Romance Reader by Pearl Abraham, page 21
The Darling by Russell Banks, page 38
By the Sea by Abdulrazak Gurnah, page 80
Empress of the Splendid Season by Oscar Hijuelos, page 95
Lost in Translation by Eva Hoffman, page 220
The Kite Runner by Khaled Hosseini, page 97
Animal Dreams by Barbara Kingsolver, page 104
Death and the Penguin by Andrey Kurkov, page 114
Remembering Babylon by David Malouf, page 182
Promised Lands by Jane Rogers, page 161
The Hacienda by Lisa St Aubin de Terán, page 241
Balzac and the Little Chinese Seamstress by Dai Sijie, page 178
The Death of Vishnu by Manil Suri, page 181
Anita and Me by Meera Syal, page 184
The Hundred Secret Senses by Amy Tan, page 187

WARANDITSAFTERMATH

Each of these books is set against the backdrop of a very different war. Tim Binding explores the occupation of Guernsey in the Second World War, while Sebastian Faulks graphically describes the bloody struggles at the Western Front during the First World War and Charles Frazier charts two journeys during the American Civil War.

Island Madness by Tim Binding, page 44
Birdsong by Sebastian Faulks, page 70
Cold Mountain by Charles Frazier, page 74

THEHOLOCAUSTANDITSAFTERMATH

In different ways, these four books explore the effects of the cataclysmic events that helped to shape the second half of the twentieth century. They range from *The Drowned and the Saved*, an attempt by Primo Levi, himself a concentration camp survivor, to understand how such atrocities came to be committed, to Ursula Hegi's novel, which depicts a small German town during the first half of the twentieth century, and traces its justification and shame at the horrors perpetrated by the Hitler's régime.

Stones From the River by Ursula Hegi, page 92
The Drowned and the Saved by Primo Levi, page 227
Fugitive Pieces by Anne Michaels, page 134
The Reader by Bernhard Schlink, page 165

MODERNTIMES

Here are several books that capture the spirit of an age which many readers will remember although the world they depict may be one foreign to most of us. From the dark underbelly of sixties London in Jake Arnott's *The Long Firm* to the claustrophobia of Franco's Barcelona in Carlos Louis Zafón's *The Shadow of the Wind*, these novels are vividly evocative of a time close to our own.

The Long Firm by Jake Arnott, page 23
Behind the Scenes at the Museum by Kate Atkinson, page 27
The Darling by Russell Banks, page 38
The Buddha of Suburbia by Hanif Kureishi, page 110
Death and the Penguin by Andrey Kurkov, page 114
Brightness Falls by Jay McInerney, page 122
In a Land of Plenty by Tim Pears, page 152
Balzac and the Little Chinese Seamstress by Dai Sijie, page 178
The Shadow of the Wind by Carlos Louis Zafón, page 199

THEPERSONALISPOLITICAL

No matter how we feel about politics and the machinations of the state, every aspect of our lives is affected by them. These books explore the power of politics on personal lives, from the unfinished business of Hannah's terrorist past in Russell Banks' *The Darling* to Anna Funder's moving investigation into the appalling effects of state mass surveillance in *Stasiland*.

The Darling by Russell Banks, page 38
Stasiland by Anna Funder, page 217
By the Sea by Abdulrazak Gurnah, page 80
Death and the Penguin by Andrey Kurkov, page 114
Balzac and the Little Chinese Seamstress by Dai Sijie, page 178
No Place Like Home by Gary Younge, page 247

CRIME

Strictly speaking, there is only one crime novel in the traditional whodunit sense among the Readers' Guides included in this book: Ian Rankin's *Black and Blue*. That said, all of the books listed below deal with a serious crime and its repercussions, and all include the attendant elements of mystery, suspense and plot.

The Long Firm by Jake Arnott, page 23
Alias Grace by Margaret Atwood, page 29
The Crow Road by Iain Banks, page 35
Midnight in the Garden of Good and Evil by John Berendt, page 205
Island Madness by Tim Binding, page 44
Black and Blue by Ian Rankin, page 158
Morality Play by Barry Unsworth, page 193
The Cutting Room by Louise Welsh, page 196
The Shadow of the Wind by Carlos Louis Zafón, page 199

DISTURBEDMENTALSTATES

Each of these books explores the effect of altered mental states, from Jonathan Coe's comic yet humane depiction of narcolepsy to Kay Redfield Jamison's brave account of her own experiences of manic depression.

The Leper's Companions by Julia Blackburn, page 47
The House of Sleep by Jonathan Coe, page 56
Skating to Antarctica by Jenny Diski, page 208
Middlesex by Jeffery Eugenides, page 67
Our Lady of the Forest by David Guterson, page 83
An Unquiet Mind by Kay Redfield Jamison, page 223
The Ninth Life of Louis Drax by Liz Jensen, page 101
The Icarus Girl by Helen Oyeymi, page 147
The Hacienda by Lisa St Aubin de Terán, page 241

ECCENTRICITYANDTHEUNUSUAL

This list encompasses both Murray Bail's *Eucalyptus*, which adopts the traditional fairytale device in which a father sets an impossible task to be achieved by his daughter's suitors, and the intense friendship which develops between a man and an angel in Elizabeth Knox's *The Vintner's Luck*. Other books include a range of eccentric characters, from Amy Tan's Kwan, who sees the spirit world through her 'yin' eyes, to the cast of bizarre individuals that people the town of Savannah, Georgia, in *Midnight in the Garden of Good and Evil*.

Eucalyptus by Murray Bail, page 33
Midnight in the Garden of Good and Evil by John Berendt, page 205
Wise Children by Angela Carter, page 53
Ghosting by Jennie Erdal, page 211
Middlesex by Jeffery Eugenides, page 67
Sheer Blue Bliss by Lesley Glaister, page 77
Our Lady of the Forest by David Guterson, page 83
The Seal Wife by Kathryn Harrison, page 89
The Vintner's Luck by Elizabeth Knox, page 107
Death and the Penguin by Andrey Kurkov, page 114
Ingenious Pain by Andrew Miller, page 138
The Icarus Girl by Helen Oyeymi, page 147
The Magician's Assistant by Ann Patchett, page 150
The Minotaur Takes a Cigarette Break by Steven Sherrill, page 168
The Hundred Secret Senses by Amy Tan, page 187

HUMOUR

If you're in need of a little light relief, humour is a strong element running through all six of these books.

Behind the Scenes at the Museum by Kate Atkinson, page 27
The Crow Road by Iain Banks, page 35
Wise Children by Angela Carter, page 53
The House of Sleep by Jonathan Coe, page 56
Death and the Penguin by Andrey Kurkov, page 114
Anita and Me by Meera Syal, page 184

THENATURALWORLD

From Jim Crace's depiction of physical decay to Barbara Kingsolver's exploration of the gulf between those who have lived harmoniously with nature for centuries and those determined to profit from it, these six novels examine the relationship between human beings and the natural world.

The Voyage of the Narwhal by Andrea Barrett, page 41
Being Dead by Jim Crace, page 58
Skating to Antarctica by Jenny Diski, page 208
Our Lady of the Forest by David Guterson, page 83
The Seal Wife by Kathryn Harrison, page 89
Animal Dreams by Barbara Kingsolver, page 104

THEROLEOFWOMEN

Although this section includes no novels traditionally perceived as feminist, in the vein of Charlotte Perkins Gilman's *The Yellow Wallpaper* or Doris Lessing's *The Golden Notebook*, all the books listed below consider women's role in society, with some, such as Margaret Forster's family history, offering a clear insight into the way in which that role has changed over the years.

The Romance Reader by Pearl Abraham, page 21
Alias Grace by Margaret Atwood, page 29
The Voyage of the Narwhal by Andrea Barrett, page 41
Hidden Lives by Margaret Forster, page 214
Cold Mountain by Charles Frazier, page 71
Giving Up the Ghost by Hilary Mantel, page 232
The World Below by Sue Miller, page 141
Girlitude by Emma Tennant, page 244

READERS'GUIDES

The books for the seventy-five Readers' Guides in this section have been chosen to generate lively discussion. They range from novels such as Ursula Hegi's *Stones From the River*, a humane and profound attempt to understand how ordinary Germans dealt with the horrors of Hitler's régime, to Anita Shreve's *The Last Time They Met*, a delicately drawn love story with a twist. In the non-fiction section you'll find John Berendt's colourful travelogue and true crime story, *Midnight in the Garden of Good and Evil*, alongside Kay Redfield Jamison's moving and brave account of her experiences of manic depression, *An Unquiet Mind* and *No Place Like Home*, Stephen Younge's exploration of his own black British idenity and what it means to be black in America.

   Each of the guides includes a brief synopsis, a background section the contents of which vary from a profile of the author, historical background to the book or what made the writer come to write it. A brief biography of the author is followed by a set of points designed to get a discussion going rather than to be followed to the letter, together with a list of useful websites. Finally, the list of suggested further reading includes books by the same author, books by other authors that may share the same major themes or elements of the book's style, and books that may provide a useful context for the book should you want to research it further. Titles in **bold type** have their own entry in this book.

FICTION

THE ROMANCE READER (1995)
Pearl Abraham

📖 About the book

As the eldest daughter of a rebbe struggling to establish his first synagogue, Rachel is expected to observe and exemplify the many exacting standards of the Hasidic community to which she belongs. As she enters adolescence, she finds herself chafing at these strictures. She loves to swim but is forbidden to wear a bathing suit in public; she wants to dress attractively but must conform to a strict dress code designed to hide her body; most of all, she loves the trashy romantic novels which give her a fascinating, if misleading, glimpse of a world which is forbidden to her. She would dearly love to escape but does not know how. As she faces the prospect of an arranged marriage she realizes that, perverse as it might seem, marriage may be the only way to attain the freedom she craves.

Background

The Romance Reader is rich in cultural references, offering an insight into a way of life far removed from the Western mainstream, for the Benjamins are members of the minority Jewish sect known as Hasids (or *Chassids* in Yiddish). The central theme of the novel is Rachel's struggle for independence in a community depicted by Pearl Abraham as insular, inward looking and regulated by strict rules. Abraham draws deeply upon her own experience of growing up in Hasidic communities, vividly evoking a claustrophobic atmosphere in which a young intelligent girl longs to reach out to the world but is faced with the agonizing choice of either losing her family or forgoing the chance of independence and a life of her own choosing.

When *The Romance Reader* was first published many reviewers drew parallels between Abraham's novel and Chaim Potok's similarly autobiographical first novel, *The Chosen*, now considered to be a classic. Set in 1940s Brooklyn Potok's novel portrays the Hasidic world from the point of view of Danny, the young son of a rebbi, as he struggles with the demands of his community to follow in his father's footsteps, his religious doubts and his secular ambitions to become a psychologist. In contrast his less Orthodox friend Reuven, a gifted mathematician and the son of a Jewish scholar, wants to become a rabbi. *The Chosen* explores the tensions between these disparate fathers and sons.

Both *The Romance Reader* and *The Chosen* offer the outsider a glimpse of a world far removed from their own, yet which share universalities with tightly knit communities of many cultures and religions. So successful is *The Romance Reader* at depicting the struggle between the deeply Orthodox and the secular in ways to which all can relate that it is now studied in American schools and universities.

About the author

For the first twelve years of her life Pearl Abraham's family moved between Hasidic communities in New York and Jerusalem. She now teaches creative writing at New York University and lives in New York City. *The Romance Reader* is her first novel.

For discussion

✪ Why do you think Pearl Abraham chose *The Romance Reader* as the title for the novel? Why is reading so important to Rachel? Why does she not read so much in Williamsburg? Rachel reads a very particular sort of book. How do you think this shapes her view of the world outside her community? She says: 'Novels are lies, lies upon lies'. What has brought her to this conclusion?

✪ What do you notice about the ways that men and women behave in the community? What are the differences? Do you think men or women have the harder life? Can you find examples to back up your ideas?

✪ What is your view of Rachel's mother? What made you come to these conclusions? What do you make of the relationship between Rachel's mother and her father? Why do you think their relationship is like this?

✪ Both Rachel and Leah have to be constantly on their guard against being found out – about reading books in English, about their lifeguard training. How do you think this affects them?

✪ Why is it so hard for Rachel to gain her independence? Do you think she should just turn her back on her family and leave? If not, why not? If so, why do you think she doesn't? She says: 'I won't be here, on their hands, for long'. Do you think she will leave? The last sentence reads: 'I wonder how high I will get before I fall.' What do you think she means by this?

✪ When Rachel and Elke talk about marriage, Elke has no qualms about her arranged marriage. What do you think of the position she takes? Rachel says: 'I think it's easier for Elke because she doesn't think about love in novels.' What questions do you think might be raised about the Western idea of romantic love as opposed to arranged marriages? Why do you think Rachel decides to marry Israel?

○ Has anyone in the group any experience as part of a minority group? If so, how do you feel about Pearl Abraham's descriptions of the response of the outside world to the Hasids? Do Rachel's struggles ring any bells?

🖥 Resources
www.bombsite.com/issues/91/articles/2728 – article by Aryeh Lev Stollman in *Bomb* ezine
www.pearlabraham.com – Pearl Abraham's website

🗺 Suggested further reading
FICTION
Disobedience by Naomi Alderman (2006); *Oscar and Lucinda* by Peter Carey (1998); *The Ladies Auxilliary* by Tova Mirvis (2000); *The Chosen* by Chaim Potok (1967); **Anita and Me by Meera Syal** (1996); *A Complicated Kindness* by Miriam Toews (2004); *Oranges are Not the Only Fruit* by Jeanette Winterson (1985)
NON-FICTION
Lost in Translation by Eva Hoffman (1989); *Boychiks in the Hood* by Robert Eisenberg (1995); *The Joys of Yiddish* by Leo Rosten (1970)
OTHER BOOKS BY PEARL ABRAHAM
Giving up on America (1998); *The Seventh Beggar* (2005)

THE LONG FIRM (1999)
Jake Arnott

📖 About the book
Narrated by five very different characters, *The Long Firm* follows the career of Harry Starks, a gangland boss with a weakness for stardom and a yearning for respectability. Each narrator tells the story of their dealings with Harry: Terry is Harry's pretty suburban kept boy; Teddy is the corrupt peer who finds himself out of his league; Jack the Hat is a freelancer who flits dangerously between Harry and the Kray twins; Ruby is a fading Rank starlet and Lenny is a criminologist whose relationship with Harry leads him into the dark realities of the criminal underworld. Set in mid-sixties London amidst enormous social change and written with a wit as sharp as the cut of a gangster's suit, *The Long Firm* explores the dark underbelly of a period often recalled as vibrant and exciting, expertly blending fact and fiction in a vivid evocation of the times.

Background

The Long Firm is the first part of a trilogy which explores the sinister underworld of gangland London. The second part, *He Kills Coppers*, examines the fallout from a brutal murder while *truecrime* sees the return of Harry Starks, still on the run, bringing his story into the 1990s and taking a swipe at those who jumped on the 'geezer chic' bandwagon with a Guy Ritchie-like film director. Jake Arnott has expressed his annoyance at 'feelgood gangster movies' whose 'slapstick violence' often result in audiences finding gangsters 'cool' rather than experiencing the sinister menace which his own novels evoke. He explains that, 'With a lot of those gangster films people did actually go and talk to Frankie Fraser, etc, and took them on their word. They went away thinking they were lovely geezers. And they can be very charming people, so you can't actually make a critical film anymore.'

The Long Firm expertly evokes the atmosphere of the mid-sixties, a time of enormous social change when a booming economy marked the beginnings of a new consumerism and youth cultures sprang into life but which also harboured a dark side. This evocation is very much the product of Arnott's meticulous research which results in a seamless blend of fact and fiction. Real events provide a newsreel-like backdrop for the action. Well known – and not so well known – personalities from the time have walk-on parts either under their own names (Peter Rachman, Joe Meek, Judy Garland) or under another such as Gerald Wilman, a thinly disguised Kenneth Williams. Others have a more prominent role the most notable of which is Jack the Hat McVitie, a freelancer murdered by the Krays (a constant shadowy presence in the novel) for which they were sentenced to life imprisonment. The student/teacher relationship between Harry and Lenny echoes that between the sociologist Laurie Taylor and John McVicar – the armed robber tagged 'Public Enemy Number 1' by Scotland Yard in the sixties and now a respected journalist – who collaborated on the book *In the Underworld*. Such verisimilitude resulted in a little embarrassment for Arnott who chose the name George Mooney for the policeman he based on certain officers in the Obscene Publications Squad convicted of corruption charges, unfortunately resulting in confusion with Harry Mooney, a former, and entirely honest, Chief Inspector in the Metropolitan Police. A polite and gracious apology was issued.

Arnott has said that Ronnie Kray was an inspiration for the character of Harry Starks; like Ronnie, Harry is open in his acknowledgement of his homosexuality. This previously unexplored aspect of gangland led to Arnott being talked of as a gay writer. Gay himself, Arnott was delighted that the book was selected as a Big Gay Read but he is wary of being labelled explaining that he doesn't 'want to be stuck in one category, either as an artist or as a human being'. With the immense talent displayed in this clever and intensely atmospheric novel Arnott should succeed in escaping attempts to slot him into any pigeonhole.

About the author

Jake Arnott was born in Aylesbury, Buckinghamshire 1961. He left Aylesbury grammar school at sixteen and has worked in a wide variety of jobs including mortuary technician, theatrical agent's assistant, artist's model, sign language interpreter and actor. He lived in a variety of squats in the eighties. In 1989 he worked for the Red Ladder theatre company in Leeds, and began writing while working part-time for Leeds Social Services as a resource centre worker. *The Long Firm*, Arnott's first novel and the first in his London gangland trilogy, met with a good deal of acclaim and was selected as a Big Gay Read. The book was later made into a four-part series by the BBC starring Mark Strong as Harry Starks and Derek Jacobi as Teddy Thursby. Jake Arnott lives in north London.

For discussion

✪ 'He looked clumsy and awkward, intimidated for all his toughness.' Harry is introduced by Terry's description of his entrance to the Casbah Lounge. What kind of man is Harry? What are the many contradictions and complexities that make up his character?

✪ Given his brutal treatment of those who cross him, how do you explain Harry's concern over Bernie the young murdered prostitute? To what extent can it be argued that Harry practises a form of morality albeit one very different from the norm?

✪ 'The gangsters were the real stars at The Stardust'. One of the themes of the novel is the link between glamour and gangsterism, a link which exists in reality. Why do you think such a link exists?

✪ Why do you think Jake Arnott chose to write his novel using five narrators? How successful did you find this structure? Which narrative did you feel worked best and why? How does Arnott convey the nature of these very different characters and the worlds in which they move? Why do you think he chose not to have Harry as a narrator?

✪ Arnott prefaces each of his narratives with a quotation. How appropriate did you find each of these? Did you find any of the quotes particularly apposite? If so which one was it and why?

✪ 'The terms he used mocked my own lost faith in a theoretical system. A faith that he himself had shattered.' How has Harry shattered Lenny's faith in the theory of criminology? What do you make of that system in comparison with Harry's own ideas?

✪ "'I'm not gay," he said sternly. "I'm homosexual but I'm not gay.'" What is Harry's attitude towards his sexuality? How surprising do you find his openness about it given the period in which the book is set and the world in which Harry moves?

✪ Arnott succeeds in vividly evoking the sixties. How does he achieve this?

✪ How does Arnott use humour in the book?

✪ What is the significance of the novel's title?

✪ *The Long Firm* has been described as a crime novel. Would you agree with this description and if not how would you describe it? What do you think are the elements of a crime novel?

🖳 Resources

www.contemporarywriters.com/authors/?p=auth166 – profile of Jake Arnott at the British Council website including a critical essay by Dr Jules Smith

www.newstatesman.co.uk/199908230035.htm – review by James Harkin published in *The New Statesman*

http://query.nytimes.com/gst/fullpage.html?res=940CE5D7153EF933A25753C1A9 6F958260 – review by the writer Henry Shukman published in *The New York Times*

http://observer.guardian.co.uk/review/story/0,,1749920,00.html – interview with the novelist and critic Peter Guttridge published in *The Observer*

www.bbc.co.uk/dna/collective/A1143433 – BBC interview conducted on the publication of truecrime the third in *The Long Firm* trilogy

www.eastlondonhistory.com/krays%20nemesis.htm – webpage at the East London History site on *The Long Firm* and the Krays

www.thekrays.co.uk – The Krays' website which includes a very detailed page on Jack the Hat McVitie

🕮 Suggested further reading

FICTION

The Burning Girl by Mark Billingham (2004); *Any Human Heart* by William Boyd (2002); *Get Carter* by Ted Lewis (1970); ***The Cutting Room* by Louise Welsh** (2002)

NON-FICTION

Inside the Firm by Tony Lambrianou (1991); *White Heat: A History of Britain in the Swinging Sixties* by Dominic Sandbrook (2006); *In the Underworld* by Laurie Taylor and John McVicar (1985)

OTHER BOOKS BY JAKE ARNOTT

He Kills Coppers (2001); *truecrime* (2003); *Johnny Come Home* (2006)

BEHIND THE SCENES AT THE MUSEUM (1995)

Kate Atkinson

📖 About the book

This is the story of Ruby Lennox told in her own voice from the moment of her conception, heralded by a few grunts and groans from her father while her mother feigns sleep. Ruby and her family live above their pet shop in the shadow of York Minster. Theirs is a story of humdrum family life in the fifties – endless housework, minor peccadilloes on the part of Ruby's father, homework, weddings and funerals. Interwoven with Ruby's story is that of her great-grandmother, her grandmother, uncles, aunts and cousins as they struggle through two world wars. But there are small gaps in the narrative, hints of something amiss. Family secrets, long hidden, begin to surface – one so devastating that it overwhelms Ruby even as it explains so much that has been puzzling in her life.

Background

Behind the Scenes at the Museum is a domestic novel with a twist. Its complicated structure draws together the many threads running through the lives of four generations of women, spilling clues and rattling skeletons kept firmly shut away in the closet. The novel requires close attention to appreciate the many hints dropped and turns taken but every loose end is satisfyingly tied in.

Kate Atkinson has described herself as 'pathologically nostalgic' and her writing as an 'act of rescuing the past, even if it's an imaginary one'; but her main aim is to entertain, something in which *Behind the Scenes at the Museum* certainly succeeds. Atkinson is a playful writer: *Behind the Scenes at the Museum* was seen by many to be a tragi-comic parody of the family saga; her second novel, *Human Croquet* poked gentle fun at magic realism; *Emotionally Weird*, a novel about storytelling, plays with different typographies for each story genre with several well-aimed digs at the academic world; and *Case Histories* stretched the boundaries of the crime genre. Her novels zig-zag back and forth in time, her characters play games with each other and with the reader, and her narrators are unreliable: all of which have earned her the rather lazy sobriquet 'post-modernist', a label which she vehemently dismisses.

When Atkinson won the 1995 Whitbread Book of the Year Award with her first novel, pipping Salman Rushdie and Roy Jenkins to the post, she found herself disparaged by the (largely male) literary establishment, although both Hilary Mantel and Joanna Trollope leapt to her defence. Atkinson attributes such criticism to the fact that she is a woman and that her novel was misinterpreted as critical of the idea of the family. She has since gone on to prove herself more than worthy of the award, a resounding and very satisfying raspberry to those who felt that she was something of a literary upstart.

About the author

Kate Atkinson was born in York in 1951. She took a master's degree in English Literature at Dundee University and went on to do further post-graduate work in American literature. While raising her two daughters she did a wide variety of jobs, from university tutor to home help. Her short stories have been published in several British magazines. *Behind the Scenes at the Museum* was her first novel and it was greeted with a storm of critical acclaim culminating in the Whitbread Book of the Year award in 1995.

For discussion

✪ Atkinson's structure is extremely complex, weaving backwards and forwards through the years, dropping clues and hints along the way. How does she mesh the two narratives together? How successful is her technique?

✪ How successful is Atkinson at capturing both time and place in the novel? What techniques does she use to achieve this?

✪ Ruby Lennox narrates half of the novel. How would you describe her voice? How does the tone of her narrative differ from the footnotes? What effect does this achieve?

✪ There are four generations of women in the book. How do their lives and circumstances differ? What are the biggest changes? What do they have in common? Many of the women have 'had enough'. What do you think they mean by this and why is the phrase never associated with the male characters?

✪ Bunty can hardly be described as the best of mothers. Do you have any sympathy with her constant irritation and if so why?

✪ What is Ruby's Lost Property Cupboard Theory of Life? How does it apply to her own life?

✪ Many secrets are revealed over the course of the book. How does this affect individual characters? How typical do you think this is of family life?

Would you describe the novel as a comedy or a tragedy, and why?

🖥 Resources

www.contemporarywriters.com/authors/?p=auth4 – profile of Kate Atkinson at the British Council website including a critical essay by Dr Jules Smith

http://www.telegraph.co.uk/arts/main.jhtml?xml=/arts/2004/08/29/boatkinson.
xml&sSheet=/arts/2004/08/29/bomain.html – interview by Helen Brown in *The
Telegraph*
www.barcelonareview.com/32/e_ka.htm – a short story by Kate Atkinson published at the *Barcelona Review* website

🖢 Suggested further reading
FICTION
The Family Tree by Carole Cadwalladr (2005); **Wise Children by Angela Carter**
(1991); **The House of Sleep by Jonathan Coe** (1997); *Crocodile Soup* by Julia
Darling (1998); *Watch Me Disappear* by Jill Dawson (2006); *David Copperfield* by
Charles Dickens (1849–50); *The Ten O'Clock Horses* by Laurie Graham (1996); *War
Crimes for the Home* by Liz Jensen (2002); **The Orchard on Fire by Shena Mackay**
(1995); *Drowning Ruth* by Christina Schwarz (2000); *Tristram Shandy* by Laurence
Sterne (1760); **Anita and Me by Meera Syal** (1996)
NON-FICTION
Hidden Lives by Margaret Forster (1995)
OTHER BOOKS BY KATE ATKINSON
Novels: *Human Croquet* (1997); *Emotionally Weird* (2000); *Not the End of the
World* (2002); *Case Histories* (2004); *One Good Turn* (2006)
Drama: *Abandonment* (2000)

ALIAS GRACE (1996)
Margaret Atwood

📖 About the book
Together with her fellow servant, James McDermott, Grace Marks has been found
guilty of the murder of their employer and his mistress. Simon Jordan, a young psychologist, is asked to assess Grace's mental state so that an application for pardon
may be made on the grounds of insanity. Dr Jordan listens to Grace's story with a
mixture of disbelief and sympathy. As he draws her towards the day of the murders,
an event which she claims not to remember, he grapples with the question that
haunts the novel – is Grace an innocent victim of circumstance or a vicious
murderer? Throughout the interviews, Dr Jordan has been troubled by his own
problems. His loneliness, his increasing sexual frustration and his puzzlement over
the enigmatic Grace begin to overwhelm him. He finds himself involved in a sexual

entanglement with his landlady and flees to avoid scandal, leaving the puzzle of Grace unsolved.

Background

Alias Grace is a fictionalized account of a celebrated Canadian murder case. Two immigrant servants, James McDermott and sixteen-year-old Grace Marks, were accused of the brutal slayings of their employer, Thomas Kinnear, and his mistress, Nancy Montgomery in 1843. Both of the accused were found guilty and sentenced to death but Grace's sentence was commuted. She was confined to Kingston Penitentiary, spending some time in the Toronto mental asylum. The novel is the product of Margaret Atwood's long fascination with the case, a fascination which was sparked off by Susanna Moodie's account of the murders in *Life in the Clearings* (1853). Moodie had visited Grace at the lunatic asylum in Toronto and at Kingston Penitentiary where we first meet her in *Alias Grace*. In Moodie's somewhat melodramatic account, written from her memory of those two meetings, Grace manipulated McDermott into committing the murders because she was sexually jealous of Nancy Montgomery; McDermott agreed in the hope of becoming Grace's lover. In her research for *Alias Grace*, Atwood found other, contradictory accounts in prison records and in newspapers (notoriously unreliable in their reporting at that time) none of which could provide a satisfactory resolution to Grace's case. Atwood contends that, despite her many historical researches, she still does not know who killed Thomas Kinnear and Nancy Montgomery.

In the 1970s, Atwood wrote a television drama, *The Servant Girl*, based Susanna Moodies's account of the notorious murder case. Twenty years later, *Alias Grace* takes her interpretation of Grace's story several steps further, filling in the many gaps that were undocumented but leaving known facts unchanged. The novel touches on many themes contemporary to the period, from the Victorian ambivalence towards women and the tensions between servants and employers, to the insatiable public appetite for scandal and the enthusiasm for spiritualism which swept Canada in the mid-nineteenth century.

About the author

Margaret Atwood was born in Ottawa, Ontario, in 1939. She was educated at the University of Toronto, Radcliffe College and Harvard. She has since lived in the United States, England, France, Italy and Germany but currently lives in her native Canada. Atwood has held a wide variety of teaching positions and has been granted many honorary degrees and literary awards. She is both a prolific and internationally acclaimed writer in a wide range of areas including fiction, poetry and children's literature. *Alias Grace*, her ninth novel, was published in 1996. It won the prestigious Canadian Giller award and was shortlisted for the Orange Prize. Often tipped as a favourite for the Booker Prize, Atwood finally won it in 2000 with her novel, *The Blind Assassin*.

For discussion

❍ *Alias Grace* is a fictionalized account of an historical event. To what extent did this affect your reading of it? What light did the extracts from the various records of the events at the time shed on the book for you? Did the Afterword change your interpretation of the novel in any way?

❍ How would you interpret the title of the book?

❍ Atwood uses the interviews with Simon Jordan as a means of telling some of Grace's story rather than having Grace speak directly to us at all times. What effect does this achieve?

❍ Mary Whitney is mentioned almost from the beginning of the novel although we do not meet her for some time. How important an influence on Grace was Mary? What do you make of her final 'appearance'?

❍ Both Simon's and Grace's dreams are recounted in great detail. To what extent did you find that their dreams illuminated the rest of the novel?

❍ Grace gives three different versions of the events surrounding the murders at the time of her trial. She continued to deny the memory of the murder. Did your opinion about Grace's guilt or innocence change during the course of the novel? What factors influenced your opinion? What conclusion did you reach by the end of the book, and why?

❍ As Margaret Atwood says in her Afterword, there was a good deal of fascination with Grace's part in the murder. Attitudes towards her reflected the Victorian ambivalence towards the nature of women. What were those attitudes? Are there other female characters that illustrate this ambivalence?

❍ How do their employers, particularly men, treat servants? In what ways do the worlds of servants and employers overlap? How do servants see their employers and vice versa?

🖳 Resources

www.litencyc.com/php/sworks.php?rec=true&UID=6784 – entry for *Alias Grace* at *The Literary Encyclopedia* website

www.randomhouse.com/resources/bookgroup/aliasgrace_bgc.html#interview – interview with Margaret Atwood about *Alias Grace*

www.salon.com/jan97/interview970120.html – interview at *Salon* internet magazine

www.contemporarywriters.com/authors/?p=auth03C18N390512635243 – profile of Margaret Atwood at the British Council website including an essay by Garan Holcombe

http://books.guardian.co.uk/departments/generalfiction/story/0,,943485.html – profile in *The Guardian* by Robert Potts

http://books.guardian.co.uk/bookerprize2000/story/0,6194,377730,00.html – profile in *The Guardian* by Katherine Viner

www.owtoad.com – Margaret Atwood's reference website

Suggested further reading

Hawksmoor by Peter Ackroyd (1985); *The Alienist* by Caleb Carr (1994); *98 Reasons for Being* by Clare Dudman (2004); *The French Lieutenant's Woman* by John Fowles (1965); *Electricity* by Victoria Glendinning (1995); *The Conversations at Curlow Creek* by David Malouf (1996); *Fortune's Rocks* by Anita Shreve (1999); **Morality Play by Barry Unsworth** (1995)

OTHER BOOKS BY MARGARET ATWOOD

Novels: *The Edible Woman* (1969); *Surfacing* (1972); *Lady Oracle* (1976); *Life Before Man* (1979); *Bodily Harm* (1981); *The Handmaid's Tale* (1985); *Cat's Eye* (1988); *The Robber Bride* (1993); *The Blind Assassin* (2000); *Oryx and Crake* (2003); *The Penelopiad: The Myth of Penelope and Odysseus* (2005); *The Tent* (2006); *Moral Disorder* (2006)

Short stories: *Dancing Girls* (1977); *Bluebeard's Egg* (1983); *Murder in the Dark* (1983); *Wilderness Tips* (1991); *Good Bones* (1992)

Poetry: *Double Persephone* (1961); *The Circle Game* (1966); *The Animals in That Country* (1968); *The Journals of Susanna Moodie* (1970); *Procedures for Underground* (1970); *Power Politics* (1971); *You Are Happy* (1974); *Selected Poems* (1976); *Two-Headed Poems* (1978); *True Stories* (1981); *Interlunar* (1984); *Selected Poems II: Poems Selected and New 1976–1986* (1986); *Morning in the Burned House* (1995)

Non-fiction: *Survival: A Thematic Guide to Canadian Literature* (1972); *Days of the Rebels 1815–1840* (1977); *Second Words* (1982); *Strange Things: The Malevolent North in Canadian Literature* (1996); *Two Solicitudes: Conversations (with Victor-Lévy Beaulieu)* (1998); *Negotiating with the Dead* (2002); *Curious Pursuits* (2005)

EUCALYPTUS (1998)

Murray Bail

📖 About the book

With his wife dead, his daughter Ellen away at school and no apparent need to make a living, Holland perfects his eucalyptus collection until he has over five hundred trees on his isolated New South Wales estate. When Ellen joins him, she passes her days walking, listening to her father's stories, occasionally yearning for city life. As she reaches marriageable age, Holland sets up a competition with Ellen's apparent acquiescence – the first man who names all his eucalypts will marry her. So begins a long parade of suitors beating a path to Holland's door, their imagination captured by stories of Ellen's beauty. Finally, one remains – Roy Cave, steeped in knowledge of eucalypts and little else. But Ellen has another suitor who appears on her daily walks, beguiling her with his storytelling. When it seems that Cave cannot fail, Ellen takes to her bed and it is left to the young storyteller to revive her with one last tale.

Background

Eucalyptus is a glorious celebration of the art of storytelling. Holland tells stories to his daughter (despite warning her to 'beware of any man who deliberately tells a story'); Ellen is enthralled by a young storyteller; the narrator tells us stories about eucalypts; even Cave, the dullest of suitors, has his story to tell, albeit brief and uneventful. The novel employs a classic device of the traditional fairytale – a father offers the hand of his daughter in marriage to the man who can complete a seemingly impossible task. Bail's language is rich in fabulous imagery and metaphor: it is only the occasional mention of motorcycles or hairdryers that reminds us that this tale is set in contemporary Australia.

Murray Bail's writing career spans several decades and yet he can hardly be described as prolific. His first collection of stories was published in Australia under the title *Contemporary Portraits* in 1975, and appeared in the UK in 1986 as *The Drover's Wife*, the collection's most highly acclaimed and widely anthologized story. Bail's fiction includes only two other novels, *Holden's Perfomance* and *Homesickness*, and a collection of three stories, *Camouflage*. Bail excels at the short story form, a talent which he demonstrates beautifully in *Eucalytus*, stringing stories along the framework of his novel like a rope of sumptuous pearls.

A Trustee of the National Australian Art Gallery for five years, Bail has also written a highly acclaimed appreciation of Ian Fairweather (1891–1974), widely regarded by both art critics and his fellow artists as Australia's greatest painter. Perhaps it is the influence of Bail's interest in art that results in the vividly evocative imagery of *Eucalyptus*, creating prose pictures that appear before the reader's eyes as if projected on a screen.

About the author

Murray Bail was born in Adelaide in 1941 and has lived in both Bombay and London. As well as being a novelist, he has written non-fiction and many short stories which have been widely published. He is also the editor of the *Faber Book of Australian Short Stories*. His first novel, *Homesickness*, won both the National Book Council Award for Australian Literature and the Age Book of the Year Award. His second novel, *Holden's Performance*, won the Vance Prize for Fiction. In 1999 *Eucalyptus* won both the Commonwealth Writers' Prize and the Miles Franklin Award.

For discussion

✪ Why do you think Holland sets up the competition? It seems the act of a tyrannical father but Holland is far from that. Why do you think Ellen goes along with it? Do you think she wants to get married? What sort of man do you think she wants to marry?

✪ What do you think of Holland's interest in eucalypts? When Cave talks about his pursuit of eucalypt knowledge he says, 'Mind you, it's given me a life of sorts.' What do you make of this? Do you think Cave and Holland have much in common besides eucalypts?

✪ What do you make of Ellen? Do you think she is happy? How do you think the loss of her mother when she was a baby has shaped her life? There are no women in Ellen's life in New South Wales. How do you think this has affected her?

✪ Each chapter is headed with the name of a eucalypt. Why do you think Bail chose this structure? Do you think it works? Can you think of other ways he might have structured the novel?

✪ *Eucalyptus* is much more about storytelling than about eucalypts. How important do you think storytelling is in our lives? Storytelling is usually associated with fiction. Do you think that it is valid to argue that non-fiction tells a story rather than simply reporting the facts and, if so, why?

✪ Do you think there is a pattern to the stories that the stranger tells Ellen? Do they share a theme? If so, what is it and why has he chosen it?

✪ Do members of the group have a favourite among the many stories in the novel? If so, which one? What was it that you particularly enjoyed about the story? Do you think it has a particular significance in the novel and, if so, what is it?

✪ Near the end, Bail writes 'the formidable instinct in men to measure, which is often mistaken for pessimism, is counter-balanced by the unfolding optimism of women, which is nothing less than life itself'. What do you think he means by this? Do you agree with this assessment of men and women? Do you think it is borne out by the male and female characters in the novel? If so, can you point to examples?

🖥 Resources

http://query.nytimes.com/gst/fullpage.html?res=9A00E4DA1439F937A35753C1A9 6E958260 – review of *Eucalyptus* in *The New York Times* by the novelist Michael Upchurch

🐚 Suggested further reading

Tales From One Thousand and One Nights C.C. Addison; *The Book of Illusions* by Paul Auster (2002); *Nights at the Circus* by Angela Carter (1984); *The Canterbury Tales* by Geoffrey Chaucer (c. 1387); *Tokyo Cancelled* by Rana Dasgupta (2005); *Periodic Table* by Primo Levi (1975); *In Babylon* by Marcel Möring (1999); *Life, a User's Manual* by Georges Perec (1978); *Lighthousekeeping* by Jeanette Winterson (2004)

OTHER BOOKS BY MURRAY BAIL

Novels: *Homesickness* (1980); *Holden's Performance* (1987)
Short stories: *The Drover's Wife and Other Tales* (1986); *Camouflage and Other Stories* (2001)
Edited: *The Faber Book of Contemporary Short Stories* (1988)
Non-fiction: *Ian Fairweather* (1981); *A Writer's Notebook* (1989); *Notebooks* (2005)

THE CROW ROAD (1992)

Iain Banks

📖 About the book

When Prentice McHoan comes home from Glasgow University to attend his grandmother's funeral, he has more than the usual family troubles to confront or, preferably, avoid. There is the widening rift between him and his father, the unsolved mystery of his uncle Rory's disappearance, his infatuation with the lovely Verity, not to mention a burgeoning sibling rivalry with his brother, Lewis. When his father dies in a freak accident, their differences still unresolved, Prentice knows it's time to shape up. He learns to deal graciously, if painfully, with Lewis's successful career and his happiness with Verity. But when his old friend Ashley uncovers some leads about his uncle Rory, Prentice cannot resist following them no matter how shocking the outcome or how dangerous the path. Set in the early 1990s, this multi-layered novel – part thriller, part family saga, part coming-of age-novel – is criss-crossed with flashbacks and leavened with humour.

Background

Laced with a dark humour which introduces itself in the first line of the novel, *The Crow Road* is one of Iain Banks's warmest and most accessible books. His work is both refreshing in its boundless originality and hugely diverse in its range. He made his name in 1984 with the publication of his first novel, *The Wasp Factory*, now regarded as a cult classic, in which the sixteen-year-old narrator, a self-confessed murderer, brushes aside his crimes as mere misdemeanours, a world away from the well-meaning, likeable Prentice who is deeply disturbed by the secret he unravels.

Banks alternates his writing between mainstream fiction and science fiction, writing roughly a book a each year and publishing his science fiction novels under the name Iain M. Banks. Although the style he adopts for each genre differs, the subject matter frequently seems to cross over, blurring the lines between the two. The strange, dreamlike world evoked by the narrator of *The Bridge*, lying in a coma after a near-fatal car accident, would not seem amiss in a science fiction novel. Conversely the themes addressed by his 'Culture' series in which fabulously intelligent machines grapple with the difficulties of attempting to establish a Utopian society, would not be out of place in a literary novel. Banks slips from one genre to the other with an ease which underlines his immense skill as a writer. Few authors have attracted such a degree of popular acclaim in both mainstream and genre fiction.

Banks has frequently disparaged 'the Hampstead novel' with its narrow pre-occupations. Given the vast range of his own work, its imaginative scope, its, often, political edge and his unfailing ability to stretch himself, it is not a tag that he need fear for his own books.

About the author

Born in Dunfermline, Fife, in 1954, Iain Banks was an only child but surrounded by a multitude of aunts, uncles and cousins. He studied English Literature, Philosophy and Psychology at Sterling University, publishing his first novel, the controversial *Wasp Factory*, in 1984. It was successful enough for him to give up his day job and to write full time. Since then he has divided his writing between science fiction and main-stream fiction, publishing his first work of non-fiction, *Raw Spirit*, a very personal guide to Scottish whisky distilleries, in 2003. In 1996 *The Crow Road* was made into a four-part television drama series by BBC Scotland. Iain Banks lives in Fife.

For discussion

⭕ Humour is an important element in *The Crow Road*. How would you describe Banks's particular brand of humour? Why do you think he uses humour?

⭕ Prentice reflects on his parents' different attitudes towards bringing up their children. How do you think these two attitudes are reflected in Prentice's character? Do you think that Kenneth was a good father and if so can you say why? If not, why not? Why do you think that the rift between Prentice and his father is so great? Why are they unable to bridge it?

⭕ How do you think Prentice changes during the book? Are there particular points in the book at which those changes take place? How would you describe Prentice's philosophy of life at the end of the novel? How do you think he has arrived at this?

⭕ Religious and political differences are crucial in the book. How would you describe Kenneth's politics? Do you think they have influenced his determined atheism or vice versa? Why do you think Hamish drops his eccentric religious views after Kenneth's death and becomes a fully fledged Christian?

⭕ The Urvills, the McHoans and the Watts all come from very different backgrounds. How are class differences portrayed in the book? How important is class as an issue in the book? How do attitudes to class change between the generations?

⭕ When Janice gives Prentice the first set of notes for Rory's book, the file is labelled 'Crow Road'. Janice explains that taking the Crow Road meant dying. Why do you think Rory chose that title? Why do you think Iain Banks uses it? How important is death in the book?

⭕ How does Banks work clues into the structure of the book? Did the plot fall into place for you at the end? If not, what did you think was unresolved?

⭕ What do you make of the relationship between Ashley and Prentice? How important do you think Ashley is in the development of Prentice's character? Were you surprised when their relationship took a different turn?

🖥 Resources

http://books.guardian.co.uk/departments/generalfiction/story/0,6000,102071,00.html – lengthy unsigned profile of Iain Banks in *The Guardian*

www.contemporarywriters.com/authors/?p=auth12 – profile of Iain Banks at the British Council website including an essay by Garan Holcombe

www.futurehi.net/phlebas/text/banksinto6.html – interview by Jayne Dowle published in *The Telegraph*

www.litencyc.com/php/speople.php?rec=true&UID=243 – profile of Iain Banks by Martyn Colebrook and Lucie Arnitt at the *Literary Encyclopedia* website

📚 Suggested further reading

The House of Sleep by **Jonathan Coe** (1997); *Everything You Need* by A.L. Kennedy (1997); *The Buddha of Suburbia* by Hanif Kureishi (1991); *The Funnies* by J. Robert Lennon (1999); *The Ice Storm* by Rick Moody (1994); *The Distance Between Us* by Maggie O'Farrell (2004); *The Catcher in the Rye* by J.D. Salinger (1951); *The Little Friend* by Donna Tartt (2002)

OTHER BOOKS BY IAIN BANKS

Fiction: *The Wasp Factory* (1984); *Walking On Glass* (1985); *The Bridge* (1986); *Espedair Street* (1987); *Canal Dreams* (1989); *Complicity* (1993); *Whit* (1995); *Song of Stone* (1998); *The Business* (1999); *Dead Air* (2002); *The Steep Approach to Garbadale* (2007)

Non-fiction: *Raw Spirit: In Search of the Perfect Dram* (2003)

Writing as **Iain M. Banks** (science fiction): *Consider Phlebas* (1988); *The Player of Games* (1988); *The State of the Art* (1989); *Use of Weapons* (1990); *Against a Dark Background* (1993); *Feersum Endjinn* (1994); *Excession* (1996); *Inversions* (1998); *Look To Windward* (2000); *The Algebraist* (2004)

THE DARLING (2004)

Russell Banks

📖 About the book

On the run for many years for her part in an extremist political movement, Hannah Musgrave reluctantly tells her story. After several years living underground in the States Hannah is co-erced by Zack, a fellow activist, into joining him in his flight to Africa. She finds a job as a medical laboratory assistant in Liberia where she marries Woodrow Sundiata, a junior minister in Samuel Doe's government. As Hannah finds herself eased into a privileged bourgeois life, her only political act is to defend her beloved chimpanzee sanctuary. When she eventually intervenes, helping Charles Taylor to escape his American prison, Liberia descends into a bloodbath that engulfs both her husband and her three sons. In this ambitious novel, Russell Banks explores a wide range of issues from the fallout from the radical politics of the sixties and seventies to the machinations of American foreign policy and the bloody politics and corruption of West Africa.

Background

Born to working class parents in Newton, Massachusetts, Russell Banks is often associated with raw, hard-hitting novels such as *Affliction* and *Continental Drift* which draw on his own experience and compassionately chart the difficulties of ordinary people trying to get by in an unforgiving world. In something of a departure, the epic *Cloudsplitter*, told the story of the renowned abolitionist and political martyr John Brown, often credited with providing the spur for the American Civil War.

With *The Darling*'s narrator Hannah Musgrave, Banks returns to the theme of political activism. As with *Cloudsplitter*, he has expertly blended meticulously researched fact with fiction, touching on a multitude of political and social issues from feminism to race, colonialism to terrorism. Hannah is a well-connected middle class radical, listed as one of the FBI's most wanted for her part in the Weather Underground, an extremist radical group, several of whose real life members have only relatively recently been released after serving sentences for their bombing campaign in the seventies in protest against racism and the Vietnam War. Hannah's flight from the law leads her eventually to Liberia, America's West African colony. Her life as the wife of one of Samuel Doe's ministers makes her an eyewitness to the corruption and bloody turmoil, orchestrated to some extent by the CIA, which eventually resulted in the terrible civil war of the early nineties. The novel ends with Hannah's final flight from a Liberia where Charles Taylor is president but the repercussions of that turbulent period continue to be played out on the world stage with Taylor's flight from Liberia in 2003, his indictment for war crimes by a United Nations tribunal in Sierra Leone and allegations of his links to al-Qaeda in Liberia.

Russell Banks' own political activism came to the fore with his outspoken criticism of The Patriot Act, passed in response to the 9/11 terrorist attacks, which was condemned as draconian by many on both the Right and the Left.

About the author

Russell Banks was born in 1940. He has twice been a Pulitzer Prize finalist and has won numerous literary prizes and fellowships. He is a both a highly acclaimed novelist and a journalist whose writing has been published in *Vanity Fair*, *The New York Times Book Review*, *Esquire* and *Harper's*. Two of his novels, *The Sweet Hereafter* and *Affliction* have been made into award-winning films.

For discussion

✪ Who is the eponymous darling? Why do you think Russell Banks chose it as the novel's title?

✪ Banks has chosen to narrate his novel from the point of view of a woman. Why do you think he did this? How successful is he at capturing a woman's voice and character?

✪ 'The truth is, most of the time, even now, I don't want to tell my story. Not to you, not to anyone'. Why does Hannah feel compelled to tell her story now? Why would she prefer not to?

✪ What did you make of Hannah's vision of the chimps when she returns to Boniface Island? Why does she want their judgement? Why do you think the chimps are so important to her?

✪ 'The very idea of revolution, which in the late sixties and seventies had seemed ready for immanence, had been turned into a comic metaphor for self-indulgent self delusion'; what do you think of Hannah's statement and her assessment of her own political activism? How would you describe Zack and Hannah's politics in the seventies? To what extent can either of them be described as 'revolutionaries'? How do Hannah's politics change?

✪ How would you describe the relationship between Hannah and Woodrow? How different are they? Were you surprised by the nature of their relationship and if so, why? Why do you think Hannah married him? Why do you think he married her?

✪ How would you describe Hannah's relationship with her mother, and with her father? She frequently disparages her mother, accusing her of narcissism. How different are the two women? How similar are they?

✪ Hannah has several personas: Hannah Musgrave, Dawn Carrington and Mrs Woodrow Sundiata. How would you describe each of these women? How would you describe Hannah at the end of the book?

✪ Liberia began as an American colony. What does the novel have to say about colonialism? What does it have to say about American foreign policy?

✪ Although fictional *The Darling* recounts actual events. How important do you think fiction is in helping us to understand history and the important issues that shape both our lives and the lives of others? How successful do you think *The Darling* is in this context?

🖳 Resources

http://pandora.cii.wwu.edu/banks/Banks_transcript.pdf – lengthy but very informative interview with Russell Banks (in PDF fromat).

http://news.bbc.co.uk/1/hi/world/africa/country_profiles/1043500.stm – BBC News Country Profile: Liberia

www.pbs.org/wgbh/globalconnections/liberia/essays/history – American Public Service Broadcasting page on Liberian history with timeline

http://www.pbs.org/newshour/bb/africa/liberia/taylor-bio.html – American Public
Service Broadcasting page on Charles Taylor
http://www.pbs.org/independentlens/weatherunderground/more.html American
Public Service Broadcasting page on the Weather Underground and other sixties
and seventies underground organizations.

📚 Suggested further reading
FICTION
The Catastrophist by Ronan Bennett (1999); *Heart of Darkness* by Joseph Conrad
(1902); *The Poisonwood Bible* by Barbara Kingsolver (1998); *The Good Terrorist*
by Doris Lessing (1985); *A Bend in the River* by V.S. Naipaul (1979); *Vida* by Marge
Piercy (1980)
NON-FICTION
The Liberian Civil War by Mark Huband (1998); *1968* by Mark Kurlansky (2005)
OTHER BOOKS BY RUSSELL BANKS
Novels: *Trailerpark* (1981); *Affliction* (1989); *The Book of Jamaica* (1986);
Continental Drift (1985); *Family Life* (1985); *Hamilton Shark* (1986); *The Relation of
My Imprisonment* (1984); *The Sweet Hereafter* (1991); *Rule of the Bone* (1995);
Cloudsplitter (1998); *The Reserve* (2008)
Short stories: *Searching for Survivors* (1975); *Success Stories* (1986); *The Angel
on the Roof* (2000)

THE VOYAGE OF THE NARWHAL (1998)
Andrea Barrett

📖 About the book
In 1855 Zeke Voorhees sets off on an ill-judged voyage in search of the remains of
the great Franklin expedition to the Arctic. Accompanying him is his future brother-
in-law Erasmus Darwin Wells, an amateur naturalist. As Zeke's enthusiasm transforms itself into a lonely despotic command of the voyage, Erasmus becomes more
and more uneasy about the outcome of the adventure. When Zeke strikes out on
his own, Erasmus has no option but to try to guide the crew of the *Narwhal*, much
depleted by the hardships of facing a winter ill prepared, to safety. On his return, he
finds himself estranged from his sister who blames him for leaving Zeke behind,
and derided by the public for the failure of his mission. When Zeke returns with two

Eskimos Erasmus is at first delighted, then appalled by his plan to stage a lecture tour featuring the Eskimos as exhibits.

Background

Exploration and an overriding desire to extend the boundaries of knowledge were two hallmarks of the nineteenth century. Too often the thirst for knowledge was accompanied by an equal thirst for glory, coupled with an enthusiastic amateurism which frequently ended in disaster. But Sir John Franklin's aim was not simply to add to the sum of human knowledge. His 1845 expedition was to find the much sought after Northwest passage which would provide a lucrative trading route between the Atlantic and Pacific oceans and further secure Britain's supremacy as a trading nation. The failure of the expedition was a blow both to Britain's mercantile ambitions and to the public's enthusiasm for such adventures. Many expeditions followed in its wake and its disappearance continues to fascinate even today with the Franklin Memorial Expedition mounted in 2003 in the hope of solving the mystery.

In *The Voyage of the Narwhal*, Andrea Barrett captures both the spirit of adventure that fired explorers and public alike and the incalculable destruction wrought in the name of discovery. Zeke's boyish excitement soon transforms itself into a fanaticism bordering on madness as the ill-prepared Narwhal encounters appalling adversity. In contrast, the gentle Erasmus continues his scholarly quest for scientific knowledge and is horrified at the exploitation of Annie and her son Tom whose exhibition, planned by Zeke, reflects the worst aspects of public interest in exploration.

Barrett's fiction reflects her interest in science and scientific discovery, and her fascination and love of the sea, both of which she attributes to her upbringing on Cape Cod. She studied biology as an undergraduate and worked in the field before taking up writing. Like any good scientist she researches her fiction thoroughly, sleeping in a tent on an Arctic ice sheet while preparing to write *The Voyage of the Narwhal*. She has said that science is 'what I know and in some sense that has always been the task of fiction, to bring the worlds that we know and are interested in to our readers in some shape that makes it possible for them to apprehend that and to be interested in that.' With its vividly evocative prose and perceptive characterization she has achieved that and more in *The Voyage of the Narwhal*.

About the author

Andrea Barrett grew up on Cape Cod, Massachusetts. She studied biology at Union College in Schenectady and has taught an MFA Program for Writers at Warren Wilson College. Her collection of short stories, *Ship Fever*, won the American National

Book Award in 1996 and *The Voyage of the Narwhal* was shortlisted for the Orange Prize in 1999. Andrea Barrett lives in Rochester, New York.

For discussion

○ Barrett has chosen an extract from *Tristes Tropiques* by the anthropologist Claude Lévi-Strauss to preface her novel. What bearing does this quotation have on the major themes of the novel? To what extent do you agree with the ideas expressed in the quotation? The quotation is dated 1955 – how much do you think things have changed since then? All the chapters are prefaced with a quotation – are there any which strike you as particularly apt and if so, which are they and why?

○ What impression do you have of Erasmus at the beginning of the book? What are the major forces that have shaped his character at this point? How does he feel about exploration by the end of the book? What has led him to these conclusions? Lavinia says of Zeke: 'He loves me ... In his own way – I know he does.' To what extent do you think Zeke is capable of love?

○ Why does Zeke become so isolated? What sort of man is he at the beginning of the book? How has he changed by the end?

○ How does Ned change? He is not much younger than Zeke, but who would make the better leader and why?

○ What part does class play in the book?

○ What light do the extracts from Alexandra's journals throw on the position of women in nineteenth-century society? How is this explored in part three of the book?

○ Officers and men alike are contemptuous of 'discovery men'. Captain Sturrock says that they 'get lost. Lose things. Franklin is lost, and his ships and his men, and Dr Kane's ship is lost, and yours and all your precious relics and specimens.' Why do you think the sailors feel this way? Do you have any sympathy with their view? If so, why are we still fascinated by people like Franklin?

○ When the *Narwhal* leaves Boothia, Zeke says of his pet fox, Sabine: 'Don't you think I'm doing well with her?' The final sentence of the chapter reads: 'As they began to move she stood and howled to her relatives back on shore.' What do you think Barrett is trying to convey about Zeke in this passage?

○ What does the book have to say about the motives of the men who mounted the great expeditions of the nineteenth century? Do you think that these ideas apply today? How did the explorers affect the Eskimos? Are there parallels today?

🖳 Resources

www.boston.com/news/globe/magazine/articles/2004/02/29/the_science_of_her _art/ – interview with Tracy Mayor originally published in the Boston Globe www.identitytheory.com/people/birnbaum35.html – interview with Robert Birnbaum published at indentity.com

www.salon.com/books/int/1998/12/cov_02inta3.html – interview with Peter Kurth at *Salon* internet magazine

www.salon.com/books/sneaks/1998/09/08sneaks.html – review by Peter Kurth at *Salon* internet magazine

www.channel4.com/history/microsites/H/history/n-s/northwest2.html – short account of Franklin's search for the Northwest passage at Channel 4's history website

Suggested further reading

FICTION

Water Music by T. Coraghessan Boyle (1982); *Heart of Darkness* by Joseph Conrad (1902); *The River Thieves* by Michael Crummey (2001); *Wegener's Jigsaw* by Clare Dudman (2003); *Rites of Passage* by William Golding (1980); **Remembering Babylon by David Malouf** (1993); *Moby Dick* by Herman Melville (1851); *The Discovery of Slowness* by Sten Nadolny (1983); **Promised Lands by Jane Rogers** (1995)

NON-FICTION

Barrow's Boys by Fergus Fleming (1998); *Arctic Dreams* by Barry Lopez (1986)

OTHER BOOKS BY ANDREA BARRETT

Novels: *Lucid Stars* (1988); *Secret Harmonies* (1990); *The Middle Kingdom* (1992); *The Forms of Water* (1994); *The Air We Breathe* (2008)

Short stories: *Ship Fever* (1996); *Servants of the Map* (2002)

ISLAND MADNESS (1998)

Tim Binding

About the book

It is 1943 and the Germans have suffered their first crushing defeat at Stalingrad. Far away in Nazi-occupied Guernsey, life goes on with its parties, love affairs and amateur dramatics. But when Isobel van Dielen, daughter of a wealthy construction magnate, is found murdered, the powder keg of resentment and suspicion that has been contained during the three years of Occupation is on the point of blowing. The Germans have taken up Occupation in every possible way – requisitioning houses, redeploying servants and, not least, monopolizing the sexual favours of every young woman with an eye to the main chance. As he goes about the unenviable task of solving the murder, Ned Luscombe, head of the local police force, begins to uncover the decadence and corruption of both occupying power and islanders alike.

Background

When the Germans invaded the Channel Islands in 1940, it was to be a 'model occupation' but as time wore on, food became scarce and a thriving black market sprang up. As the line between co-operation and collaboration began to blur, resentment and suspicion flourished on both sides. Ostensibly a murder mystery, *Island Madness* explores this sensitive episode in British history and investigates the psychology of Occupation from both points of view.

Britain proudly proclaims that she has resisted invasion for almost a millennium yet her borders were breached during the Second World War with the Occupation of the Channel Islands which were largely left to their own devices by a British government intent on preventing a German presence on the mainland. Though many remained staunchly loyal, some determined to protect the Islands' few Jewish inhabitants and help the foreign forced labourers, betrayal and collaboration were an almost inevitable consequence of fear and starvation. The Occupation remains a painful chapter in British history. While Jersey appears to have faced up to its past, commemorating the contribution of the Jewish islanders' protectors, Guernsey seems to have more difficulty in doing so, only erecting a small plaque to the memory of the three Jews who were deported from the island and who died in concentration camps, in 2001.

Tim Binding's fiction is characterized by a fascination with British twentieth century history. *A Perfect Execution* is a vivid portrayal of one of Britain's last executioners while *Anthem* traces the increasingly intertwined lives of small group of neighbours during the Falklands War. *Man Overboard* tackles the Cold War with its fictionalized account of war hero Buster Crabb whose corpse may, or may not, have turned up in 1957 after his disappearance during Khrushchev's first visit to the West. *Island Madness*, his third novel, exemplifies Binding's writing: an uncharacteristic and sometimes overlooked slice of British history combined with a compelling story which both entertains and enlightens.

About the author

Tim Binding was born in Germany in 1947. He has been an editor with Penguin Books and a part-time commissioning editor with the publishers Simon & Schuster. As well as being an editor and a novelist he has written scripts for the BBC, co-writing the comedy drama series *The Last Salute* with Simon Nye. His second novel, *A Perfect Execution*, was shortlisted for the *Guardian* Fiction Prize in 1996. Tim Binding lives in Kent.

For discussion

✪ Right at the beginning of the book, Binding describes Hitler's fixation on the islands as 'island madness'. Is the title of the novel open to more than one interpretation? Are there particular characters who fall into the grip of island madness and, if so, who are they and why? The American edition of the novel was published under the title *Lying with the Enemy*. Which do you find more appropriate?

✪ What is Major Lentsch's attitude towards Hitler when the book opens? What does he see as the main aims of the war? How has his attitude changed at the close of the novel and what has brought this about?

✪ When Zepernick returns from taking a phone call at Lentsch's welcome-back party, Binding describes him as 'in so many ways the epitome of the Occupation'. What traits and behaviour seem to epitomize the Occupation for you?

✪ How have the inhabitants of Guernsey been changed by the Occupation? Have particular relationships changed and, if so, how? Have there been any benefits and, if so, what are they?

✪ Why is Veronica so eager to acquire a German officer as a boyfriend? What are the contradictions in her relationship with Captain Zepernick and her relationship with Peter, the young slave labourer? Binding writes of Veronica and Zepernick '[he] began to recognize a part of him in her, just as while listening she became aware of a part of her within him'. What is it that Veronica and Zepernick recognize in each other? How does Veronica redeem herself?

✪ How would you describe Ned Luscombe's character? What particular difficulties does he face as head of the island's police force and how does he deal with them?

✪ How satisfying do you find the dénouement when Isobel's killer is revealed?

✪ The issue of collaboration during the five-year Occupation of the Channel Islands has remained very sensitive. Who do you consider to be a collaborator in the novel and who is merely co-operating to ensure their survival? Where would you draw the line between the two?

🖥 Resources

http://partners.nytimes.com/books/00/01/02/reviews/000102.02furstt.html – review of *Lying with the Enemy*, the title of the American edition of *Island Madness*, by novelist Alan Furst published in *The New York Times*

www.bbc.co.uk/guernsey/content/articles/2004/07/19/occupation_timeline_193
9_feature.shtml – the BBC's timeline of the Occupation
www.guardian.co.uk/Columnists/Column/0,5673,1130297,00.html – article on the
legacy of Occupation in the Channel Islands by Madeline Bunting, author of *The
Model Occupation*, published in *The Guardian*

⛁ Suggested further reading
FICTION
Captain Corelli's Mandolin by Louis de Bernières (1994); *Charlotte Gray* by
Sebastian Faulks (1998); **Stones From the River by Ursula Hegi** (1995); *Mephisto*
by Klaus Mann (1936); *The Sword of Honour Trilogy* by Evelyn Waugh, published
separately as: *Men at Arms* (1952), *Officers and Gentlemen* (1955), *Unconditional
Surrender* (1961)
NON-FICTION
The Model Occupation by Madeline Bunting (1965); *The German Occupation of
the Channel Islands* by Charles Cruickshank (2004); *The Channel Islands at War*
by G. Forty (1999)
OTHER BOOKS BY TIM BINDING
Novels: *The Kingdom of Air* (1993); *A Perfect Execution* (1996); *Anthem* (2003);
Man Overboard (2005)
Non-fiction: *On Ilkley Moor* (2001)

THE LEPER'S COMPANIONS (1999)
Julia Blackburn

📖 About the book
Devastated by grief having suffered the loss of her beloved, a woman escapes into
a strange and fascinating world, sometimes watching, occasionally involving herself in the life of a fifteenth century English village. The villagers have their own
griefs to solace: a young girl loses her husband to an obsession with the mermaid
he brought ashore only to have her disappear; a shoemaker's wife watches as her
dear husband regains his sight only to lose his wits; a young woman mourns her
grandmother whose peaceful death follows a long slow scrutiny of the life that
rushed past her as she lived it. When a leper arrives in the village, he finds himself
miraculously recovered from his affliction and joins the villagers who have been

inspired to make a pilgrimage to Jerusalem, a pilgrimage he once undertook alone. Our unnamed narrator joins them on their journey. Written in marvellously poetic prose, *The Leper's Companions* is a strange but beguiling novel that conjures captivating dreamlike images of a lost world.

Background

Although slim in volume *The Leper's Companions* is not a book to be gulped down in one sitting but rather one to be savoured; a book whose exquisite language and images linger, working their magic on the reader's mind rather as the leper's map induced a wanderlust in Sally after she had eaten it.

Julia Blackburn is an author whose work defies categorization. Her books often straddle several genres, expressing very personal views while commanding a great deal of respect for the quality of her writing. They have all pursued historical themes, although only two are novels. Of her four best known works of non-fiction all but *With Billie* (a biography of Billie Holiday) have interwoven fact with meditative speculation and a degree of what might be termed fiction. *Daisy Bates in the Desert* blends research into the life of Daisy, based on her own records, with a reconstruction of her time with the Australian Aborigines told from Daisy's point of view. In *The Emperor's Last Island*, an exploration of Napoleon's last days on St Helena, Blackburn weaves historical details through descriptions of her own journey to the island, and the thoughts that journey provoked. Similarly *Old Man Goya* is a sweeping biography of the artist in which Blackburn leavens her meticulous research with very personal reflections, both of the life of the artist and on her own life. Blackburn's other novel, *The Book of Colour*, could be accused of having one toe in family history as it explores the lives of a nineteenth century family, blighted by racial prejudice, who travels from Mauritius, from which her own family originated, to England. Each of these books is marked by Blackburn's characteristic idiosyncrasy, and each is very different from the others, but they all share the shimmering prose and mastery of language that is so captivatingly displayed in *The Leper's Companions*.

About the author

A graduate of York University, Julia Blackburn was born in London in 1948. Her family was originally from Mauritius. She is the author of several non-fiction works and of two Orange Prize-shortlisted novels: *The Leper's Companions* and *The Book of Colour*. The daughter of the poet Thomas Blackburn, she has also edited a collection of his poems.

For discussion

✪ 'She whimpered like a little child, the noise so close and intimate it sounded like my own voice.' The world that the narrator conjures into being is never explained to the reader: it could be an hallucination, the narrator's means of escape from her pain, a fable, a parable, a 'psychotic episode' as one critic has suggested, or simply an exercise in beautifully evocative writing. How did you interpret the narrative? Why did you choose this interpretation?

✪ What kind of world does Blackburn depict? How does it compare with our own? How do the villagers make sense of their world? How important is religion to them?

✪ 'The sadness that I carried inside me is eating through my skin and it has turned me into a leper'. Who might the leper be or who might he symbolize? What is his effect on the village?

✪ In what way does the narrative change when the pilgrimage begins?

✪ '"I was thinking of the meal we had on the day we left the village", the priest said and with that they both shared the same recollection of cold rain, the cry of marsh birds and a long journey only just begun.' What have the leper and each of his companions taken from the pilgrimage? How important is the pilgrimage both to them and to the narrator?

✪ How appropriate did you find the quotation from Stevie Smith's poem 'Away Melancholy' which prefaces the novel? Why do you think Julia Blackburn chose it?

✪ Blackburn's use of language and imagery is both vivid and idiosyncratic. How would you describe the language that she uses? Were there particular passages that struck you and if so, what were they and why did you find them striking?

🖥 Resources

www.nytimes.com/books/99/04/18/reviews/990418.18bawert.html – review by literary critic Bruce Bawer published in *The New York Times*

www.salon.com/books/review/1999/04/26/blackburn – review by Alex Abramovich published at *Salon* internet magazine

🥢 Suggested further reading

The Bridge by Iain Banks (1986); *The Canterbury Tales* by Geoffrey Chaucer (c. 1387); *Flying to Nowhere* by John Fuller (1984); **The Vintner's Luck by Elizabeth Knox** (1999); **Ingenious Pain by Andrew Miller** (1997); *Perfume* by Patrick Süskind (1985); **Morality Play by Barry Unsworth** (1995)

OTHER BOOKS BY JULIA BLACKBURN

Fiction: *The Book of Colour* (1997)

Non-fiction: *The White Men* (1979); *Charles Waterton, 1782–1865* (1989); *Daisy Bates in the Desert* (1994); *The Emperor's Last Island* (1991); *With Billie* (2005) Edited: *Selected Poems* by Thomas Blackburn (2001)

VISIBLE WORLDS (1998)

Marilyn Bowering

📖 About the book

In 1960 Nate Bone, national football star and local hero, dies in a freak accident playing football in his hometown of Winnipeg. Nate held the key to the story which links three neighbouring families with Fika, a young woman who is using the full force of her will and endurance to cross the Arctic snows from Russia to Canada. When Albrecht finds a map of Siberia, dated 1951, in Nate's boot he immediately recognizes it as his twin brother's work. But Gerhard has been missing since 1945. Albrecht tells the story of the three families whose lives have become so entwined over two wars and a multitude of misfortunes that each has become a part of the other. Fighting for survival as she crosses the Polar ice cap, Fika tells her own story. As each narrative unfolds, small details coincide, family links become clear until, finally, Fika finds her way to safety and the two stories become one.

Background

Visible Worlds is a complex, tightly plotted novel. Two narratives alternate, each full of clues to the connections which bind three Canadian families both to each other and to a young woman determinedly struggling across the Arctic snows. Although slim in volume, the novel is epic in scale. It covers both the Second World War and the Korean War, humanizing the political forces that shaped the twentieth century by filtering them through the lives of the Storrs, the Bones and the Fergussons.

Marilyn Bowering is a playwright and a poet as well as a novelist, and she has brought to bear talents from all three forms in the writing of *Visible Worlds*. Her language is elegant and exact, her descriptions evocative; each word has been carefully and precisely chosen to fit its purpose. She marshals her perceptively-drawn characters, setting their scenes beautifully and directing them upon a vast world stage. The novel encompasses many remarkable incidents and ideas, some of which, such as Personal Magnetism, may seem fantastical but she has explained that all are rooted in reality including Fika's astonishing feat of endurance. Since writing the book she has learned of several similar crossings but the original inspiration for Fika's trek was her meeting in the Broken Islands off Vancouver with a man who had travelled overland from Siberia to Canada.

While she has acknowledged the importance of research, storytelling lies at the root of the novel, a long established tradition in her Newfoundland paternal family. She has said that 'In *Visible Worlds* I was trying to grasp the interplay between the personal and the cultural as I feel it myself. It was done through the fingertips, so to speak. I was asking, "What is really going on behind the events of our lives and why do I feel about them the way I do?"' In answering those questions she has written a novel which transports her readers to other worlds, offering them marvellous insights along the way.

About the author

Marilyn Bowering was born in Winnipeg, Manitoba, and grew up in Victoria, British Columbia. She is widely traveled and has lived in Greece, Scotland and Spain. She now lives in British Columbia where she teaches part-time at the University of Victoria. In addition to being a novelist, she is one of Canada's leading poets. Her first book of poetry, *The Liberation of Newfoundland*, was published in 1973. She is also a playwright and was commissioned to write the critically acclaimed *Anyone Can See I Love You ...*, a play about Marilyn Monroe, for BBC Radio Scotland. Her first novel, *To All Appearances a Lady*, was published in 1989.

For discussion

✪ The literary critic Alberto Manguel said of *Visible Worlds*, the reader 'reaches the end with the sense of having undertaken a long, complex, enthralling journey in the company of a throng of tragic, ordinary, brave human beings whom he has grown to love'. How did you feel when you reached the end of the novel? Do you agree with Manguel and, if so, why? If not, what didn't work for you?

✪ Why do you think Wilhelm is so wedded to the idea of Personal Magnetism? How does it affect his life? Do you think other characters in the novel have unorthodox personal philosophies? If so, who are they and how do they try to explain the world to themselves?

✪ The novel is made up of two narratives: Albrecht's and Fika's. Did you find this effective? How does Bowering establish links between the two narratives?

✪ There are many references to the natural world in both Albrecht's and Fika's narratives. Why do you think Bowering makes these references? What do you think she is saying about the relationship between humans and nature?

✪ Danger is a strong presence in the novel – floods, bitter cold, animals, war. Why do you think Bowering lays so much emphasis on danger? How do her characters react to it? Does their suffering change them and, if so, how?

✪ There are a variety of different attitudes towards war in the novel. How would you describe the attitudes of Wilhelm, Friedl, Fritz, Nate, Pietor, Albrecht and Mary? Why do you think they have reached these conclusions?

✪ Albrecht says: 'I am a twin without his other half. I am less than myself.' How would you describe the relationship between Albrecht and Gerhard? How do they differ from each other? What do you think Albrecht means by 'I am less then myself'?

✪ In the final passage of the book, when Fika finds Albrecht, he thinks 'I have a feeling of something about to happen, pins and needles of the brain, and at the same time I know it doesn't matter, there is no forever'. What do you think he means by 'there is no forever'? Why does he think it at this point? How do you think it relates to what has happened in the book?

💻 Resources

http://webcontent.harpercollins.com/text/guides/pdf/0006481256.pdf – background information published at HarperCollins website on Marilyn Bowering which includes an interview

www.marilynbowering.com/index.html – Marilyn Bowering's website

📚 Suggested further reading

Catch-22 by Joseph Heller (1961); *A Prayer for Owen Meany* by John Irving (1989); **Fugitive Pieces by Anne Michaels** (1997); *The Book of Lights* by Chaim Potok (1981); *The Story of My Disappearance* by Paul Watkins (1997)
OTHER BOOKS BY MARILYN BOWERING
Fiction: *To All Appearances a Lady* (1989); *Cat's Pilgrimage* (2004)
Poetry: *The Alchemy of Happiness* (2002); *Green* (2007); *What it Takes to be Human* (2007)

WISE CHILDREN (1991)

Angela Carter

📖 About the book

On her seventy-fifth birthday, Dora Chance sits down to write her memoirs. She and her twin are the illegitimate daughters of the renowned Shakespearean actor Sir Melchior Hazard, whose one-hundredth birthday is to be honoured at a magnificent party that evening. Both the Chances and the Hazards are show business to the core but while the Hazards are members of the theatrical aristocracy, the Chances were chorus girls. As Dora looks back over her life a tale unfolds of unacknowledged paternity, mistaken identities, twins at every turn, Shakespeare, Hollywood, music hall, discarded wives, glorious love and rollicking good times. Despite the social gulf that divides them and the refusal of Melchior to acknowledge the twins as his daughters, the paths of the Hazards and the Chances criss-cross throughout their lives until the glorious finale, worthy of a Shakespearean comedy, when all the players are assembled, identities revealed and more than a few home truths told.

Background

Wise Children is steeped in show business, from the Hazard Shakespearean dynasty to the music hall turns of the Chances. The story revolves around issues of paternity and legitimacy. It is packed with Shakespearean references with a plot worthy of one of the Comedies and written in language which is earthy, vivid and memorable. With its vibrant depictions of the sassy Chance sisters, two old women who would surely have eschewed the more genteel term 'elderly', *Wise Children* offers a lively alternative to the stereotype of the ageing woman mourning her lost youth. In her review published in *The Guardian*, the novelist Ali Smith recounts the story told to an interviewer of Angela Carter's Aunt Kitty: 'an alarmingly too-soubrette young thing who, Carter's grandmother thought, might "go on the halls" but who was forced to become a clerk instead since "going on the halls" was a bit too close to "going on the streets". Kitty, she told Bailey, eventually went mad, and died. "I thought, you know," she told him, "I'd send her on the halls." Another generous resurrection.' The original jacket for the publication of the novel depicted the real-life music hall twins known as The Dolly Sisters who were hugely successful on both sides of the Atlantic.

Wise Children was Angela Carter's last novel, published the year before her death from lung cancer in 1992. Hers had been a long and prolific career, beginning with her first novel *Shadowdance* published 1966, a year after leaving Bristol

University. She was a novelist, poet and essayist whose strikingly original work met with both popular and critical acclaim. Her fiction often drew upon the themes and symbolism of both fairytale and myth, underpinned by feminism and sometimes coupled with a rich humour. Her literary influences were many, from Mary Shelley to Borges, Blake to Shakespeare, clearly apparent in *Wise Children*. She had a passion for film, born in childhood when her father took her regularly to the cinema, and a love of medieval texts with their romance, folk tales and bawdy comedy. She was a writer who drew enormous respect from her fellow authors, from Salman Rushdie to Margaret Atwood, many of whom she counted as her friends. She was regarded as outstanding amongst her generation in the scope of her imagination, her playful but erudite allusions, her lively humour and the marvellous vividness of her prose. Her passing was much mourned.

About the author

Angela Carter was born in 1940. After studying English at Bristol University, she spent two years in Japan. She lived and worked extensively in both Australia and the United States. In 1976 she was appointed Fellow in Creative Writing at Sheffield University, a position she held until 1978. Her second novel, *The Magic Toyshop* (published in 1967), won the John Llewellyn Rhys Prize and was adapted for a BBC television dramatisation. Neil Jordan filmed *The Company of Wolves*, taken from her collection of short stories, *The Bloody Chamber*, in 1984. Angela Carter died in 1992.

For discussion

✪ How would you describe Angela Carter's writing style? Can you see ways in which her style fits her subject matter? Were there passages in the book which you found particularly striking and, if so, which were they?

✪ Grandma's motto, often quoted by Dora, is 'Hope for the best, expect the worst'. How is this philosophy illustrated in the book? Do you think it was helpful to Dora and Nora, and, if so, in what way? At one point, Nora says that Grandma's ghost is trying to tell them something – 'Expect the worst, hope for the best'. Why do you think the order of the phrases is reversed here?

✪ What does the book have to say about illegitimacy? Because they are illegitimate, Nora and Dora are excluded from the 'legitimate' theatre and confined to music hall, although the two seem to come together in Hollywood. What do you think this says about attitudes in different types of culture?

✪ The issue of paternity is an important theme in the book. What do you think the book is saying about fatherhood? Does it also have something to say about motherhood and, if so, what?

○ Dora says, 'It's a characteristic of human beings, one I've often noticed, that if they don't have a family of their own, they will invent one.' Do you think this is true and, if so, can you think of reasons why? How is this illustrated in the book?

○ We often expect twins to share similar traits. Why do you think Melchior and Perry are presented as such different characters? What are the main differences between them?

○ Nora and Dora are seventy-five, strong and lively. What do you think the book has to say about ageing and in particular about the ageing of women?

🖳 Resources

http://books.guardian.co.uk/departments/generalfiction/story/0,6000,102086,00. html – writer and academic Lorna Sage's obituary of Angela Carter published in *The Guardian*

www.centerforbookculture.org/interviews/interview_carter.html – interview by academic Anna Katsavos published at the Centre for Book Culture website

www.litencyc.com/php/speople.php?rec=true&UID=5060 – profile of Angela Carter by Linden Peach at the *Literary Encyclopedia* website

📚 Suggested further reading

FICTION

An Awfully Big Adventure by Beryl Bainbridge (1991); *Nicholas Nickleby* by Charles Dickens (1839); *The Sword Cabinet* by Robert Edric (1999); *Carter Beats the Devil* by Glen David Gold (2001); *The Final Confession of Mabel Stark* by Robert Hough (2002); *Niagara Falls All Over Again* by Elizabeth McCracken (2001) *Juggling* by Barbara Trapido (1995)

NON-FICTION

The Dolly Sisters by Gary Chapman (2006); *White Cargo* by Felicity Kendal (1998)

OTHER BOOKS BY ANGELA CARTER

Novels: *Shadow Dance* (1966); *The Magic Toyshop* (1967); *Heroes and Villains* (1969); *The Infernal Desire Machines of Dr Hoffman* (1974); *Nights at the Circus* (1984); *Love* (1987); *The Passion of New Eve* (1993)

Short stories: *Fireworks* (1974); *The Bloody Chamber* (1979); *Black Venus* (1985)

Essays: *The Sadeian Woman: An Exercise in Cultural History* (1978); *Nothing Sacred* (1982); *Expletives Deleted* (1992); *American Ghosts and Old World Wonders* (1993)

Edited: *Wayward Girls and Wicked Women* (1986); *The Virago Book of Fairy Tales* (1990); *The Second Virago Book of Fairy Tales* (1993)

THE HOUSE OF SLEEP (1997)

Jonathan Coe

📖 About the book

In Ashdown, a university hall of residence, Sarah is about to break up with Gregory, fed up with being treated like his research subject rather than his lover. He is fascinated by her narcolepsy, a sleep disorder which occasionally results in dreams so vivid that she is convinced that they are real. Among the other residents, Robert, hopelessly in love with Sarah, looks on in mute despair as she becomes drawn into a relationship with a woman, while Terry is immersed in his obsession with cinema and his spectacular, fourteen-hour, Technicolor dreams. Twelve years later Terry, now chronically insomniac, hears that Ashdown has become a sleep disorder clinic. He books himself in and through a number of strange coincidences, finds himself reacquainted with his old housemates. With more than a touch of comedy, the intricately plotted narrative loops backwards and forwards through twelve years, spilling a multitude of clues at every turn, and neatly resolving every one of them.

Background

What a Carve-up!, a scathing social satire on the Thatcherite 1980s, marks the beginning of Jonathan Coe's serious career as a novelist with his three preceding experimental novels barely mentioned by critics considering his work. All four of his major novels are lengthy with complex constructions (particularly evident in *The House of Sleep*) that require attentive reading. Narratives, strewn with clues and hints, loop back and forth. There are stories within stories and a multitude of perspectives. Such cinematic narrative techniques demonstrate Coe's interest in film, which is particularly evident in *What a Carve Up!* and *The House of Sleep*, both in the structure of the novels and in the preoccupations of their main protagonists. All four novels share a concern with the state of modern Britain, coupled with a humour which is sometimes leavened with pathos, sometimes downright slapstick. This concern has led one interviewer to ask him if he minded being described as a 'State of the Nation' writer to which he replied: 'It seems to me that you would have to write a novel on a very small, intimate scale for it not to become political. As soon as you start writing about how human beings interact with each other socially, you're into politics, aren't you?'

Of these four novels, *The House of Sleep* is by far the most gentle; aside from the megalomaniac Gregory, its characters share an emotional depth and concern for each other. The many intricacies of the novel hinge upon the misunderstandings, sometimes comic, sometimes devastating, which result from Sarah's inability to distinguish her extraordinarily vivid narcoleptic dreams from reality. It is a novel that demands close attention: many apparently insignificant details are crucial to the resolution of the plot. As the novel draws to its conclusion, its many conundrums are satisfyingly solved as the links between each character become clear.

About the author

Jonathan Coe was born in Birmingham in 1961. He was educated at Trinity College Cambridge and completed a PhD on Henry Fielding's *Tom Jones* at Warwick University. He taught English Poetry at Warwick, before working as a professional musician, writing music for jazz and cabaret. He also worked as a legal proofreader before becoming a freelance writer and journalist, spending some time as the film critic for the New Statesman. He has written biographies of both James Stewart and Humphrey Bogart. His novel *What a Carve Up!* won the John Llewelyn Rhys Prize in 1995. *The Rotters' Club*, set in 1970s Birmingham where Coe grew up, was adapted for BBC television in 2004 and its companion novel, *The Closed Circle*, was published the following year. Coe's fascination with the author B.S. Johnson, author of the 1970s cult novel *Christie Malry's Own Double-Entry* led him to write Johnson's biography *Like a Fiery Elephant* which won the BBC4 Samuel Johnson Prize for Non-Fiction in 2005. *The House of Sleep* won both the 1997 Writers' Guild Award (Best Fiction) and France's Prix Médicis Etranger in 1998.

For discussion

✪ Jonathan Coe has worked as a film critic as well as a novelist. Can you see ways in which cinema has influenced his writing style? Are there particular passages in the book which seem to you to be cinematic?

✪ Although it has a number of serious themes running through it, *The House of Sleep* is a comic novel. How would you describe the humour? Were there any passages that you found particularly funny? How does the humour of these passages work?

✪ Dr Dudden is often portrayed in the book as someone to be laughed at but he has some disturbing traits. Why do you think Coe chose to make him a comic figure?

✪ What does the book have to say about modern society? Can you think of specific examples?

✪ What did you think of the way the novel ended?

✪ The main characters, Dr Dudden, Sarah, Terry and Robert, are present in both the 1983–84 and the 1996 narratives? How does each of the characters change?

✪ *The House of Sleep* is constructed around the different stages of sleep. How far do you think each section reflects its equivalent stage as described by Dr Dudden?

🖥 Resources

www.contemporarywriters.com/authors/?p=auth22 – profile of Jonathan Coe at the British Council website including an essay by Daniel Hahn

www.salon.com/books/sneaks/1998/04/02sneaks.html – review by Charles Taylor at *Salon* internet magazine

http://query.nytimes.com/gst/fullpage.html?res=9B00E1D61638F93AA15750C0A96 E958260 – review by the novelist Suzanne Berne published in *The New York Times*

www.threemonkeysonline.com/threemon_article_jonathan_coe_closed_circle_ interview.htm – interview by Alex Mitchell on the publication of *The Closed Circle* published at *Three Monkeys Online* website

📚 Suggested further reading

Emotionally Weird by Kate Atkinson (2000); ***The Crow Road* by Iain Banks** (1992); *The Road to Wellville* by T. Coraghessan Boyle (1993); *The Last Picture Show* by Larry McMurty (1966); *The Treatment* by Daniel Menaker (1998); *253* by Geoff Ryman (1998)

OTHER BOOKS BY JONATHAN COE

Fiction: *The Accidental Woman* (1987); *The Dwarves of Death* (1991); *A Touch of Love* (1997); *What A Carve Up!* (1994); *The Rotters' Club* (2001); *The Closed Circle* (2004); *The Rain Before it Falls* (2007)

Non-fiction: *Like a Fiery Elephant: The Story of B.S. Johnson* (2004)

BEING DEAD (1999)

Jim Crace

📖 About the book

On a beautiful afternoon a couple lie dead on a beach, their bodies bloody and battered. They have been married for almost thirty years and even in the throes of a violent death they appear devoted, as Joseph's hand is curved around Celice's shin. In acknowledgement of their death, Jim Crace tells us that the novel is to be a 'quivering', a retelling of their lives in an expiation of grief in accordance with an ancient custom. So begins the narrative of Joseph and Celice's life from their first meeting and when they had made love for the first time on that same beach, to their brutal murders. Woven into their story are the details of what happens to their bodies as they lie undiscovered for six days on the deserted beach. Written in language that is graphic yet poetic, Crace makes the unbearable and the inevitable into something to be looked in the face.

Background

Written in his distinctive rhythmic, sometimes lyrical, poetic style, Jim Crace's novels are set in worlds that, although resembling our own, are oddly disconcerting – dubbed Craceland by some critics. Craceland ranges from the imaginary seventh continent which echoes the developing world in his first book, *Continent* to *Six's* contemporary City of Kisses, superficially attractive yet on the edge of violent political disruption; both very far removed from the calm of suburban Birmingham where he has lived for many years. He has said that, unusually for his work, *Being Dead* sprang from an event in his own life. His father, a lifelong atheist, had recently died and his family, determined to honour his father's request, had resisted having a funeral of any kind. Crace regretted the lack of a ritualized goodbye and wrote *Being Dead* as a response to this regret and to his dissatisfaction with his own atheism, seeking comfort in a world where death means the end of everything.

The novel reflects Crace's fascination with science and with natural history. He has said: 'I'm very aware that no matter what I've said about my views on religion, there's a deep ambiguity, in me and my books, that shows through about spirituality. There's a spirituality that comes across in a very old fashioned and biblical way. But then I deny the existence of God. All I'm doing is replacing God with natural history.' However, he is quick to point out that the passages in the novel describing the two corpses' decay was not researched but based on his observations of animal decomposition when out walking. He is adamant that writing fiction is about making things up (the ritual of the 'quivering' is also fabricated), rejecting the modern preoccupation with absolute factual accuracy in novels. He has expressed his amusement at some critics' reactions to such an idea, explaining that although he makes up the epigraphs that appear in his novels, he has sometimes found them attributed to some 'sadly neglected aphorist'. For many years a journalist, Crace has proved himself to be a consummate storyteller whose thoughtful and reflective work is entirely the product of his own fertile imagination.

About the author

Jim Crace was born in Enfield, North London, in 1946. After taking his degree in English Literature at Birmingham he went to the Sudan as part of a Voluntary Service Overseas programme, where he worked in Khartoum as an assistant for educational television. On his return he worked for sixteen years as as a freelance journalist for *The Sunday Times* and *The Daily Telegraph* magazine. His first novel, *Continent*, was published in 1986 and went on to win both the Whitbread First Novel Award and *The Guardian* Prize for Fiction. *Quarantine*, published in 1997, won the Whitbread Novel of the Year Award. *Being Dead* was also shortlisted for the Whitbread Fiction Prize.

For discussion

✪ The book deals with disturbing details of death and physical decay. What did you think of this as subject matter for fiction? What was your reaction to Crace's graphic descriptions of bodily corruption and decay? Why do you think he chose to describe this so explicitly?

✪ Joseph dies with his hand on Celice's leg, a detail that is referred to frequently in the novel. How important is this as a signal of the state of their relationship. How does your view of the relationship between the couple change from the opening chapter to the end of the book? How does Crace convey the nature of the relationship between Joseph and Celice, the details of their characters and their lives?

✪ How would you describe Crace's style and tone? The narrative has a strong authorial voice. What effect does this have? What did you think of his use of language? Can you give examples of passages that you found particularly effective?

✪ What would you say was the central message of the book? What does it say about death and attitudes towards death in modern society? How does Crace convey this?

✪ Crace writes of Joseph and Celice: 'Both know that life and death are inextricably entwined, the double helix of existence.' How does the book illustrate this idea?

✪ Nature and science are closely intertwined throughout the book – both Joseph and Celice are scientists who specialize in the natural world. What do you think Crace is saying about the links between science and nature?

✪ When *Being Dead* was published, it was noted by experts that many of the scientific details were inaccurate. How much does this matter in a work of fiction?

✪ The relationship between Syl and her parents is, at best, an uneasy one. When it becomes clear that something is wrong and Syl goes back to her parents' home, Crace asks, 'Why had Syl come?' Why do you think she went home? What is her reaction to her parents' death? Why do you think she feels this way?

✪ The novel ends with the sentence 'These are the everending days of being dead'. Why do you think Crace chose the word 'everending' which can so easily be read as 'neverending'? How does a misreading of this word change the meaning of the sentence?

🖥 Resources

www.salon.com/books/review/2000/03/30/crace/ – review by Gary Krist at *Salon* internet magazine

www.beatrice.com/interviews/crace/ – interview by Ron Hogan published at Beatrice.com

www.contemporarywriters.com/authors/?p=auth24 – profile of Jim Crace at the British Council website including an essay by Sean Mathews

http://books.guardian.co.uk/departments/generalfiction/story/0,6000,541326,00.html – lengthy interview by Sally Vincent published in *The Guardian*

www.powells.com/authors/crace.html – interview by Dave Weich published at Powell's bookshop website

http://threemonkeysonline.com/threemon_article_jim_crace_interview.htm – interview by Andrew Lawless published at *Three Monkeys Online* website

📖 Suggested further reading

FICTION

As I Lay Dying by William Faulkner (1930); *One True Thing* by Anna Quindlan (1994); **The Death of Vishnu by Manil Suri** (2000); *Blackwater Lightship* by Colm Tóbín (1997)

NON-FICTION

Paula **by Isabel Allende** (1995); *Iris and Her Friends* by John Bayley (1999); *A Year of Magical Thinking* by Joan Didion (2005); **Hidden Lives by Margaret Forster** (1995); *The Shadow Man* by Mary Gordon (1996); *Father and Son* by Edmund Gosse (1907); *Remind Me Who I Am, Again* by Linda Grant (1998); *Seeking Rapture* by Kathryn Harrison (2003); *My Ear at His Heart* by Hanif Kureishi (2004); *The Undertaking: Life Studies from the Dismal Trade* by Thomas Lynch (1997); *On the Death of a Parent* edited by Jane McLaughlin (1994); **And When Did You Last See Your Father? by Blake Morrison** (1993); *A Voyage Around My Father* by John Mortimer (1971); *How We Die* by Sherwin Nuland (1996)

OTHER BOOKS BY JIM CRACE

Continent (1986); *The Gift of Stones* (1988); *Arcadia* (1992); *Signals of Distress* (1994); *Quarantine* (1997); *The Devil's Larder* (2001); *Six* (2003); *The Pesthouse* (2007)

A HOME AT THE END OF THE WORLD (1990)

Michael Cunningham

📖 About the book

When Jonathan Glover meets Bobby Morrow at high school, he is desperate to impress and falls more than a little in love. But what seems to be the essence of cool to Jonathan, is really the stunned, trance-like state of a young boy in deep shock, the result of an appalling tragedy. Bobby watched his brother die in his mother's arms after a freak accident and his mother died of an overdose shortly after. While the two boys experiment with sex and drugs, Jonathan's mother, Alice, realizes that Bobby desperately needs a family, and when Jonathan goes to university, Bobby stays behind with the Glovers. In New York, Jonathan meets Clare, spiky and eccentric, with whom he shares an apartment and fantasies of family life. When Bobby joins them, the family is almost complete and the birth of Rebecca makes it so. But the country idyll that they build for themselves in upstate New York is at best precarious and, finally, blown off course.

Background

A Home at the End of the World was published a decade after Michael Cunningham's debut novel, *Golden States*. Although he had continued to write, supporting himself by teaching creative writing courses, he met with little success until, planning to demonstrate to his new partner the difficulties of the writer's life, he sent a short story to the *New Yorker*, only to have it accepted. The story, *White Angel,* became the third chapter of *A Home at the End of the World* and went on to be included in the annual anthology, *Best American Short Stories* for 1989. Well reviewed on publication, *A Home at the End of the World* marked the beginning of Cunningham's career as a highly respected novelist.

The novel is a thoughtful examination of what can constitute a family in a society where the conventional nuclear family of the twentieth century was already something of a rarity. Relationships shift and transform themselves yet the yearning for a family of some sort runs deep: Clare, Bobby and Jonathan even play the game of happy families as the Hendersons. Some readers may feel that the book ends on an ambivalent note yet Cunningham has said that he feels that all his books end happily, that 'I seem to be interested in whatever love and hope – the love of life that hope implies – can survive.'

Cunningham is an openly gay writer but prefers not to be labelled as such but rather as a writer who happens to be gay. His novels all feature characters who are either gay or whose sexuality is ambivalent – both Jonathan and Bobby in *A Home at the End of the World*, Billy the son of the dysfuntional Stassos family in his wonderfully sprawling saga, *Flesh and Blood*, and several characters in *The Hours*, his most widely acclaimed novel to date. All his characters, gay or straight, are wonderfully rounded: their complexity, their unhappinesses and their happiness depicted with humanity and sensitivity that endears them to his readers.

About the author
Michael Cunningham was born in Cincinnati, Ohio, in 1952 and grew up in Pasadena, California. He took degrees from both Stanford University and the University of Iowa. His work has been widely published in magazines such as *Esquire*, *The New Yorker* and *Vogue*. In 1999, he was awarded the prestigious Pulitzer Prize for fiction for his novel *The Hours*, which was inspired by Virginia Woolf's *Mrs Dalloway*. It was adapted for the cinema by David Hare. *A Home at the End of the World* was made into a film for which Cunningham wrote the screenplay in 2004. Michael Cunningham lives in New York City

For discussion
❍ The novel is narrated in four different voices, Jonathan's, Bobby's, Alice's and Clare's. How does the writing style of each narrative reflect the character? How successful did you find this structure?

❍ Alice says, 'This is what you do. You make a future for yourself out of the raw material at hand.' What do you think of Alice's philosophy? How has it worked for her? Does she change it at any stage and, if so, how?

❍ The novel opens in the 1960s when Jonathan and Bobby are children. How much have their characters been shaped by the time in which they grew up? How is Alice's life shaped by the social climate of that period? How much do you think Alice's and Clare's experiences differ because of the generation into which they were born?

❍ Why do you think Clare, Bobby and Jonathan play the Hendersons game? How do the characters each of the players take on match their own characters? Do you think this changes throughout the course of the book? How far do you accept Clare, Bobby and Jonathan as a family?

❍ What do you think of Clare's final decision?

❍ On the last page Jonathan says, 'I was merely present, perhaps for the first time in my adult life.' What do you think he means by this and why does he feel it at that point?

⊙ When Jonathan says he is in love with both Bobby and Clare, what do you think he means? Clare also says she is in love with both Jonathan and Bobby, do you think she means the same thing as Jonathan?

Resources
www.barnesandnoble.com/writers/writerdetails.asp?cid=1015986 – interview by barnesandnoble.com which includes a profile by Amanda H. Reid
http://books.guardian.co.uk/departments/generalfiction/story/0,6000,103050,00.html – interview by the writer Nicholas Wroe on winning the 1999 Pulitzer Prize for fiction with *The Hours*
www.pbs.org/newshour/bb/entertainment/jan-june99/pulitzer_4-13.html – transcript of an interview by Elizabeth Farnsworth broadcast by the American organization PBS
www.powells.com/authors/cunningham.html – interview by Dave Weich published at Powell's bookshop website

Suggested further reading
Love Invents Us by Amy Bloom (1997); *The Short History of a Prince* by Jane Hamilton (1998); *The Hotel New Hampshire* by John Irving (1981); *Equal Affections* by David Leavitt (1989); *The Ice Storm* by Rick Moody (1994); **The Magician's Assistant by Ann Patchett** (1998); *A Regular Guy* by Mona Simpson (1996)
OTHER BOOKS BY MICHAEL CUNNINGHAM
Fiction: *Golden States* (1984); *Flesh and Blood* (1995); *The Hours* (1999); *Specimen Days* (2005)
Non-fiction: *Land's End: A Walk through Provincetown* (2004)

TALKING TO THE DEAD (1996)
Helen Dunmore

About the book
Nina, going to help her sister Isabel after the difficult birth of her first child, finds Isabel, weak from the birth, caught up in a fearful love for her new son and in retreat from the rest of the world. Both Nina and Isabel's husband Richard are deeply concerned for her mental and physical welfare but eventually find themselves drawn into an obsessive affair. As the heat of the summer intensifies so do relationships within the household. Nina begins to remember scenes from her

childhood with Isabel, in particular disturbing memories of their brother Colin, who died at three months supposedly of cot death. The pace of the narrative quickens as it works towards its shocking climax when Isabel goes missing.

Background

For such a slim volume, *Talking to the Dead* is a richly complex book. On one level it has the pace of a thriller with clues scattered throughout the plot. On another and almost contradictory level, it is a long prose poem written in language which is as sensuous and languorous as the heat which seems to permeate every page. On yet another level it is packed with insight into the complications of family life and the secrets which may lie hidden for years but which can both shape and destroy our lives. Despite the very different nature of Helen Dunmore's fiction which ranges from *The Siege's* painfully sensitive depiction of the quiet desperation of a young woman, her father and her lover during the siege of Leningrad to the tangled and destructive relationships between two brothers in *With Your Crooked Heart*, these are the themes that run through many of her novels.

She has said that poetry is a more natural medium for her than fiction (although she excels at both) and her sensuous descriptions of both food and sex, particularly evident in the descriptions of the preparations for the feast in *Talking to the Dead*, are written in richly poetic language. She also uses that language to firmly anchor her novels, imbuing them with a sense of place: *Zennor in Darkness*, her first novel, offers a marvellous evocation of Cornwall at the outbreak of World War One.

She has explained that *Talking to the Dead* evolved from a conversation while taking her baby for a walk around Firle churchyard where Vanessa Bell, the sister of Virginia Woolf, is buried. Bell had lived at Charleston House and Woolf had been a regular visitor; those who know the area will instantly recognize Dunmore's descriptions of the house in her novel. Woolf's relationship with her sister was overshadowed by the death of their mother when they were both children. When Bell died Woolf lost her substitute mother, and later drowned herself.

About the author

Helen Dunmore was born in Beverley, Yorkshire, in 1952. After studying English at York University, she spent two years teaching in Finland. She is a children's writer and an award-winning poet as well as a novelist and short story writer. In 1996 she was the first winner of the Orange Prize for Fiction, open only to women novelists, for *A Spell of Winter*. The Siege was shortlisted for the Whitbread Novel of the Year in 2001, and for the Orange Prize in 2002. She lives in Bristol.

For discussion

○ How would you describe the relationship between Nina and Isabel at the beginning of the novel? How has your view changed by the end? Were there significant points at which your view changed?

○ The story is told through Nina's voice. Do you feel that you gain as strong a view of Isabel's character as you do of Nina's? How would you describe Isabel? Does your view of her change? If so, why?

○ Edward says to Nina: 'There's something missing in you.' Do you think this is true? If so, what is it? What reasons do you think there might be?

○ Why do you think Nina sleeps with Richard? Do you find their affair shocking? If so, why? What does Isabel's attitude to the affair seem to be? How does your view of Richard change? Do you think the nature of their affair changes?

○ In Chapter 9, Nina describes her preparation of the celebratory meal and the meal itself. What does this chapter tell us about each of the characters? Do you think that it is an important event in the development of the novel? If so, why?

○ How do you think Colin died? Do you believe Isabel's version of events? Do you think the ending of the novel is ambiguous?

○ Nina has several dreams which throw light on the past. Why do you think Dunmore has used this method to elucidate Nina and Isabel's childhood relationship?

○ Do you think that Dunmore's writing style reflects the fact that she is a poet? If so, can you find examples of language, imagery and metaphor in the novel to support this?

○ Nina says: 'People do strange things when it's as hot as this.' Heat is present in the book almost as a character – do you think this has a purpose? If so, what do you think it is?

🖥 Resources

www.bbc.co.uk/communicate/archive/helen_dunmore/page1.shtml – 'Live Chat' discussion of *Talking to the Dead* at the BBC's website

http://readers.penguin.co.uk/nf/Document/DocumentDisplay/0,,P100000002_RPT, 00.html – transcript of interview by a readers' group at the Institute of Cancer Research at the Penguin Readers' Group website

www.contemporarywriters.com/authors/?p=auth103 – profile of Helen Dunmore at the British Council website including a critical essay by Dr Jules Smith

www.charleston.org.uk – Charleston House website

🕮 Suggested further reading

***Behind the Scenes at the Museum* by Kate Atkinson** (1995); *Sleep with Me* by
Joanna Briscoe (2005); *The Game* by A.S. Byatt (1967); *Telling Liddy* by Anne Fine
(1998); *Limestone and Clay* by Lesley Glaister (1993); *Sleepwalking* by Julie
Myerson (1994); *The Distance Between Us* by Maggie O'Farrell (2004)
OTHER BOOKS BY HELEN DUNMORE
Novels: *Zennor in Darkness* (1994); *Burning Bright* (1995); *A Spell of Winter* (1996);
Your Blue-eyed Boy (1999); *With Your Crooked Heart* (1999); *The Siege* (2001);
Mourning Ruby (2003); *The House of Orphans* (2006); *Counting the Stars* (2008)
Short stories: *Love of Fat Men* (1998); *Ice Cream* (2000)
Poetry: *Apple Fall* (1983); *The Sea Skater* (1986); *The Raw Garden* (1988); *Short
Days, Long Nights: New and Selected Poems* (1991); *Recovering a Body* (1994);
Bestiary (1997); *Bouncing Boy* (1999); *Out of the Blue* (2001)

MIDDLESEX (2003)

Jeffrey Eugenides

📖 About the book

In the tiny hamlet of Bithynios, tucked away in a corner of the crumbling Ottoman
Empire, Desdemona and Lefty Stephanides are the only remaining members of
their family. Surviving the catastrophic burning of Smyrna, they flee to America in
1923 and during the voyage brother and sister transform themselves into husband
and wife. The couple begin their new life in their married cousin's home in Detroit
and when both women become pregnant on the same night their children seemed
destined for each other. Driven to distraction by her guilty secret Desdemona looks
on, increasingly frightened by the consequences of such a union, consequences
which surface in her grandchild: brought up as a longed-for daughter the sexually
confused adolescent Calliope discovers she is a hermaphrodite. Comparable in its
scope to an Homeric epic, *Middlesex* explores a multitude of themes, from race,
war and religion to love, sexuality and gender, as Cal tells both his own story and
the story of his family set against a backdrop which encompasses the Second
World War, the Detroit race riots and the Turkish invasion of Cyprus.

Background

Jeffrey Eugenides was inspired to write *Middlesex* after reading *Memoirs of a 19th
Century French Hermaphrodite*, the diary of Herculine Barbin discovered by

Michel Foucault in the archives of the French Department of Public Hygiene. Expecting to be gripped by the book, Eugenides was left disappointed by its wooden melodramatics but wanting to write a novel that would bring the story to life. Researching genetics and genetic mutation as he began to develop his ideas for *Middlesex*, Eugenides realized that he would need to tell the story of Calliope/ Cal's genetic history. A mutation such as Calliope/Cal's is most likely to originate in small, close-knit communities similar to the Greek villages which Eugenides' own ancestors would have known and this together with the origins of the hermaphrodite, Tiresias, in Greek mythology lead him to write a novel which is both Calliope/Cal's story and the story of the Greek-American Stephanides family.

Almost a decade passed between the publication of Jeffrey Eugenides' acclaimed debut *The Virgin Suicides* and that of *Middlesex*, a delay surely accounted for by the complexity of a novel which explores terrain as diverse as genetic mutation, gender identity and explosive racial tension while tracing a turbulent family history which spans nearly a century. While *The Virgin Suicides* dealt with male voyeurism as the gradual demise of five sisters is obsessively charted by a group of young boys, *Middlesex* is narrated from both a female and a male point of view in the voice of one person. Through his narrator Eugenides explores the social as well as the biological construction of identity but the complexity of Calliope/Cal's identity is reflected not just in the construction of sexual identity or the multitude of themes addressed by the novel but also in the sheer breadth and depth of the history it charts.

About the author

Jeffrey Eugenides was born in Detroit, Michigan in 1960. Educated at Brown and Stanford Universities, Eugenides received an MA in English and Creative Writing from Stanford in 1986. The first of his short stories, which have appeared in *The New Yorker*, *The Paris Review* and *Best American Short Stories*, was published two years later. In 1996 he was named as one of *Granta*'s Best Young American Writers. *The Virgin Suicides*, Eugenides' first novel, was published to great critical acclaim in 1993. In 1999, Sofia Coppola made her much-praised directorial debut with a film based on the novel. Ten years in the writing, *Middlesex* won the 2003 Pulitzer Prize for fiction. Jeffrey Eugenides now lives in Berlin with his wife and daughter.

For discussion

❍ 'Not me but somebody like me might have been made that night. An infinite number of possible selves crowded the threshold, me among them but with no guaranteed ticket' How important are both chance and fate in the novel? Does one or the other seem to be more important to Cal?

✪ 'If you were going to devise an experiment to measure the relative influences of nature versus nurture, you couldn't come up with anything better than my life'. How does Cal's life illustrate this debate? Where do you stand in it?

✪ '"This is America", Lefty said. "We're all *Amerikandhes* now."' To what extent does either Desdemona or Lefty become American? Are Milton and Tessie more American than Greek? What about Cal and Chapter 11?

✪ Desdemona finds a refuge from her fears in both superstition and religion. To what extent do the two seem to overlap? What are Milton's views? How important is science in the novel?

✪ 'What's the matter with you people?' asks Milton of Morrison who buys cigarettes from him during the 1967 race riots. To which Morrison replies 'The matter with us ... is you'. What part does race play in the novel? How does Milton interpret this remark?

✪ Middlesex is described in elaborate detail in the chapter of the same name. What do you think the house symbolises?

✪ 'Here's a question I still can't answer: Did I see through the male tricks because I was destined to scheme that way myself? Or do girls see through the tricks too, and just pretend not to notice?' To what extent does Cal combine what are traditionally seen as female qualities with male traits? Why does Cal decide to live as a man rather than a woman? What does he find difficult about changing gender? What regrets does he have? To what extent does he become reconciled to his new identity?

✪ How important is social conditioning in Calliope/Cal's gender identity? How do people react to his hermaphroditism?

✪ Why do you think Dr Luce told Cal's parents one thing, but wrote an entirely different report?

✪ What does the book have to say about sexuality and desire?

✪ Calliope is named after the muse of epic poetry. How appropriate does this name seem to be for *Middlesex*'s narrator? How important is Greek myth and literature in the novel? Milton dons his Greek tragedy and comedy cufflinks before the final appointment with Dr Luce. Does either or both seem appropriate to the novel and why?

✪ How would you describe the tone in which Cal narrates *Middlesex*? How does it change and when? Would the novel have worked if it had been written in the third person? How would it have been different?

✪ In American law Chapter 11 provides a protective shield for failing companies on the verge of bankruptcy. Why do you think Cal refers to his brother as Chapter 11?

🖳 Resources

www.powells.com/authors/eugenides.html – interview by Dave Weich published at Powell's bookshop website

www.bombsite.com/issues/81/articles/2519 – interview by Jonathan Safran Foer at *Bomb* ezine

http://books.guardian.co.uk/departments/generalfiction/story/0,6000,805334,00. html – interview by Geraldine Bedell in *The Observer*

http://arts.telegraph.co.uk/arts/main.jhtml?xml=/arts/2002/10/06/boeug06.xml – review by Kathryn Hughes in *The Telegraph*

http://books.guardian.co.uk/print/0,3858,4514554-110738,00.html – review by Mark Lawson in *The Guardian*

www.nybooks.com/articles/15794 – review by Daniel Mendelsohn in *The New York Review of Books*

🥬 Suggested further reading
FICTION

Behind the Scenes at the Museum by Kate Atkinson (1995); *Birds Without Wings* by Louis de Bernières (2004); *Flesh and Blood* by Michael Cunningham (1995); *James Miranda Barry* by Patricia Duncker (1999); **Empress of the Splendid Season by Oscar Hijuelos** (1999); *The Odyssey* by Homer ; *Midnight's Children* by Salman Rushdie (1981); *Misfortune* by Wesley Stace (2005); *Tristram Shandy* by Lawrence Sterne (1759)

NON-FICTION

Genome by Matt Ridley (1999)

OTHER BOOKS BY JEFFREY EUGENIDES

The Virgin Suicides (1993)

BIRDSONG (1994)

Sebastian Faulks

📖 About the book

When Stephen Wraysford is sent to Amiens in 1910 to learn what he can of the French textile business, he finds himself obsessed with his host's wife. The couple begin an affair so passionate that it rocks both their lives. Six years later, Stephen is again in Picardy, fighting as an officer in the British army. Possessed by a seemingly invincible will to survive, he lives through some of the fiercest battles of the Western Front. Sixty years after the war, his granddaughter Elizabeth begins a journey into the past as she tries to understand both the grandfather she never knew and the terrible events which shaped his life. *Birdsong* tells the harrowing story of men who lived in conditions which are barely imaginable, witnessing the gruesome deaths of friends and enemies alike, trying to find ways to survive in a world fractured by one of the bloodiest wars of the twentieth century.

Background

Although not originally intended as a trilogy, three of Sebastian Faulks's novels – *Birdsong, The Girl at the Lion D'Or* and *Charlotte Gray* – are linked through location, history and several minor characters. *Birdsong* and *Charlotte Gray* are set in the arenas of war, but in both novels Faulks vividly depicts his characters' personal lives so that we never forget that they are ordinary people whose lives have been thrown into chaos by cataclysmic events. *Birdsong* is largely set at the Western Front of the First World War. It contains graphic scenes of bloodshed which, while gut-wrenching, are wholly necessary to the novel's themes which address the terrible cost that warfare exacts as well as the human propensity for love.

The war chapters, which follow the fortunes of the three main protagonists Stephen, Jack Firebrace and Michael Weir, span the years from 1916 to 1918, covering the ferocious battles of the Marne, Verdun and the Somme. Losses were appalling, the carnage beyond imagination for the generations that came after. In the Somme campaign alone, around one million casualties were sustained out of an estimated three million participants. At the outset many had hoped that the First World War would be the last, the War to End All Wars as it was sometimes known. Sadly, as *Birdsong* portends, the Treaty of Versailles (1919), which all but crushed Germany, carried the seeds of the Second World War which would follow just two decades later.

Championed by William Hague, *Birdsong* appeared on the top twenty-one titles on the BBC's Big Read list and was finally ranked at number thirteen. Speculating as to what will be considered a classic fifty years from now can be dangerous, but surely *Birdsong*, with its grand sweep and its painful yet humane depictions of what we do to each other in wartime, deserves to stay the course.

About the author

Sebastian Faulks was born in Newbury, England, in 1953. He graduated from Cambridge University in 1974 and took a job teaching in a London school. He wrote freelance book reviews for a variety of papers and in 1978 left teaching to become a reporter for *The Daily Telegraph*, later becoming a feature writer for *The Sunday Telegraph*. His first novel, *A Trick of the Light*, was published in 1984 and in 1986 he became literary editor at the newly established *Independent* newspaper. His second novel, *The Girl at the Lion D'Or*, was published in 1989, and in 1991 he left journalism to write fiction full time. *Birdsong* has remained a consistent bestseller since its publication in 1994. Something of a Francophile, Faulks and his family spent 1996 in France but now live in London.

For discussion

✪ What do you think of Faulks's descriptions of the relationships between his male and female characters? How do they compare with his descriptions of the relationships between the male characters in the novel?

✪ Why do you think Isabelle leaves Stephen, having sacrificed home, family and reputation for him? What do you think the consequences are for both of them?

✪ Stephen Wraysford is described by various characters as 'cold' or 'strange'. How would you describe his character? Does he have traits which help him to deal with the horrors that he experiences and, if so, what are they? How is he changed by the war?

✪ Stephen is one of the few characters to survive the war, virtually the only character who has continuously fought at the Front. Why do you think he survives when others don't? Is it simply chance or does something else sustain him? Are there significant points at which his view of the war changes?

✪ How would you describe Firebrace's character? How is he changed by the war? Are there other events that change him, and if so what are they and how do they change him? Why does he seem relieved to die?

✪ How would you describe the relationships between officers and men? What are the different ways in which the officers try to motivate the men while dealing with their own horrors?

✪ How would you compare the experiences of the officers with those of the men at the Front? How do both officers and men try to cope with what would seem to be intolerable horror? How successful do you think Faulks is in conveying the state of mind of the forces at the Front?

✪ Firebrace reflects that 'None of these men would admit that what they saw and what they did were beyond the boundaries of human behaviour.' Why do you think this is so? The letters home on the eve of the first attack of the Somme are optimistic to the point of being almost anodyne, despite the horrors which surround the men. Why do you think this might be so?

✪ Why do you think Faulks introduces Elizabeth into the story? What purpose does she serve both in the development of the story and in any message that you feel Faulks is trying to convey?

✪ Stephen's life is ultimately saved by a German soldier. How significant is this? Why do you think Faulks chose a German Jew to save Stephen's life?

✪ How important do you think fiction is in helping us to understand history and the important issues that shape our lives? How successful do you think *Birdsong* is in this context?

🖥 Resources

www.contemporarywriters.com/authors/?p=auth3 – profile of Sebastian Faulks at the British Council website including a critical essay by Dr Jules Smith

http://observer.guardian.co.uk/magazine/story/0,,1552740,00.html – profile by Kate Kellaway published in *The Observer* magazine August 2005

www.firstworldwar.com/index.htm – website devoted to the First World War

www.bbc.co.uk/history/worldwars/wwone – BBC History's World War One webpages

🖥 Suggested further reading

FICTION

The Regeneration Trilogy by Pat Barker, published separately as: *Regeneration* (1992), *The Eye in the Door* (1994), *The Ghost Road* (1995); *Birds Without Wings* by Louis de Bernières (2005); *Anthem* by Tim Binding (2003); *Grey Souls* by Philippe Claudel (translated by Adriana Hunter) (2005); *A Very Long Engagement* by Sebastien Japrisot (translated by Linda Coverdale) (1991); *All Quiet on the Western Front* by Erich Maria Remarque (1930); *The Crimson Portrait* by Jody Shields (2007); *War and Peace* by Leo Tolstoy (1805)

AUTOBIOGRAPHY

Undertones of War by Edmund Blunden (1928); *Testament of Youth* by Vera Brittain (1933); *Goodbye to All That* by Robert Graves (1929)

FIRST WORLD WAR HISTORY

The Donkeys by Alan Clark (1991); *The First World War* by Martin Gilbert (1994); *The Somme* by Lyn Macdonald (1983)

OTHER BOOKS BY SEBASTIAN FAULKS

Novels: *A Trick of the Light* (1984); *The Girl at the Lion D'Or* (1989); *A Fool's Alphabet* (1992); *Charlotte Gray* (1998); *On Green Dolphin Street* (2000); *Human Traces* (2005); *Engleby* (2007)

Non-fiction: *The Fatal Englishman: Three Short Lives* (1990); Edited (with Jorg Hensgen): *The Vintage Book of War Stories* (1997); *Pistache* (2006)

COLD MOUNTAIN (1997)

Charles Frazier

📖 About the book

Set in North Carolina during the American Civil War, *Cold Mountain* tells the story of Inman and Ada, separated at the beginning of a tentative love when Inman enlists in the Confederate army. Four years later, weary of a war whose brutality and bitterness have left him so changed that he hardly knows himself, Inman decides to leave his hospital bed and walk home to Cold Mountain where he hopes to find his sweetheart. His journey takes him through a country as changed as he is: farms in ruins, terrible poverty, lawlessness and degradation. At home, Ada's ladylike education has left her ill-equipped to run a farm or deal with the depredations of war. Her relationship with Ruby, a young woman well versed in the practicalities of life, has literally saved her from starvation. As Ada learns to master the skills she needs to survive so she, too, is irrevocably changed by the war.

Background

Cold Mountain is the story of two journeys. Inman's journey is homeward. It takes him through a stricken land, shattered by the brutality of the American Civil War. His sweetheart Ada's journey is one of self-discovery as she learns that the love of knowledge and beauty cherished by her father has left her lamentably unprepared for survival. Charles Frazier alternates their stories, drawing them ever closer in a novel that is as much about the human ability to adapt and endure as it is about love.

The character of Inman was based in part on Frazier's great great uncle and in part on his great grandfather, both of whom he has said were stricken by 'war fever' and enlisted in the first few months of the war. He points out, however, that although his great great uncle shares the name Inman with *Cold Mountain*'s fictional character, Frazier knew little about him: 'It's just a little fragment of a family story about this guy'. What had captured Frazier's imagination was his ancestor's journey home from the war, 'what he was getting away from and what he was walking toward', and it was this that led him to base *Cold Mountain*'s structure on Homer's *Odyssey* in which Odysseus has many encounters on his way home to Penelope from the Trojan Wars.

The character in *Cold Mountain*, like the Inman on whom he is loosely based, would have had no interest of his own in the war. Fought between 1861 and 1865, the American Civil War was ostensibly about the abolition of slavery: neither Inman were likely to have been slave owners. Frazier suggests that men like Inman went to war to 'because they thought they were repelling an invasion of their homeland.' In his researches for the novel he has said that he found the diaries and letters of 'very intelligent, headstrong, opinionated, strong women', women who were far from the familiar Southern belle stereotype but were the sort of woman that Ada became.

Frazier writes vividly about nature and the terrain Inman crosses on his way home, summoning up a world that has long passed. Sadly, when Anthony Minghella came to film his adaptation of *Cold Mountain* modern development prevented him from locating it in the landscape that Frazier had so memorably evoked. Instead it was filmed in the mountains of Romania.

About the author

Charles Frazier was born in North Carolina in 1950. He took degrees at Chapel Hill and Appalachian State followed by a PhD in twentieth-century American literature at the University of South Carolina. He has taught at the University of Colorado and North Carolina State University. *Cold Mountain* is Charles Frazier's first novel and won the American National Book Award in 1997. The film version starring Nicole Kidman, Jude Law and Renée Zelweller was adapted and directed by Anthony Minghella in 2003.

For discussion

❍ How would you describe Inman's character before he went to war? How has he been changed by the war? How does Frazier illustrate this?

❍ Why do you think that Inman thinks of Cold Mountain as a place where 'all his scattered forces might gather'?

❍ Throughout the war and his journey home, Inman has taken comfort from the book by Bartram that he carries with him. How has the book sustained him and what does it tell you about him?

❍ A traveller tells Inman that the road is 'a place apart, a country of its own ruled by no government but natural law, and its one characteristic was freedom'. How is this idea either illustrated or disproved in the book?

❍ What effects has the war had upon the country Inman walks through? What do people's attitudes seem to be to the war? How have they been affected by it?

❍ How would you describe the relationship between Ada and Ruby? Which of them is changed most by it and how?

❍ Ada writes to her cousin Lucy that she has found something 'akin to content-ment'. How would you describe that contentment and how do you think she has achieved it?

✪ What do you think of Monroe and the way that he has brought up Ada?

✪ A young man gestures to the battlefield and says to Inman: 'Right there's what mostly comes of knowledge.' Are there similar comments or illustrations of this attitude to knowledge in the book and, if so, what do you think Frazier means by it?

✪ Many critics commented on Frazier's use of language when the book was published in America, saying he had captured the speech patterns and vernacular of those who lived in the southern Appalachians in the Civil War period. How important did you find language when reading the novel? To what extent did it add to your enjoyment? How might the response of an American reader differ from that of a British reader?

✪ Slavery was a central issue of the American Civil War. Do you think that this is evident in *Cold Mountain*? What do you think the book says about slavery?

🖥 Resources

www.salon.com/july97/colddiary970709.html – essay by Charles Frazier on what prompted him to write *Cold Mountain* published at *Salon* internet magazine

www.bookbrowse.com/author_interviews/full/index.cfm?author_number=239 – interview published at bookbrowse.com

http://en.wikipedia.org/wiki/American_civil_war – entry on the American Civil War in Wikipedia online encyclopedia

🍃 Suggested further reading

March by Geraldine Brooks (2006); *The Red Badge of Courage* by Stephen Crane (1895); *Birdsong* **by Sebastian Faulks** (1983); *On the Occasion of My Last Afternoon* by Kaye Gibbons (1998); *That Summer* by Andrew Greig (2000); *Oldest Living Confederate Widow Tells All* by Alan Gurganus (1990); *The Widow of the South* by Robert Hicks (2005); *The Odyssey* by Homer; *Enemy Wome*n by Paulette Jiles (2002); *Gone with the Wind* by Margaret Mitchell (1936); *All True Travels and Adventures of Lidie Newton* by Jane Smiley (1998)

OTHER BOOKS BY CHARLES FRAZIER

Thirteen Moons (2006)

SHEER BLUE BLISS (1999)

Lesley Glaister

📖 About the book

Connie Benson is plucked from the isolation of her Norfolk home when a retrospective exhibition of her work is mounted at the National Portrait Gallery in London. The centrepiece of the exhibition is the final portrait of her lover, Patrick Mount, who mysteriously disappeared in 1965. Mount was an eccentric whose theory of the Seven Steps to Bliss has sunk into obscurity. But for Tony, a disturbed and beautiful young man who stalks Connie in the hope of finding the key to the elixir of bliss, Mount is still a heroic figure. Tony is haunted by his obsession, desperately trying to suppress his dark and fearful childhood memories, which are in stark contrast to the startlingly vivid memories which Connie summons of her own youth. Their narratives are interwoven as each draws inexorably towards the other until the two merge in a gripping dénouement.

Background

Lesley Glaister alternates the voices of a deeply disturbed young man and an elderly woman trying to cope with the disruption and excitement of having her work exhibited at the National Portrait Gallery. Tony's obsessive nature becomes apparent in a narrative suffused with unease and menace. Connie's memories of her youth, in poignant contrast to the pain and sheer hard work of old age, are threaded through the narrative of her trip to London. The two strands are drawn together, and the pace of the novel quickens, as it moves towards its taut climax.

Although perhaps more benign, in many ways Connie epitomizes Glaister's female characters: an elderly somewhat eccentric woman, with a stock of memories to draw upon, some joyous, some deeply damaging, dealing with a difficult old age and living on the edge of society. Her novels are characterized by their claustrophobic, edgy atmospheres in which her characters are bedevilled with obsessions, some, such as Trixie Bell in *The Private Parts of Women* teetering on the edge of psychosis disguised as eccentricity for the public eye. There are dark secrets lurking below the surface waiting to be chiselled out. A taut thread of tension runs through all her novels, tightening to a thin wire as they move inexorably towards denouements that never fail to deliver a sting, yet she neatly side-steps the clichéd territory of the airport thriller as she probes the strangeness that so often bubbles away beneath the apparently smooth surface of everyday life. All this leavened with a dark humour which occasionally verges on farce

Glaister's fiction has earned her a great deal of respect from her fellow writers. Ruth Rendell, with whom she has been compared by several critics, has described Glaister as writing with 'mastery' and a 'gift for character delineation', while Hilary Mantel, an early champion of Glaister's writing, has described her work as 'witty, macabre and beautifully constructed' (a description equally appropriate for Mantel's own writing). So impressed was Mantel by Glaister's work that when Glaister attended a course at the Arvon foundation in 1989, Mantel recommended her to a literary agent thus kick-starting the career of one of our most original literary authors.

About the author

Lesley Glaister was born in Wellingborough in 1956 and grew up in Suffolk. She is a graduate of both the Open University and of Sheffield University. She has also tutored at the Arvon Foundation and teaches creative writing at Sheffield Hallam University. She is an occasional book reviewer and has contributed to the *Spectator* and *The Times*. In 1991 her novel *Honour Thy Father* won a Somerset Maugham and a Betty Trask award. In 2003 she staged a play, *Bird Calls*, which was commissioned by the Crucible Theatre in Sheffield. Lesley Glaister lives in Sheffield and Orkney with her husband, the writer Andrew Greig, and her three sons.

For discussion

✪ An atmosphere of unease pervades *Sheer Blue Bliss* almost from the beginning. How does Lesley Glaister achieve this?

✪ How would you describe Tony? How does Glaister convey Tony's character? Why is he so disturbed? Why do women upset him so much? The only woman with whom he seems remotely comfortable is Donna. Why is this?

✪ Connie's memories of her youth are very vivid. How do you think she feels about getting older? Are her feelings about ageing different in London and, if so, why? What do other people's attitudes to Connie say about the way we see older people in contemporary society?

✪ What does the way Connie is treated in London say about the modern perception of celebrity? How does Connie feel about it?

✪ A year after the deaths of her family, Connie reflects: 'There are those who have suffered and those who haven't and that is the biggest difference between people.' How is this idea reflected in the rest of the novel? What do you think of it?

✪ How does the loss of her family shape Connie's life? How do Sacha and Patrick help her through her grief? To what extent does Sacha become a mother figure for Connie?

✪ What do you think about Patrick's 'phytosophical principle' and the Seven Steps to Bliss? Would Mount's memoir seem out of place in a bookshop today? Why do you think Tony is so attracted to Patrick's ideas?

✪ How big is the difference between Tony's view of Patrick and Connie's view of him? Red describes Patrick as a bully but Connie disagrees. What do you think?

✪ What do you think of Patrick's attitude towards sex? Would you describe Connie's sexual relationship with Patrick as a betrayal of Sacha? Do Patrick and Sacha truly have an 'open marriage'? How does Patrick feel about Connie having other lovers? What do you think of this?

🖥 Resources

www.newstatesman.com/199902050044 – review by Francis Gilbert in *The New Statesman*

www.contemporarywriters.com/authors/?p=auth183 – profile of Lesley Glaister at the British Council website including a critical essay by Dr Jules Smith

www.bloomsbury.com/Ezine/Articles/Articles.asp?ezine_article_id=619 – lengthy profile of Lesley Glaister's work by Simon James, published at her publisher's, Bloomsbury, website

📚 Suggested further reading

The Blind Assassin by Margaret Atwood (2000); *The Chymical Wedding* by Lindsay Clarke (1989); *Nothing Natural* by Jenny Diski (1983); *Burning Bright* by Helen Dunmore (1994); *Enduring Love* by Ian McEwan (1997); *The Artist's Widow* by Shena Mackay (1998)

OTHER BOOKS BY LESLEY GLAISTER

Honour Thy Father (1990); *Trick or Treat* (1991); *Digging to Australia* (1992); *Limestone and Clay* (1993); *Partial Eclipse* (1994); *The Private Parts of Women* (1996); *Easy Peasy* (1997); *Now You See Me* (2001); *As Far as You Can Go* (2004); *Nina Todd Has Gone* (2007)

Edited: Short story anthology *Are You She?* (2004)

BY THE SEA (2002)

Abdulrazak Gurnah

📖 About the book

Saleh Omar is an elderly asylum seeker from the east coast of Africa. Told not to reveal his ability to speak English by the man who sold him his ticket, Saleh finds himself, after weeks of maintaining his silence, finally blurting out a sentence to his kindly refugee worker when she tells him she has found an interpreter. But when he learns the proposed interpreter is Latif Mahmud, Saleh realises that they are already bound together by an intricate web of events which brought about the downfall of Latif's family and the imprisonment of Saleh. When Latif visits Saleh, each tells his story, both of which have been swathed in rumour and speculation in their homeland and each crucially different from what the other had believed. Written in delicately wrought evocative prose, *By the Sea* unravels the complexities of each man's past offering hope of redemption.

Background

Abdulrazak Gurnah's page at the University of Kent's website describes his academic interest as 'colonial and postcolonial discourses', and it is with colonialism, postcolonialism and the immigrant experience that much of his own fiction is concerned. His first three novels, *Memory of Departure*, *Pilgrims Way* and *Dottie*, all explore what it means to be an immigrant in contemporary Britain while *Admiring Silence* tells of a young man who leaves Zanzibar for England where he builds a life but finds himself shaken by a visit home twenty years later. *Paradise* is set in colonial East Africa during the First World War and *Desertion* is set against a backdrop of imperialism and the struggle for independence. Narrated by an asylum seeker and an immigrant, with flashbacks to a country struggling with the legacy of imperialism *By the Sea* continues Gurnah's exploration of these twin themes.

To some extent Gurnah's fiction can be said to reflect his own experience. Once the centre of the spice and slave trades Zanzibar, Gurnah's homeland and the homeland of both Saleh and Latif in *By the Sea*, had been influenced by many different cultures although it was the Arab traders who were to become paramount bringing Islam with them. After the abolition of the slave trade Zanzibar became a British protectorate, gaining its independence in December 1963 only to have its government overthrown in a violent coup one month later in January 1964. Gurnah left Zanzibar to study in the UK in 1968 but did not receive the welcome that an intelligent young man taught to look to Europe for a bright future might have expected. Instead, arriving on the eve of Enoch Powell's infamous speech on immigration Gurnah was shocked 'to discover the loathing in which I was held: by looks, sneers, words and gestures, news reports, comics, on TV, teachers, fellow students. Everybody did their bit and thought themselves tolerant, or perhaps mildly grumbling, or even amusing. At the receiving end, it seemed constant and mean. If there had been anywhere to go to, I would have gone. But I had broken the law in my own country and there was no going back.'

Although he has said that he was not an asylum seeker or refugee himself he has written passionately about the plight of those who flee persecution and torture hoping to find safety in this country. Gurnah has lived in Britain for several decades but still feels a deep attachment to Zanzibar saying to one interviewer 'I think about it every day, several times a day. Places don't live just where they are, they live within you.'

About the author

Abdulrazak Gurnah was born in 1948 on the island of Zanzibar off the East Coast of Africa. He came to England as a student in 1968 and now teaches at the University of Kent where he is Professor of English and Postcolonial Literatures. His fourth novel *Paradise* was shortlisted for both the 1994 Booker and Whitbread prizes. *By the Sea* was longlisted for the Booker Prize and shortlisted for the *Los Angeles Times* Book Award. Desertion was shortlisted for a Commonwealth Writers Prize.

For discussion

✪ 'I know about the hardships of being alien and poor, because that is what they went through when they came here, and I know the rewards. But my parents are European, they have a right, they're part of the family.' What do your think of Kevin Edelman's view of Saleh's right to come to Britain? Saleh is a refugee, an asylum seeker. Did reading the novel change your opinions of asylum seekers and if so, how?

✪ What does Saleh's story of the ud-al-qamari tell us about the British Empire and its relationship with Zanzibar? What does it tell us about Saleh? What kind of man is he? What does he think of the British?

✪ 'Part of his story I knew very well, only too well, but that was when he was a son, and a youth and called a different name. The story of the rest of his life, his real life, I knew only by rumour.' What part does rumour play in both Saleh and Latif's story? How important is storytelling in *By the Sea*?

✪ 'Someone called me a grinning blackamoor on the street, speaking out of a different time' How important is race in the novel? Why does Latif later call Saleh a 'grinning blackamoor'?

✪ Who is most to blame for Rajab Shaaban Mahmud's ruin – Saleh, Hussein or Rajab himself? Did your opinion change as you read the book and if so how?

✪ 'I had decided on the plane. I would not use the name I had been given, but would be Latif, for its gentleness and the softness of its modulations.' Why does Latif decide to shed his old identity? To what extent does he succeed?

✪ '"I took your father's name to save my life," I said "There was a certain sweet irony in that, after your father had so very nearly succeeded in destroying it."' What does Saleh mean by this?

✪ How would you describe the relationship between Saleh and Latif when it begins? How does that relationship change, and how is each changed by it?

✪ 'There were witnesses, and I am not sure who is worse in such moments, the criminal or the innocents who stand by and watch and act as if nothing is taking place' Saleh muses as he remembers his beatings. What do you think?

✪ The novel is narrated by both Saleh and Latif. How does the tone of the narrative change as it shifts between the two? How does Gurnah convey the two narrator's characters?

📖 Resources

http://books.guardian.co.uk/reviews/generalfiction/0,6121,495855,00.html – review by the writer Maya Jaggi published in *The Guardian*

www.nytimes.com/books/01/06/10/reviews/010610.10pyelt.html – review by the writer Michael Pye published in *The New York Times*

www.guardian.co.uk/immigration/story/0,,1421456,00.html – piece by Gurnah on the experience of refugees published in *The Guardian*

http://news.bbc.co.uk/1/hi/world/africa/country_profiles/3850393.stm – page on Zanzibar at the BBC website

📚 Suggested further reading

Welcome to Paradise by Mahi Binebine (translated by Lulu Norman) (1999); *The Kite Runner* by Khaled Hosseini (2003); *Embers* by Sandor Marai (translated by Carol Brown Janeway) (2002); *In the Country of Men* by Hisham Matar (2006)

OTHER BOOKS BY ABDULRAZAK GURNAH

Memory of Departure (1987); *Pilgrims Way* (1988); *Dottie* (1990); *Paradise* (1994); *Admiring Silence* (1996); *Desertion* (2005)

OUR LADY OF THE FOREST (2003)

David Guterson

📖 About the book

Sexually abused, homeless, an outcast given to bouts of drug abuse, sixteen-year-old Ann Holmes hardly seems a candidate for divine revelation but when gathering chanterelles in the woods Ann has a vision of the Virgin who proclaims to her that she will appear on four successive days. Ann confides in the sceptical Carolyn who takes her under her wing, spotting an opportunity to find a way out of her hand-to-mouth life. Word gets around and the rundown mill town of North Fork finds itself the focus of thousands of pilgrims and camp followers. Some of the townspeople are more troubled than others, not least the young priest Father Collins who becomes involved in the ecclesiastical investigation, and Tom Cross, the angry self-loathing father of a young paralysed man, struggling with his own kind of piety and guilt. David Guterson's thoughtful, intelligent novel explores the terrain of religious faith, doubt, credulity and the possibility of redemption.

Background

In his acceptance speech for the prestigious PEN/Faulkner award David Guterson acknowledged a debt owed to Harper Lee for paving the way to success for *Snow Falling on Cedars* with her novel *To Kill a Mockingbird*. Guterson is unafraid of tackling serious issues. While his first novel dealt with the racist treatment of a Japanese family in a small Northwestern community during the aftermath of the Second World War, his second, *East of the Mountains*, explored the dilemma of a retired heart surgeon faced with the prospect of a prolonged and painful death from cancer, or with taking his own life.

Our Lady of the Forest, a book that he hopes will prompt readers to ask themselves questions about spirituality, begins with a young girl's vision of the Virgin and offers many views of religion, spirituality, scepticism and credulity through a wide variety of characters. Guterson had long been interested in the cult of the Virgin Mary which he felt seemed to fulfil a need for a feminine element to the idea of the divine. Born to Jewish parents and brought up in 'an atmosphere of secular humanism' Guterson describes himself as an agnostic whose 'spiritual and religious journey is a permanent one'.

Part of Guterson's spirituality seems to be a reverence for nature which pervades this novel and is an ever-present element in his writing. Ann's experience is firmly rooted in the beautiful forests surrounding North Fork. But the forests do not escape controversy; the logging company's avaricious attitude towards the forest clashes with the environmentalists' determination to conserve it without thought to the loggers' need to make a living. Such tensions reflect those of the Pacific Northwest in which Guterson has lived for many years just as his lyrical descriptions of the forest reflect his abiding love of the natural beauty of the area.

About the author

David Guterson was born in Seattle in 1956, the son of a distinguished criminal lawyer. After receiving his MA in literature from the University of Washington, he taught English at high school and began writing journalism for *Sports Illustrated* and *Harper's* magazine for which he is now a contributing editor. His highly acclaimed bestselling first novel, *Snow Falling on Cedars*, won the PEN/Faulkner award in 1995 and was made into a film starring Ethan Hawke and Sam Shephard. David Guterson now writes full-time and has lived for many years on Bainbridge Island in Puget Sound.

For discussion

✪ 'Ann in ecstasy, Carolyn thought, was something like a theatrical performance that even Ann believed in.' How convincing did you find Ann's claims of divine visitation? Tom Cross, Carolyn, Father Collins and Father Butler all have very different reactions to Ann's claims. With which did you identify? Did the final chapter confirm what you had thought about Ann throughout the book?

✪ What kind of person is Ann? What qualities within her convince her o er vision and made her determined to carry out the Virgin's wishes? How might her experience have predisposed her towards the idea of a religious vision, and in particular a vision of the Virgin?

✪ How would you describe the community of North Fork at the beginning of the novel? What are the various tensions running through the town? How do its inhabitants react to Ann's claims and the pilgrims she attracts? In what ways has the town changed by the end of the book?

✪ '... it all felt to Tom like a witches' coven or a sylvan gathering of warlocks. It all felt dangerously supernatural and disconnected from God'. Tom Cross is an important character in the novel. How would you describe him? How would you describe his attitude to religion? How does it compare with those of other characters? What is his reaction to Ann's claims? In what ways has he changed by the end of the book and what has brought about those changes?

✪ What kind of priest is Father Collins? How do his views compare with those of

Father Butler's? Whose side of their various debates did you find yourself taking and why?

✪ Ann's visions attract thousands of people to North Fork. What makes so many people travel to the town? What needs does their belief in Ann's vision fulfil within them? How different is the faith of Father Collins to that of the pilgrims and camp followers?

✪ What is Carolyn's role in Ann's visionary experience? In what ways is she changed by it? What do you make of her discussion with Father Collins in the final chapter?

✪ 'The girl was pornographic in ecstasy, a male projection of female religious passion, as if God had entered her'. Sexuality and religion are often linked in the novel: Ann frequently masturbates, including two instances before her first vision; Father Collins is troubled by his desires. Why do you think Guterson chose to make such a strong link? What was your reaction to it?

✪ 'Was there any difference, he asked himself, between legitimately, actually seeing the Virgin and believing to have seen the Virgin?' What conclusions, if any, does Father Collins draw? What would your answer be?

✪ How important is humour in the book and how would you describe that humour? Why do you think Guterson uses it?

✪ Descriptions of landscape in the novel are both vivid and detailed. To what extent does Guterson tie Ann's experience to the landscape? How important is the book's setting?

🖥 Resources

http://books.guardian.co.uk/reviews/generalfiction/0,6121,1075058,00.html – review by Stephen Amidon in *The Guardian*

http://seattlepi.nwsource.com/books/141494_guterson27.html – interview with David Guterson in the *Seattle Post-Intellingencer*

http://www.bookreporter.com/authors/au-guterson-david.asp – interview with David Guterson at bookreporter.com

http://members.aol.com/UticaCW/Mar-link.html – AOL's Marian Apparitions and Catholic Apocalypticism Links page

http://www.gonorthwest.com/Visitor/webs/wildlife.htm – Pacific Northwest nature links page

🥢 Suggested further reading

FICTION

Monsignor Quixote by Graham Greene (1986); *Mariette in Ecstasy* by Ron Hansen

(1991); *The Vintner's Luck* **by Elizabeth Knox** (1998); *Mr Wroe's Virgins* by Jane Rogers (1981); *Empire Falls* by Richard Russo (2002); *Lying Awake* by Mark Salzman (2001)

NON-FICTION

Ann the Word by Richard Francis (2000); *The Devils of Loudon* by Aldous Huxley (1953)

OTHER BOOKS BY DAVID GUTERSON

Novels: *Snow Falling on Cedars* (1994); *East of the Mountains* (1999)

Short stories: *The Country Ahead of Us, the Country Behind* (1989)

DISOBEDIENCE (2000)

Jane Hamilton

About the book

When seventeen-year-old Henry Shaw stumbles upon an email correspondence that reveals his mother's passionate affair, all the certainties of his life are thrown into question. Unable to resist his electronic eavesdropping, Henry's emotional confusion spills over into his own first love affair and continues to haunt the adult Henry as he looks back, a decade later, over the year of his mother's infidelity. Meanwhile, Elvira, Henry's sister, strides around wearing the regimental uniform of a nineteenth-century drummer boy, obsessed with re-enacting Civil War battles – much to her mother's horror and her father's delight. Elvira's ambitions to take part in a re-enactment at the historic site of Shiloh are shattered when she is violently unmasked and her gender revealed. It is this traumatic event that pulls the family back together as both parents, each in their own way, come to the defence of their beleaguered daughter.

Background

Coming as she does from a background where women were determined to write, it must have seemed natural for writing of some kind to form an important part of Jane Hamilton's life. Her mother was both a poet and a journalist and so determined was her grandmother to write that, according to Hamilton, she 'got herself into a retirement home when she was fifty-eight. She was in perfect health but wanted to write books, not mess around with housework.' Although she could not find an opening on a writing course after graduating from college in 1979, Hamilton was undeterred. She began with short stories and in 1982, *Harper's Magazine* accepted a piece for publication. She became a regular contributor to *Harper's* which no doubt eased the way to finding an agent for her first novel, *The Book of Ruth* published in 1989.

It is Hamilton's empathy, compassion and understanding of the bleakness that can sometimes descend on modern family life that have drawn comparisons with writers such as Jane Smiley, Annie Proulx and Carol Shields. When reviewing Hamilton's third novel *A Short History of a Prince* for *The Times*, the novelist and critic Amanda Craig described her as 'one of the most profound writers we have'. When asked about the qualities she looks for in other authors she has said 'a writer's wisdom, his invention, his grace, his penetrating gaze, his fluid sentences, his sense of humour' – qualities that she herself has in abundance.

With their themes of tangled family relationships, small domestic tragedies and the darker side of family life, Jane Hamilton's work made her an obvious choice for the Oprah Winfrey book club. Indeed she was one of the few writers to have two novels chosen by Oprah: both *The Book of Ruth* and her second novel, *A Map of the World*, appeared on Oprah's list.

About the author

Jane Hamilton was born in 1957 in Oak Park, Illionis. She grew up in Illinois and studied English Literature at Carleton College, Minnesota and at Edinburgh University. In 1989 her first book, *The Book of Ruth*, was awarded the PEN/Hemingway Foundation Award for best first novel. Both her first novel and her second, *A Map of the World*, were selected for Oprah Winfrey's book club while her third, *The Short History of a Prince*, was shortlisted for the 1999 Orange Prize. She lives and works in her orchard farmhouse in Rochester, Wisconsin.

For discussion

✪ What is the significance of the title of the book? Which of the characters have been disobedient and what form has that disobedience taken? What do you think of Hamilton's choice of the word 'disobedience'?

✪ How has the young Henry's electronic eavesdropping shaped the adult Henry? For instance, how do you think it contributes to the kind of relationships he has with women, which we learn about from hints and asides in his narrative? Do you think his knowledge of the affair or the way that he gained that knowledge was more damaging? Do you think his behaviour was excusable?

✪ What kind of parents are Beth and Kevin Shaw? Their main point of conflict appears to be Elvira's passion for Civil War re-enactment. Why does Kevin think it is acceptable whereas Beth, despite her apparent unconventionality, does not? What does their disagreement and the different way that they handle the situation tell us about their characters?

✪ Henry is looking back over the year of the affair nearly ten years later. Why do you think Hamilton chose to have him do this rather than reporting the events as they happen? What difference does it make to your interpretation of events?

✪ Henry says: 'As a child I had no idea that the Shaws, the four of us, were removed from our century.' Elvira's removal is obvious but how are the others 'removed from our century'?

✪ Henry refers on several occasions to the 'ironic sensibility' of his generation. How does this manifest itself in his narrative? Do you think the use of irony adds to, or detracts from, the telling of the Shaws' story?

✪ Do you think that Henry would have behaved differently if he had been a girl and, if so, in what way?

✪ Henry refers to the Oedipal myth when he says: 'I was married to my mother, without having had to murder my father or pluck out my eyeballs.' Are there traces of Oedipus in Henry and, if so, how does this come out in his narrative?

✪ When his mother takes him and Elvira to meet Richard, Henry feels that he has had an epiphany, that he understands that his mother is having an affair because she is facing a 'blank' future when he leaves home. Do you think that this is what lies behind the affair or do you agree with Karen's assessment that this is the last sexual fling of a soon-to-be menopausal woman? What other reasons might there be for the affair?

✪ When the parents finally quarrel about Elvira shaving her head, Beth says that the boys who counted Elvira as one of them will 'feel hurt and ashamed and silly and embarrassed and betrayed' when they find she is a girl. Kevin replies that it will be 'a good training for what future women will do to them'. Does this prove to be the case? To what extent does this idea resonate through the rest of the novel? How significant is gender in the novel?

✪ What did you think of the book club scenes?

💻 Resources

www.salon.com/books/int/2000/10/16/hamilton – interview by the writer David Bowman at *Salon* internet magazine

www.onmilwaukee.com/buzz/articles/janehamilton.html – interview by Bobby Tanzilo at the On Milwaukee website

www.cwreenactors.com – the Civil War Reenactors website

📔 Suggested further reading

The Crow Road **by Iain Banks** (1992); *A Crime in the Neighbourhood* by Suzanne Berne (1997); *Crooked Hearts* by Robert Boswell (1987); ***Cold Mountain* by Charles Frazier** (1997); *Exposure* by Kathryn Harrison (1994); *The Ice Storm* by Rick Moody (1994); *A Thousand Acres* by Jane Smiley (1991); *Anna Karenina* by Leo Tolstoy (1874–6)

OTHER BOOKS BY JANE HAMILTON

The Book of Ruth (1989); *A Map of the World* (1994); *A Short History of a Prince* (1998); *When Madeline was Young* (2007)

THE SEAL WIFE (2002)
Kathryn Harrison

📖 About the book

In 1915 a twenty-six-year-old meteorologist finds himself posted to the new settlement of Anchorage, Alaska. One day while picking up supplies, he spies an Aleut woman: self-possessed, silent and intriguing. Bigelow follows her to her house and is soon in the grips of an obsession in which mere physical gratification cannot satisfy his desperate urge to possess this strange, unyielding woman. When she leaves the town, Bigelow is desolate, his only consolation is the building of a kite large enough to track the storms that bedevil the north. Neither a gambler nor a drinker, Bigelow is an outsider in this masculine town. Trying to fill the emotional chasm left by the Aleut woman, he finds himself first robbed by a female pickpocket then tricked by the local storeowner and his daughter. When the Aleut woman reappears, a small hope springs in Bigelow and eventually a hard-won but still silent agreement is reached. Written in spare yet vivid prose, Kathryn Harrison's novel explores the nature of erotic obsession and its near-hypnotic power.

Background

Kathryn Harrison is an author unflinching in her honesty. Born to eighteen-year-old parents she was brought up by her maternal grandmother after her mother suffered what her family referred to as a 'nervous collapse'. Her father was persuaded by his deeply unhappy young wife's parents to leave her and their child for whom her grandparents would take all responsibility. Harrison didn't see her father again until her twentieth birthday. Vulnerable and lonely, she found herself embroiled in a sexual relationship with him which was to last four years and which later became the subject of her searingly honest memoir *The Kiss*, perhaps the book for which she is best known. Several of her novels have explored the nature of sexual obsession. Both her first and second novels (*Thicker than Water* and *Exposure*) coupled this study in obsession with an exploration of the psychological frailty of damaged young women. Like *The Seal Wife*, her third and fourth novels are both set against a vividly realised historical background: *A Thousand Orange Trees* is set in seventeenth century Spain in thrall to the Inquisition, and *The Binding Chair* follows the fortunes of May born in turn-of-the-century Shanghai. *The Seal Wife* is the first of Harrison's novels in which a male protagonist takes centre stage but two of the themes she addresses through Bigelow run through all her novels: the balance of power between men and women and the way in which love is so often accompanied by suffering. Harrison's wonderfully spare, graceful prose conjures a bleak but often beautiful landscape in which the weather is all-powerful echoing the power which the Aleut woman exerts over Bigelow. Just as they succeed in finding a way to measure the tumultuous elements by rebuilding the kite together so Bigelow and the woman seem to have reached a mutual accommodation at the close of the novel.

About the author
Kathryn Harrison was born in Los Angeles, California in 1961. She is a graduate of both Stanford University and the Iowa Writers' Workshop. She lives in New York with her husband, the novelist Colin Harrison, and their children.

For discussion
❍ 'He's getting what he hoped, he tells himself, but it isn't at all what he expected, and a desolation seizes him. He's not joined to her, he can't reach her.' What is it about the Aleut woman that Bigelow so desires but can't have? Why does she withhold herself from him, or is this simply Bigelow's interpretation of her behaviour? How would you describe her?

❍ 'The woman nods, a brisk gesture, eyebrows raised as if to say she's not so ignorant – so savage – that she doesn't recognise mosquito netting.' To what extent does Bigelow, a white educated scientist, assume he knows what's best?

❍ Anchorage is a settlement of 'nearly three thousand men … 486 females'. How does that ratio shape the character of the town, and in particular relationships between men and women?

❍ Bigelow finds himself in a state of disorientated and painful limbo in Anchorage. What has contributed to that state of mind?

○ Violet submits to being gagged at a price, Miriam is so handicapped by her stutter that she cannot speak and the Aleut woman never speaks, yet Bigelow talks more to her than he has ever done with anyone else. What is the significance of speech in the novel?

○ 'Is there anything to be understood from the pictures she selects?' What do you think? Why does the Aleut woman reject Bigelow's presents yet appear to covet the images in a magazine?

○ What did you make of the end of the novel?

○ What is the significance of the title, *The Seal Wife*?

○ How would you describe Kathryn Harrison's use of language in the novel? Are there particular passages that struck you?

○ Although written in the third person *The Seal Wife* is a tale of erotic obsession written by a woman from a male point-of-view. How well did Harrison capture that point-of-view?

💻 Resources

http://query.nytimes.com/gst/fullpage.html?res=9C07EEDC153EF936A35756C0A9 649C8B63 – review by Maria Russo published in *The New York Times*
http://query.nytimes.com/gst/fullpage.html?res=9C0CE7D81F3EF933A05757C0A9 649C8B63 – review by Michiko Kakutani published in *The New York Times*
http://query.nytimes.com/gst/fullpage.html?res=9C0CE7D81F3EF933A05757C0A9 649C8B63 – Kathryn Harrison's website

🌿 Suggested further reading

Servants of the Map by Andrea Barrett (2002); *The French Lieutenant's Woman* by John Fowles (1969); *Enduring Love* by Ian McEwan (1998); *The Last Time I Saw Jane* by Kate Pullinger (1996); ***Promised Lands* by Jane Rogers** (1995)
OTHER BOOKS BY KATHRYN HARRISON
Fiction: *Thicker Than Water* (1991); *Exposure* (1993); *A Thousand Orange Trees* (1995); *The Binding Chair* (2000); *Envy* (2005)
Non-fiction: *The Kiss* (1997); *Seeking Rapture* (2003); *Saint Therese of Lisieux: A Short Life* (2003); *The Road to Santiago* (2003); *The Mother Knot* (2004)

STONES FROM THE RIVER (1994)
Ursula Hegi

📖 About the book

Trudi Montag is a *zwerg*, a dwarf, living in the small German town of Burgdorf and struggling to bridge the gulf between the way she sees herself and the way others see her. Burgdorf is engaged in its own struggle as it tries to deal with the crushing defeat of the First World War and ever-worsening economic conditions. As Trudi becomes an adult, a target for the insecurities and prejudices of those around her, she empathizes with the humiliations inflicted upon her Jewish neighbours when the newly established Nazi regime begins to flex its muscles. At great risk to themselves, Trudi and her father provide a hiding place for Jews, friends and strangers alike. When the war is finally over, the people of Burgdorf are faced with the shame and guilt, not only of a second defeat, but also of the atrocities of the Holocaust and the implications of their own part in it.

Background

Spanning the years from 1915 to 1952, *Stones From the River* is a complex and searching portrait of a small German town seen through the unflinching gaze of Trudi Montag. As it struggles to deal with the blow to its pride inflicted by the humiliating defeat of the First World War, Burgdorf represents a microcosm of Germany, ripe for the rise of a political party fired by nationalistic fervour. In its examination of the effects of the Nazi regime on a small German community, the novel is a humane and profound attempt to understand how such a thing could happen and why silence descended when it ceased.

Ursula Hegi spent the first eighteen years of her life in Germany, before emigrating to the United States. She was born in 1946, one year after the war ended, and grew up in a small village near Dusseldorf. She has said that when she arrived in America she 'realized the Americans of my generation knew a lot more about the war than I did.' The history of the war years was not taught in German schools when Hegi was a child. An impenetrable silence surrounded the war and the horrors of the death camps. Through her writing, both fiction and non-fiction, Hegi has explored that silence in an effort to understand her parents' generation and their inability to confront what had been perpetrated by their country. In her book *Tearing the Silence* she interviewed fifteen fellow immigrants, born in Germany during the war years, discovering a legacy of shame and guilt made worse by the taboo imposed by their parents. When researching *Stones From the River*, Hegi bravely summoned the courage to ask her grandmother what her own father had done in the war: she was told that he had fought on the Russian front.

Stones From the River can be seen as a 'prequel' to Hegi's second novel *Floating in My Mother's Palm*, which was set in 1950s Burgdorf. Two characters from the fringes of *Stones from the River*, Stefan Blau and Helene Montag, reappear in her fifth novel, *The Vision of Emma Blau*.

About the author

Ursula Hegi was born in Germany and moved to the United States in 1965. She has been a regular reviewer for *The New York Times*, *The Los Angeles Times* and *The Washington Post*. She has also taught both creative writing and contemporary literature at Eastern Washington University. *Stones From the River* was chosen for Oprah Winfrey's Book Club in 1997.

For discussion

❍ Why do you think Hegi makes her principal character a *zwerg* or dwarf? How do other characters respond to her 'otherness'? How does she cope with the cruelty of other children and how does it change her? Would this still happen today?

❍ When Trudi was fourteen years old she was dragged into a barn and assaulted by four young boys, one of whom was her first real friend. How does Hegi use this incident to develop Trudi's character, both immediately after the attack and throughout the rest of the book? Does she ever come to terms with it and, if so, how?

❍ Trudi collects stories about the people of Burgdorf, storing them up for future use. Why does she do this? How does the way she uses those stories change over the years? How does this illustrate the changes in Trudi's character?

❍ How do the Jewish members of the community fit in before the war? At what point does this begin to change? Were there signs of prejudice before the war and if so what were they?

❍ Frau Blau and Trudi discuss the possibility that Herr Immer's grandmother may have been Jewish. Trudi thinks: 'Until now, she'd never thought of the butcher as afraid. She'd only seen his loathing for the Jews, his malice, but now she wondered if all of that was just fear and, perhaps, contempt for himself.' To what extent do you think this idea can explain prejudice? What other reasons might people have for hating those who can be described as 'other'?

❍ How do Hegi's characters react as Nazism begins to take hold? Are particular characters more receptive than others? If so, who are they and why? Conversely, are there characters whose resistance surprises you?

⭘ Trudi and her father show enormous courage in helping Jews during the war. How does this change Trudi? How does it change the way people respond to her?

⭘ When Herr Pastor Beier and Sister Agathe are discussing her feelings of guilt, after the war, he says: 'Don't say that. That would make us all accomplices.' She replies: 'But we are. Don't you see?' What does she mean by this, and to what extent do you agree with her?

⭘ Given Hegi's German background, why do you think she decided to write Stones From the River? How difficult do you think it is for post-war generations in Germany to deal with the emotional aftermath of the Second World War? How do the people of Burgdorf cope with it? What changes happen in the community? Why won't Trudi let things rest? What is the community's attitude towards the Jews and their experiences in the camps?

⭘ Has the book helped you to understand how such an atrocity as the Holocaust could take place? If so, how has it done that?

🖥 Resources

http://seattlepi.nwsource.com/books/44152_book26.shtml – interview by Andrew Engelson published in the *Seattle Post-Intellingcer*

www.barnesandnoble.com/writers/writerdetails.asp?cid=883353 – interview at barnesandnoble.com which includes a short essay by Ursula Hegi

📚 Suggested further reading

FICTION

Beautiful Dreamer by Christopher Bigsby (2002); *My Father's Country* by Wibke Bruhns (translated by Shaun Whiteside) (2007); *The Archivist* by Martha Cooley (1998); *Middlemarch* by George Eliot (1872); *Everything is Illuminated* by Jonathan Safran Foer (2002); *The Tin Drum* by Günter Grass (1959); *A Prayer for Owen Meany* by John Irving (1989); *Schindler's Ark* by Thomas Keneally (1982); *The Time of Light* by Gunnar Kopperud (1998); *The Twins* by Tessa de Loo (1993); *Fugitive Pieces* **by Anne Michaels** (1997); *The Reader* **by Bernhard Schlink** (1997); *The Dark Room* by Rachel Seiffert (2001); *Sophie's Choice* by William Styron (1979); *A Model Childhood* by Christa Wolf (1976)

NON-FICTION

The Past is Myself by Christabel Bielenberg (1970); *Anne Frank: The Diary of a Young Girl* by Anne Frank (1947); *The Drowned and the Saved* by Primo Levi (1986)

OTHER BOOKS BY URSULA HEGI

Novels: *Intrusions* (1981); *Floating in My Mother's Palm* (1991); *Salt Dancers*

(1995); *The Vision of Emma Blau* (2000); *Sacred Time* (2004); *The Worst Thing I've Done* (2007)

Short stories: *Unearned Pleasures and Other Stories* (1998); *Hotel of the Saints* (2002)

Non-fiction: *Tearing the Silence: On Being German in America* (1997)

EMPRESS OF THE SPLENDID SEASON (1999)

Oscar Hijuelos

📖 About the book

Lydia is a Cuban cleaning lady living in New York with her family, just about getting by. Anyone who passes her on the street might think of her, if they notice her at all, as just another dowdy drudge. But Lydia has a very different view of herself. After a terrible quarrel with her father when she was sixteen, she left the trappings of a well-to-do family in Cuba but has never relinquished her sense of superiority. Married to Raul, a waiter struck down by a heart attack at the age of forty-one, Lydia has had to go back to work. From her ambitions for her children, her cherished memories of her youthful beauty and vibrant sexuality, to her tentative feelings of friendship for one of her kindly employers, and the uncovering of the secrets of others, Oscar Hijuelos tells Lydia's story through a series of closely linked vignettes.

Background

Although his writing has been compared with that of Gabriel Garcia Marqez, Hijuelos would like to feel that it is more akin to two of his favourite writers, the poet William Butler Yeats and Flann O'Brien, to whom he paid tribute in naming the characters of his third novel, *The Fourteen Sisters of Emilio Montez O'Brien*. In interviews he has said that he would prefer his writing not to be seen simply in terms of his ancestry: 'I consider myself a New York writer of Cuban parentage, with different influences ... My background is an important element, the most important, but not the only one.' However, each of Hijuelos's novels draws extensively on his Cuban roots. Memory and the celebration of Cuban music are particularly important elements in his fiction, both of which seem inextricably bound into his heritage. Of memory Hijuelos has said: 'Latins are predisposed to thinking about the past...' '... Catholicism has a lot to do with it because Catholicism is a con-templation of the past, of symbols that are supposed to be eternally present.'

It is a poignant strand which runs through Lydia's life in *Empress of the Splendid Season*. The novel is a tender portrayal of the life of a Cuban immigrant in New York whose pride never lets her forget that she has come down in the world. Although both Lydia and her husband are proud to be Cuban, their aspirations for their children are based on the American Dream. Through the España family, Hijuelos gently explores the difficulties of building a life in a new country without losing touch with the old. Lydia's story is told through a series of closely-linked vignettes which criss-cross the years from the 1950s to the 1980s. They provide snapshots of her employers' lives and a vibrant portrait of the immigrant community of Spanish Harlem as well as a touching, sometimes heart-wrenching, narrative of Lydia's life.

About the author

Oscar Hijuelos was born the son of working-class Cuban immigrants in New York in 1951. He took a BA and a Masters at New York's City College where he studied writing under the novelist Donald Barthelme. Before taking up writing full-time, Hijuelos did a series of odd jobs from raising insects in Wisconsin and selling shoes in Macy's to writing advertisements for display in New York City subway cars. His first novel, *Our House in the Last World*, won him the American Academy Arts and Letters 1985 Rome Prize, enabling him to spend a year in Italy where he began the Pulitzer Prize-winning *The Mambo Kings Play Songs of Love*, later made into a film. Oscar Hijuelos still lives in New York City.

For discussion

❍ Although not written in the first person, the novel attempts to give us an insight into Lydia and her world. How successful is Hijuelos at portraying a woman's perspective?

❍ How would you describe Lydia? Are there contradictions in her character and, if so, what are they? How does the Lydia at the beginning of the book differ from Lydia at the end?

❍ How does their position as the children of working-class immigrants shape the characters of Lydia's children, in particular Rico? How have their adult relationships with their parents been affected?

❍ What does the book say about social divisions in America? Are these divisions along the lines of race, class, money or all three? How does Lydia maintain her self-respect despite the change in her status from upper-middle-class Cuban to working-class American?

Tulsa City-County Library
Central Library

Checked Out Items 9/28/2017 13:32
XXXXXXXXXX5778

Item Title	Due Date
Book clubbed / Lorna Barrett.	11/13/2017
Bloomsbury essential guide for reading groups / Susan Osborne.	11/13/2017
The book club companion : a comprehensive guide to the reading group experience / Diana Loevy.	11/13/2017

To renew:
www.tulsalibrary.org
918-549-7444

We value your feedback.
Please take our online survey.
www.tulsalibrary.org/Z45

❂ How would you describe the relationship between Lydia and the Ospreys? How do you think they feel about her? Why is Lydia so drawn to them?

❂ How does Lydia feel about Cuba? Do you think she feels Cuban, American, or neither? Are her feelings different from Raul's and, if so, how does this manifest itself?

❂ Much of the novel is written as a series of linked vignettes from Lydia's life. What effect does this have? What is Hijuelos trying to achieve by italicizing passages in the novel and regularly placing comments in brackets? How successful do you find this technique?

💻 Resources

www.nytimes.com/books/99/02/21/reviews/990221.21klint.html – review in *The New York Times* by the writer Verlyn Klinkenborg

www.nytimes.com/books/99/02/21/specials/hijuelos-unease.html – interview by Esther B. Fein published in *The New York Times*

📖 Suggested further reading

The Infinite Plan by Isabel Allende (1994); *Dreamland* by Kevin Baker (1999); *Tortilla Curtain* by T. Coraghessan Boyle (1995); *For Kings and Planets* by Ethan Canin (1998); *This Side of Brightness* by Colum McCann (1998); *Accordion Crimes* by Annie Proulx (1996); *The Hundred Secret Senses* **by Amy Tan** (1995)

OTHER BOOKS BY OSCAR HIJUELOS

Our House in the Last World (1983); *The Mambo Kings Play Songs of Love* (1989); *The Fourteen Sisters of Emilio Montez O'Brien* (1993); *Mr Ives' Christmas* (1995); *A Simple Habana Memory* (2002)

THE KITE RUNNER (2003)
Khaled Hosseini

📖 About the book

One chilly Afghan winter's day in 1975 Amir, the son of a wealthy Pashtun merchant, witnesses a dreadful act that irrevocably changes both his life and the life of his dear friend, Hassan, the son of his father's Hazara servant. It is not simply Amir's presence during Hassan's humiliation that scars him; it is his failure to act. Fleeing the Russian invasion, Amir and his beloved father seek refuge in the United States, building a life for themselves in the Afghan community of San Francisco. Still haunted by guilt, Amir is unable to enjoy either his success as a novelist or his marriage until a phone call offers him the chance to gather his courage, confront his demons and find 'a way to be good again'. In his remarkable first novel Khaled Hosseini explores the nature of friendship, of forgiveness and of redemption, set against the turbulent background of his native Afghanistan.

Background

Khaled Hosseini's accomplished storytelling may well seem noteworthy given that *The Kite Runner* is a debut novel but the fact that he wrote it in the early hours before setting off for his 'day job' as a doctor makes it all the more remarkable an achievement. Brought up in a tradition of storytelling, Hosseini has described it as first and foremost what writing novels is about.

Assailed with media images of war-torn Afghanistan, firstly during the Soviet occupation and then under the Taliban warlords, Hosseini wanted to give the West a glimpse of the country he remembered from childhood and to dispel some of the misconceptions that some of his adopted countrymen had about it. Women, for instance, had not suffered repression before the Taliban seized power; their rights were confirmed in a new constitution in the mid-1970s. He depicts 1970s Kabul as a bustling cosmopolitan city but does not romanticize it, evoking the ethnic tensions and injustices of the time by making Amir a Pashtun, the dominant Afghan group, and Hassan a member of the persecuted Hazara minority.

It would be tempting then to assume that the novel is largely autobiographical: Hosseini's family sought asylum in the United States after the invasion and suffered the same discomfiting adjustments as Amir and his father; Hosseini, like most Afghan sons, reveres his father (but not, he is quick to point out, as desperately as Amir reveres his); and Hosseini loved both reading and writing as a child. Unlike Amir, however, Hosseini returned to Afghanistan after a twenty-seven year absence, following the fall of the Taliban, to satisfy a yearning to see his homeland again and to find out how it was faring rather than to assuage a terrible feeling of guilt. While Hassan, in turn, is based on a thirty-year-old man named Khan whom Hosseini taught to read and a servant who he learned had been abused, he too, is a work of fiction. Yet just as Hassan finally awoke something noble in Amir, his experience with Khan awoke Hosseini to social injustice and the iniquities of racism. One of Hosseini's aims in writing *The Kite Runner* was to humanise the country that so many know only from desperate images of war and with his poignant humane storytelling he has succeeded.

About the author

Khaled Hosseini was born in 1965 in Kabul where his father was a diplomat and his mother taught Farsi and history. After the 1978 coup and the subsequent Russian invasion, the Hosseinis fled Afghanistan for the United States, receiving political asylum in 1980. The family settled in San Jose, California where his father found work as a driving instructor. Hosseini is now a physician and lives with his wife and two children in Northern California. *The Kite Runner*, Hosseini's first novel and, reputedly, the first to be written in English by an Afghan, met with great critical and popular acclaim when it was published in 2003.

For discussion

❍ The novel begins 'I became what I am today at the age of twelve'. To what is Amir referring? Is his assertion entirely true? What other factors have helped form his character? How would you describe Amir?

❍ Amir had never thought of Hassan as his friend, despite the evident bond between them, just as Baba did not think of Ali as his friend. What parallels can be drawn between Amir and Hassan's relationship, and Baba and Ali's? How would you describe the relationship between the two boys? What makes them so different in the way they behave with each other? What is it that makes Amir inflict small cruelties on Hassan? Had you already guessed at the true relationship between them? If so, at what point and why?

❍ It is Amir's dearest wish to please his father. To what extent does he succeed in doing so and at what cost? What kind of man is Baba? How would you describe his relationship with Amir, and with Hassan? How does that relationship change and what prompts those changes?

❍ Khaled Hosseini vividly describes Afghanistan, both the privileged world of Amir's childhood and the stricken country under the Taliban. How did his descriptions differ from ideas that you may already have had about Afghanistan? What cultural differences become evident in the American passages of the novel? How easy do the Afghans find it to settle in the US?

❍ After Soraya tells Amir about her past, she says 'I'm so lucky to have found you. You're so different from every Afghan guy I've met'. What do you think of the reasons that Amir puts forward for this? Could there be others? How do Afghan women fare in America? Are they any better off than they were in Afghanistan before the Taliban seized power?

❍ On the drive to Kabul Farid says to Amir 'You've always been a tourist here, you just didn't know it.' What is Farid implying? What do you think of his implication? Amir feels that he is 'home again' but how well does he know or understand his country?

✪ How does Hosseini succeed in bringing the horror of the Taliban to life? Why did he choose the role for Assef that he did?

✪ 'There is a way to be good again' promises Rahim Khan, a phrase which resonates throughout the novel. Does this prove to be the case for Amir? How important is Rahim Khan to him?

✪ After reading Amir's story Rahim Khan writes to him: 'the most impressive thing about your story is that it has irony.' It is surely an irony that Hassan, whose ignorance Amir pillories, points out that there was no need for the man to kill his wife to weep tears, he could simply have smelled an onion. How important is irony in the book? Were their other instances that particularly struck you?

✪ How significant is the tale of Rostam and Sohrab? What does it mean to Hassan, and to Amir?

✪ How important is religion in the book? What attitudes do the main characters have to it? How do they compare to the popular Western idea of Islam?

✪ What is the significance of kites in the book? What do you think they symbolise? Who is the eponymous kite runner?

🖥 Resources

www.bloomsbury.com/Authors/microsite.asp?id=480&section=1&aid=863 – conversation between Hosseini and Riverhead Books, his American publisher

http://afghanmagazine.com/2004_06/profile/khosseini.shtml – conversation with Farhad Azad at afghanmagazine.com

www.sfgate.com/cgi-bin/article.cgi?file=/chronicle/archive/2003/06/08/RV140807.DTL – interview by Dair Lara of the *San Francisco Chronicle*

http://books.guardian.co.uk/reviews/generalfiction/0,6121,1036891,00.html – review in *The Guardian* by Amelia Hill

http://query.nytimes.com/gst/fullpage.html?res=9504E0DF123FF930A3575BC0A9659C8B63 – review by novelist Edward Hower in *The New York Times*

www.khaledhosseini.com – the author's website

🗏 Suggested further reading

FICTION

Amber by Stephan Collishaw (2004); **By the Sea by Abdulrazak Gurnah** (2001); *The Mulberry Empire* by Philip Hensher (2002); *The Swallows of Kabul* by Yasmina Khadra (2004); *The Fortress of Solitude* by Jonathan Lethem (2004); **The Orchard on Fire by Shena Mackay** (1995); *In the Country of Men* by Hisham Matar

(2006); *So Long, See You Tomorrow* by William Maxwell (1980); *Fugitive Pieces by Anne Michaels* (1996)

NON-FICTION

West of Kabul, East of New York by Tamim Ansary (2002); *The Bookseller of Kabul* by Asne Seierstad (2003)

ALSO BY KHALED HOSSEINI

A Thousand Splendid Suns (2007)

THE NINTH LIFE OF LOUIS DRAX (2004)

Liz Jensen

📖 About the book

Nine-year-old Louis Drax is a deeply disturbed child to whom violence is a commonplace. He is engaged in a constant battle with his schoolmates who call him 'Wacko Boy' and his visits to a child psychologist leave the man baffled but admiring of Louis's precocious intelligence. His saving grace is his beautiful mother Natalie who rescues him from his many dangerous mishaps. Now in a coma after a disastrous birthday picnic, Louis lies in his hospital bed reflecting on what has brought him there. His doctor, under the spell of the distraught Natalie, begins to doubt her version of Louis's accident and the alleged guilt of her missing husband. As Louis finds his own way to communicate, the chilling truth emerges. In this taut psychological thriller Liz Jensen explores the many ways in which people can manipulate others, from perverting the close bonds of a mother-son relationship to the exploitation of pity and sexual attraction.

Background

The Ninth Life of Louis Drax marks something of a departure for Liz Jensen whose previous books have all been black comedies albeit with a serious edge. *Egg Dancing*, her first novel, lampooned both genetic engineering and Christian evangelicalism, while her second, *Ark Baby*, was a social satire which explored evolutionary theory and genetics. *The Paper Eater* took a swipe at consumerism in an imagined dystopia run by a computer while in *War Crimes in the Home* the endlessly wise-cracking Gloria's long buried secrets remain sealed even from herself as she slides into dementia. Although, as she has pointed out, *The Ninth Life of Louis Drax* contains flashes of humour it is a very much darker book than her previous novels. She has said that the ambivalence of parenthood is rarely explored, that she wanted 'to write about a very sick parent-child relationship, its neediness and interdependency. I had to confront the things that I'm most scared of, and the things that we don't talk about in families.'

The inspiration for Jensen's novel came from within her own family. Her nineteen-year-old uncle disappeared on a family holiday near Lake Lucerne in 1937 after arguing with his mother. A search party was organized after he failed to reappear but was called off after three days. Leaving her remaining children, including Jensen's eleven-year-old mother, at their hotel his distraught mother set of to search for him herself. Her body was later found lying at the bottom of a ravine. No one knew whether she had fallen or had jumped and her son was never seen again, a mystery which remained unresolved and which continued to haunt Jensen's mother.

All five of Jensen's novels have met with critical acclaim but *The Ninth Life of Louis Drax* with its much publicized film deal announced even before the book's publication, together with its selection by Richard and Judy finally brought the popular acclaim that had eluded her but which she thoroughly deserves.

About the author

The daughter of a Danish father and an Anglo-Moroccan mother, Liz Jensen was born in Wheatley in Oxfordshire in 1959. She won a scholarship to Somerville College, where she studied English before working as a journalist in Hong Kong then becoming a graduate trainee at the BBC where she worked in news and current affairs before making features for Radio 4. She moved to Lyon with her husband where she worked for some time as a sculptor. Jensen's fourth novel, *War Crimes in the Home* was adapted for the stage and *The Ninth Life of Louis Drax* was the subject of a fierce battle between Miramax and Time Warner for film rights to the book. Miramax emerged triumphant and Anthony Minghella plans to both adapt and direct the film. Liz Jensen lives in London.

For discussion

○ Why do you think Liz Jensen chose to preface her novel with a quotation from Paul Broks's *Into the Silent Land*? How would you interpret it in relation to Louis?
○ 'But look, before I plunge further into the story of Louis, let me tell you that I was a different man then.' How is Dr Dannachet changed by what happens? How would you describe him before and after? How does Jensen convey his character?
○ How successful is Jensen at capturing the voice of a deeply disturbed nine-year-old? What techniques does she use to convey Louis's character? How does Louis view the adult world? How has that view been shaped?

○ The novel is narrated by Louis and by Dr Dannachet. How effective did you find this structure?

○ Jensen chooses an almost supernatural means of revealing the truth about Louis's accident. How successful is this device?

○ When Dr Dannachet reveals his doubts about Natalie, Jacqueline says 'It's not something that crosses your mind though, is it? Why would it cross anyone's mind?' Had the possibility of Louis's abuse crossed your mind and if so at what point? To what extent did you sympathize with Dr Dannachet's feelings for Natalie, even when faced with what she has done?

○ What do you make of Natalie's last words: 'I always saved him ... I never let him die. You have to protect your child. I love my son. I love my son more than anything in the world.'?

○ At what point did you guess Gustave's identity and why?

○ When reflecting on Natalie's manipulation of men Detective Charvillefort says 'Men want to think the best of women, especially if they're attractive. Isn't there some truth in that? That we attribute moral goodness to attractive people?'. What do you think of this statement? What does the novel have to say about assumptions about male and female roles?

○ 'If you make a choice, and it's wrong, you have to live with it. Everyone has to live with the consequences. You chose, Louis. It was your choice.' To what extent do you agree with Natalie's assertion that Louis made a choice? What do you think of his choice for his ninth life?

○ 'I still tend towards optimism, still believe just as firmly in the power of hope.' thinks Dr Dannachet, despite all that has happened. What grounds, if any, does he have? Does the book end on a note of optimism?

○ The novel can be described as a psychological thriller. How does Jensen maintain suspense and momentum in her narrative?

○ Jensen has described this as her first 'grown up' novel. What do you think she means by that?

○ Jensen has said that she thought her book would be impossible to film yet Anthony Minghella (director of *The English Patient* and *Cold Mountain*) has chosen to direct the film version. What difficulties do you think he will have encountered in adapting the book? Who would you cast for the film?

Resources

www.bookbrowse.com/author_interviews/full/index.cfm?author_number=1088 – interview with Joel Rickett originally published in *The Bookseller*

http://findarticles.com/p/articles/mi_qn4158/is_20040702/ai_n12798594 – interview with Julie Wheelwright in *The Independent*
http://books.guardian.co.uk/reviews/crime/0,6121,1263666,00.html – review by Stephanie Merrit in *The Observer*
www.telegraph.co.uk/arts/main.jhtml?xml=/arts/2004/06/13/bojens13.xml&sSheet =/arts/2004/06/13/bomain.html – review by Katie Owen in *The Telegraph*

🗐 Suggested further reading

FICTION

Behind the Scenes at the Museum by Kate Atkinson (1995); *The House of Sleep* by Jonathan Coe (1997); *White Oleander* by Janet Fitch (1999); *Mouthing the Words* by Camilla Gibb (1999); *The Curious Incident of the Dog in the Night Time* by Mark Haddon (2003); *Last Things* by Jenny Offil (1999); *Vernon God Little* by D.B.C. Pierre (2003); *The Lovely Bones* by Alice Sebold (2003); *The Miracle Life of Edgar Mint* by Brady Udall (2002)

NON-FICTION

Into the Silent Land: Travels in Neuropsychology by Paul Broks (2003); *Awakenings* by Oliver Sacks (1990)

OTHER BOOKS BY LIZ JENSEN

Egg Dancing (1995); *Ark Baby* (1998); *The Paper Eater* (2000); *War Crimes in the Home* (2002); *My Dirty Little Book of Stolen Time* (2006)

ANIMAL DREAMS (1991)

Barbara Kingsolver

📖 About the book

Adrift in her own life, Codi Noline returns to the small community of Grace, Arizona, to take care of her father whose dementia is worsening. She feels an outsider in Grace, yet everyone seems to know and welcome her. Lonely and missing her sister who has gone to help the struggling farmers of Nicaragua, Codi finds solace with her old high school friend, Emelina, and in her job as a science teacher. Her relationship with Loyd Peregrina, a Native American, awakens her to a new way of looking at the natural world. When she and her students discover the extent to which the local mining company has contaminated the river, she is shocked into action, enlisting the help of the matriarchs of the Stitch and Bitch Club to raise funds to combat the company. As Codi opens up to the community she comes to a hard-won realization both of her own place in the world and of the things which are ultimately important in her life.

Background

In *Animal Dreams*, Barbara Kingsolver explores the dislocation of the rootless metropolitan life that Codi, the central character, has left behind and the inter-dependence of those who live in the small community of Grace. Interweaving Native American beliefs with the discovery of an impending environmental disaster, Kingsolver highlights the gulf in attitudes towards the natural world between those who have lived off it for centuries and those to whom profit is paramount. These are themes dear to Kingsolver's heart. She laments the inexorable move from the land to the city in her collection of essays, *Homeland* writing: '... I find that this exodus from the land makes me unspeakably sad. I think of the children who will never know, intuitively, that a flower is a plant's way of making love, or what silence sounds like, or that trees breathe out what we breathe in', and that 'what we lose in our great human exodus from the land is a rooted sense, as deep and intangible as religious faith, of why we need to hold on to the wild and beautiful places that once surrounded us'.

Kingsolver's commitment to social justice, ecology and the importance of community is an important element in all her novels. Her fiction combines a vivid empathic storytelling with a strong desire to awaken her readers to the important matters of the world. In her essay *Jabberwocky* she wrote: 'A newspaper could tell you that one hundred people, say, in an airplane, or in Israel, or in Iraq, have died today. And you can think to yourself, "How very sad," then turn the page and see how the Wildcats fared. But a novel could take just one of those hundred lives and show you exactly how it felt to be that person rising from bed in the morning, watching the desert light on the tile of her doorway and on the curve of her daughter's cheek.' From dangers of tinkering with the balance between man and nature evident in *Prodigal Summer* to the concern for the injustices of colonialism in *The Poisonwood Bible*, Kingsolver's fiction is both emphatically humane and the work of a consummate storyteller.

About the author

Barbara Kingsolver was born in Annapolis, Maryland, in 1955. She grew up in rural Kentucky where her father was the local physician but spent some time in both the Congo and St Lucia where her father practised medicine. She won a scholarship to DePauw University, Indiana, where she majored in biology, took a creative writing course and became active in the last anti-Vietnam War protests. After graduating in

1977, she lived and worked in a variety of places including France and Greece. In the early 1980s she took a masters degree in biology and ecology at the University of Arizona in Tucson. She took up a position as a science writer at the university, and went on to write features for journals and newspapers such as *The New York Times* and *Smithsonian*. Kingsolver took up writing fiction when she suffered from insomnia while pregnant. Her first novel, *The Bean Trees*, was published in 1988. She remains keenly interested in ecology, a recurrent theme in her novels, and is an active environmentalist and human rights supporter. Her fourth novel, *The Poisonwood Bible* was shortlisted for both the Pulitzer and PEN/Faulkner Awards.

For discussion

✪ Codi and Hallie are very different from each other. How would you describe Hallie's attitude to life? How does it differ from Codi's approach? What are the most important factors in shaping that approach and why?

✪ Why does Codi feel such an outsider when she comes back to Grace? How do those feelings change and why?

✪ The natural world is an important theme in *Animal Dreams*. Codi asks her class: 'Do you, or do you not, think the world was put here for you to use?' What do you think Loyd's answer to this question would be, and why? How do you think the board of the Black Mountain mining company would answer? What would your answer be?

✪ Arizona was originally in Spanish hands and was only incorporated into the United States early in the twentieth century. It is also home to some of the largest Native American communities in the US. How important are cultural differences in *Animal Dreams*? How do the different cultures of Grace get along together?

✪ Would you describe *Animal Dreams* as a political novel and, if so, which aspects of the novel meet this description? Is the book successful in conveying a message and, if so, how does it achieve this and what is the message?

✪ Why do you think Kingsolver chose to call the novel *Animal Dreams*? How important are Codi's dreams?

✪ What kind of parent do you think Codi's father was, and why? Why is their relationship so difficult? How does Kingsolver convey their difficulties? Do you think they understand each other better by the end of the book and, if so, how has this come about?

✪ Both Homero and Codi have difficulties in remembering things. How does Kingsolver use Homero's loss of memory to develop the novel? How does it illuminate our understanding of his feelings for his daughters? Why does Codi seem to have so few memories of her early life in Grace? What is the effect of her recovering those memories?

○ Apart from Homero and Loyd, the male characters in the novel seem to fade into the background. Do you think this is a deliberate choice and, if so, why? How do reactions to the contamination of the river by the Black Mountain mining company divide along gender lines? To what extent do you think this is accurate and why?

🖥 Resources

www.litencyc.com/php/speople.php?rec=true&UID=2518 – profile of Barbara Kingsolver by Kimberly Koza at the *Literary Encyclopedia* website
www.salon.com/16dec1995/departments/litchat.html – interview at *Salon* internet magazine
www.pbs.org/newshour/gergen/kingsolver.html – transcript of interview with David Gergen originally aired on the American Public Broadcasting Service
www.kingsolver.com/home/index.asp – Barbara Kingsolver's website

📖 Suggested further reading

FICTION
The Monkey Wrench Gang by Edward Abbey (1975); *Reservation Blues* by Sherman Alexie (1995); *A Friend of the Earth* by T. Coraghessan Boyle (1999); *The Beet Queen* by Louise Erdrich (1986); *Goodnight Nebraska* by Tom McNeal (1998); *The Grass Dancer* by Susan Power (1994)
NON-FICTION
The Jaguar Smile by Salman Rushdie (1987)
OTHER BOOKS BY BARBARA KINGSOLVER
Novels: *The Bean Trees* (1988); *Pigs in Heaven* (1993); *The Poisonwood Bible* (1999); *Prodigal Summer* (2000)
Short stories: *Homeland and Other Stories* (1989)
Non-fiction: *High Tide in Tucson: Essays from Now and Forever* (1995); *Small Wonder* (2002); *Animal, Vegetable, Miracle* (2007)

THE VINTNER'S LUCK (1999)

Elizabeth Knox

📖 About the book

This is the tale of Sobran Jodeau and Xas, the angel into whose arms he quite literally falls one midsummer night. When the two decide to share a bottle of wine and exchange news on the anniversary of their first meeting, a relationship begins that will span fifty-five years, intensifying as each year passes. Life in Sobran's village in Burgundy goes on, its small tragedies, marriages and affairs punctuated by the turbulent years of the Napoleonic Wars. The murders of two young girls remain unsolved for many years until Sobran thinks he has found the key to the crimes. His family continues to burgeon and his wine to improve. His friendship with the mistress of the neighbouring château provides the villagers with fuel for speculation, as does his strange behaviour on a certain midsummer evening every year. But when one day Xas arrives unannounced and terribly injured, the relationship between angel and man changes irrevocably.

Background

The Vintner's Luck was something of a departure for Elizabeth Knox. Her previous novels are all set in contemporary Wellington, her hometown. Three in particular, *Paremata*, *Pomare* and *Tawa* which form the trilogy *The High Jump: A New Zealand Childhood*, are highly autobiographical. All are very far removed from the fantastical. She has said that she likes fantasy, but that 'I think of my fantasy as fantastic naturalism, a fantastic element in a world that is very real, and so the fantastic things have to be very real too', something that holds true for *The Vintner's Luck*. Although the potentially ethereal relationship between an angel and a vintner is central to the novel, it is firmly rooted in the earthy reality of a nineteenth-century French village. The angel Xas is a physical, muscular presence, insatiably curious about the world. He and Sobran share theological debates along with their wine just as Sobran and the Comte's niece debate new ideas emerging from scientific advances.

Knox has said that the idea for the novel came from a dream she had when delirious with pneumonia, contracted after nursing her young asthmatic son through four sleepless nights. On waking she recognized the potential for a good story but put the idea aside for a year. Since the success of *The Vintner's Luck* Knox has continued to write fiction set in other worlds and other times: *Black Oxen* is set in 2022 and peopled with a host of outlandish characters; *Billie's Kiss* takes place on a remote Scottish island in the nineteenth century; while her gothic novel *Daylight* has been compared to the novels of Anne Rice. Knox has extended her writing to include novels for young adults, fiction which also explores the fantastical.

About the author

Elizabeth Knox was born in New Zealand in 1959. She studied at Victoria University of Wellington. She lives with her husband and family in Wellington. Her first novel to be published in the United Kingdom, *The Vintner's Luck* has won several awards including New Zealand's Montana Book Awards Deutz medal for fiction in 1999 and was longlisted for the Orange Prize. Elizabeth Knox lives with her family in Wellington.

For discussion

✪ 'Could a stone escape the laws of gravity? Impossible. Impossible for evil to form an alliance with good' (Comte de Lautréamont). Why do you think Knox chose this epigram to start her book?

✪ How difficult did you find it to suspend your disbelief when embarking on a novel in which the principal character was an angel? Did you find Xas convincing? How does Knox develop his character? How does he differ from traditional depictions of angels?

✪ Why does Sobran think that Xas visits him in the early years of their relationship? What difference does this make to his life? How is he affected by Xas's revelation of his fall from grace? Why does he decide to see Xas again?

✪ Early in the book the Comte describes Sobran as 'a sharp-tongued, high-handed bully'. To what extent do you agree with the Comte and why? How is Sobran changed over the years and what changes him? How would you describe him, at his death?

✪ Why does Xas visit Sobran? What does he mean when he says: 'I had to have you – someone I could lose forever.' How is Xas's friendship with Apharah different from his relationship with Sobran? How is Xas changed after Lucifer's visit and how does this affect his relationship with Sobran?

✪ Aurora is a determined atheist. Does her relationship with Xas change her views at all and if so, how? What are Xas's views on faith?

✪ Does Xas change other characters in the book besides Sobran and Aurora? If so, who are they and how are they affected?

✪ The relationship between Sobran and Aurora seems more important than his relationship with his wife. What is its basis? How does Knox develop the relationship? How important is it in the development of the novel?

✪ *The Vintner's Luck* is set at a time when many long-held beliefs were being challenged. How important is theology in the book? How does science begin to change the world in which Sobran lives?

✪ How does Knox root her story so firmly in its period?

💻 Resources

www.nytimes.com/books/99/02/21/reviews/990221.21aubet.html – review by Nina Auerbach published in *The New York Times*

www.bookcouncil.org.nz/writers/knoxelizabeth.html – entry for Elizabeth Knox in *The Oxford Companion to New Zealand Literature* (1998) edited by Roger Robinson and Nelson Wattie, published at the New Zealand Book Council website

📚 Suggested further reading

The Leper's Companions by Julia Blackburn (1999); *The Rationalist* by Warwick Collins (1993); *Quarantine* by Jim Crace (1997); *A Case of Curiosities* by Allen Kurzweil (1992); *Ingenious Pain* by Andrew Miller (1997); *Paradise Lost Books 1 and 2* by John Milton (1667); *Lemprière's Dictionary* by Lawrence Norfolk (1991); *Perfume* by Patrick Süskind (1985)

OTHER BOOKS BY ELIZABETH KNOX

Black Oxen (2001); *Billie's Kiss* (2002); *Daylight* (2003)

THE BUDDHA OF SUBURBIA (1990)

Hanif Kureishi

📖 About the book

It's the seventies: velvet flares, Emerson, Lake and Palmer and transcendental meditation are the height of cool. The son of an English mother and an Indian father, Karim is seventeen and only too well aware that Beckenham is not where it's at. Life is dull but secure so when his father begins donning a red and gold waistcoat to impart the wisdom of Eastern philosophy to assorted suburbanites in his friend Eva's living room, Karim feels unsettled not to mention embarrassed. When his father moves in with Eva, Karim joins them, half in love with Eva's beautiful son Charlie who is intent on a glorious future in the music biz, regardless of talent. Eva takes Karim under her wing and when they all move to London, Karim's life begins to take off, yet confusion and unhappiness are never far away. Poignant yet extremely funny, Hanif Kureishi's semi-autobiographical coming of age novel satirizes English race relations in the seventies while exploring Karim's struggle for identity.

Background

Race relations in 1970s' Britain were under immense strain. Immigration on a large scale had begun shortly after the Second World War when people from the then-colonies were invited to fill the yawning gaps in the labour market. Many did not receive the welcome they had expected. The Notting Hill race riots of 1958 were followed by the introduction of an immigration quota system in 1962. Enoch Powell's infamous 1968 Rivers of Blood speech calling for repatriation struck a chord with some and by the 1970s the National Front, the new British fascists, had gained an alarming degree of support. Born in 1954, Hanif Kureishi would have been all too familiar with the casual racism of everyday life, and, worse, with bootboys on the march. The seventies was also a time of sexual experimentation for many, a time when hedonism was not only something to be embraced but almost an obligation, as Pyke and Marlene so graphically demonstrate. In *The Buddha of Suburbia* Kureishi captures the spirit of the times, injecting a wickedly satirical humour, while exploring Karim's often painful struggle to make sense of his life.

Kureishi gained something of a reputation as a chronicler of social change in Britain through his films, his plays and his novels. Apart from *The Buddha of Suburbia* which brought his work into the nation's living rooms with its 1993 BBC dramatization, he became well known through films such as *My Beautiful Launderette* (1985), *When Sammy and Rosie Get Laid* (1987) and *London Kills Me* (1991), all of which explored the complex terrain of a troubled Britain. In later years some of Kureishi's work has taken a more personal turn. His novel *Intimacy* explored the pain of a man about to leave his partner and their young children, something which Kureishi himself experienced. In 2004 he published *My Ear At His Heart* after finding the manuscript of his father's abandoned novel, years after his death, in which Kureishi appears as a character. This deeply personal, sometimes raw memoir explores Kureishi's own development as a writer and the often confused relationship he had with his father, a confusion echoed in Karim's relationship with Haroon. For those wanting a deeper understanding of Karim, or of Kureishi himself, *My Ear At His Heart* is highly recommended.

About the author

Hanif Kureishi was born in Bromley, Kent in 1954 and read philosophy at King's College, London. As well as being an acclaimed novelist he is an award-winning playwright, screenwriter and film-maker. His first play, *Soaking the Heat*, was performed at the Royal Court Theatre in London in 1976, followed in 1980 by *The Mother Country*, for which he won the Thames TV Playwright Award. In 1981 his play *Outskirts* won the George Devine Award and in 1982 he became Writer in Residence at the Royal Court Theatre. His screenplay for *My Beautiful Laundrette*, directed by Stephen Frears, was nominated for an Academy Award. His film *My Son the Fanatic*, adapted from a short story included in his collection *Love in a Blue Time*, was first shown at the 1997 Cannes Film Festival. Published in 1990, *The Buddha of Suburbia*, Kureishi's first novel, won the Whitbread First Novel Award and was adapted for the BBC's 1993 four-part television series.

For discussion

○ 'My name is Karim Amir, and I am an Englishman born and bred, almost.' Karim's mother is English and is father Indian. What difficulties does this present him with? How have attitudes towards mixed race couples and their children changed since the seventies?

○ 'He'd spent years trying to be more of an Englishman, to be less risibly conspicuous, and now he was putting it back in spadeloads' What do you make of Haroon's transformation? Which other characters transform themselves in the novel and to what effect?

○ 'Maybe there were similarities between what was happening to Dad, with his discovery of Eastern philosophy, and Anwar's last stand. Perhaps it was the immigrant condition living itself out through them.' Does this seem to be true? How do both Anwar and Haroon change in their attitudes towards England and India? How is the 'immigrant condition living itself out through them'?

○ 'She claimed to be doing it only for Jeeta, but there was real wilful contrariness in it, I suspected.' Why do you think Jamila finally marries Changez? What do you think of the way she runs the marriage?

○ 'Surely love had to be something more generous than this high-spirited egotism-à-deux?' What do you think? What are the repercussions of Haroon and Eva's relationship for those close to them? How does it effect Karim? How else is love portrayed in the novel?

○ 'But he earned this appreciation with his charm, which was often mistaken for ability. He could even charm himself, I reckoned.' What do you make of Charlie? What effect does he have on people and on Karim in particular? How does he achieve that effect?

○ 'She didn't realise it was in the blood and not on the skin; she didn't see there could be nothing more suburban than suburbanites repudiating themselves.' What does Karim mean by suburban? In what ways are suburbanites so different from Londoners, or from the punk estate kids Charlie takes of with?

○ 'Pyke conceded. "I think it may revolve around the only subject there is in England ... Class"' How important is class in the novel?

○ What did you think of Tracey's reaction to Karim's performance as Anwar? Was she right to question Karim's less than complimentary portrayal of an Indian man to a largely white audience or was Karim right when he insisted that it was simply a portrait of 'one old Indian man'?

○ 'What's the point of even discussing the soul?' asks the *Furnishings* photographer. Haroon replies: 'This failure, this great hole in your way of life defeats me. But ultimately it will defeat you.' What do you think of this?

○ Allie is an absent character throughout most of the novel but voices strong opinions in the final chapter saying 'And I hate people who go on all the time about being black, and how persecuted they were at school, and how someone spat at them once. You know: self-pity.' How would you compare his attitudes with Karim's and with Jamila's? What do you think of them?

○ *The Buddha of Suburbia* is set during the 1970s, a period of tense race relations in Britain. What is Karim's response to this? How politically aware is he?

○ Throughout the novel Karim is beset by confusion about his identity, both racial and sexual, and what he wants to do with his life. To what extent does he succeed in resolving that confusion?

○ How would you describe the novel's humour? Were there particular passages that amused you and if so what were they?

○ Hanif Kureishi has written several screenplays as well as novels. To what extent can his writing style be described as cinematic? Are there particular passages that fit this description?

🖥 Resources

www.contemporarywriters.com/authors/?p=auth57 – profile of Hanif Kureishi at the British Council website including a critical essay by Dr Jules Smith

http://books.guardian.co.uk/reviews/biography/0,6121,1301809,00.html – review of by Peter Bradshaw *My Ear At His Heart* published in *The Guardian*

📚 Suggested further reading

Brick Lane by Monica Ali (2003); *Maps for Lost Lovers* by Nadeem Aslam (2004); *The Rotters' Club* by Jonathan Coe (2001); *Buddha Da* by Anne Donovan (2003); *The Namesake* by Jhumpa Lahiri (2003); *White Teeth* by Zadie Smith (2000); ***Anita and Me* by Meera Syal** (1996)

OTHER BOOKS BY HANIF KUREISHI

Novels: *The Black Album* (1995); *Intimacy* (1998); *Gabriel's Gift* (2001)

Short stories: *Love in a Blue Time* (1997); *Midnight All Day* (1999); *The Body and Other Stories* (2002); *Something to Tell You* (2008)

Plays: *Borderline* (1981); *Birds of Passage* (1983); *Outskirts and Other Plays* (1983); *Sleep with Me* (1999); *When The Night Begins* (2004); *Venus* (2007)

Screenplays: *My Beautiful Laundrette* (1986); *Sammy and Rosie Get Laid* (1986); *London Kills Me* (1991); *My Son, the Fanatic* (1998); *The Mother* (2003)

Non-fiction: *Dreaming and Scheming: Reflections on Writing and Politics* (2002); *My Ear At His Heart* (2004); *The Word and the Bomb* (2005)

Edited: *The Faber Book of Pop* (editor with Jon Savage) (1996)

DEATH AND THE PENGUIN (2001)

Andrey Kurkov (translated by George Bird)

📖 About the book

Viktor longs to be a writer but has never quite made it. He consoles himself with bits and pieces of journalism until he has a mysterious summons from the Editor-in-Chief at *Capital News* who sets him the task of writing obituaries, a task at which Viktor excels. More than enough money is rolling in for Viktor and his doleful penguin Misha but life becomes increasingly puzzling for him: he finds himself the guardian of a gangster's daughter; is asked to make Misha available for funerals and comes upon a set of files of his obituaries marked with dates for publication. Even the unworldly Viktor can see that things are fast closing in on him. Written in stripped-down deadpan prose, *Death and the Penguin* is both an amusing black comedy and a chilling portrayal of post-Soviet Ukraine.

Background

Andrey Kurkov is one of few Ukrainian writers successful outside his country but that success was hard won. He spent fifteen years trying to be published, even producing his own books and selling them on the street. *Death and the Penguin* was his first novel to be translated into English and it established him as a bestselling author in the West.

With his skills as a reporter and his literary credentials well established Kurkov became the man the British media turned to for an explanation of the events of the Orange Revolution which overturned the Yanukovych government in favour of Viktor Yuschencko, the people's choice, in November 2004. The Ukraine he reported on then is somewhat different from the country portrayed in *Death and the Penguin* which was published in Russian in 1996. The mafia is no longer the force it once was. As Kurkov has said 'it was a factor in 1992–1995. I know that one of my first films (because I was a film script writer) was financed by mafia. The mafia started the first banks in Kiev'. He has explained that Viktor is very much a product of his time describing him as typical of 'post-Soviet young intelligentsia lads who were very infantile. I mean, they were semi-dissident in the Soviet time, but they inherited genetically all this Soviet passivity, lack of initiative and readiness to accept anything that comes. So, for me, he is quite typical, representative of this generation.'

Kurkov is of the same generation and describes himself as 'shaped by the Soviet school, by some kind of strange cynical attitude towards everything happening around you, by almost genetic mistrust in the government, in the system'. As a young man he avoided being assigned to the KGB as it would have meant that he couldn't travel for twenty-five years serving instead as a prison guard in Odessa, a city he describes as a 'very cultural, literary place'. It was there that he wrote several of his children's books yet to be translated into English.

Kurkov is optimistic about the literary future of his country. Although he says that Ukraine has no authors in their thirties, there is a new generation of enthusiastic writers in their twenties pointing to writers such as Irena Karpa, Taras Prokhasko, Lubko Deresh and Serhiy Zhadan, writers unknown to us now but clearly names to look out for.

About the author

Andrey Kurkov was born in St Petersburg in 1961. He studied at the Kiev Foreign Languages Institute and worked for some time as a journalist before completing his military service as a prison warder at Odessa. He went on to become a film camera-man, a writer of screenplays and an acclaimed novelist whose work is translated from Russian into many languages. Andrey Kurkov lives in Kiev.

For discussion

○ Andrey Kurkov prefaces his novel with a joke. How important is humour in the novel and how would you describe that humour? Why do you think Kurkov decides to portray such a dangerous chaotic world in a humorous manner?

○ 'Everyone will know your real name some day – if you want ... But for now, best keep to the *Group of Friends* that no one knows.' Viktor is employed as an obituarist for *Capital News* but what is his real function? Who are the *Group of Friends*? What is happening in the city and why are so many obituaries required?

○ 'And even now, life around him was still dangerously unfathomable, as if he had missed the actual moment when the nature of events might have been fathomed.' Why do you think Kurkov chose to portray Viktor as such an unworldly character? What effect does this achieve?

○ 'But their psychology, you understand, is far more complex then, say, a dog or a cat's. They're more intelligent, more secretive; capable of concealing feelings and affections.' Does this seem to be an apt description of Misha? Why do you think Kurkov chose to make him the only creature to whom Viktor can show affection? Do you think Misha is a metaphor, and if so what does he stand for?

○ What do you make of the way in which the book ends?

○ How would you describe the style in which the book is written? What effect does that style achieve?

○ What impression do you get of early 1990s post-Soviet Ukraine from Kurkov's novel? How does it compare with any ideas that you might have had about it before you read the book?

💻 Resources

http://query.nytimes.com/gst/fullpage.html?res=9D05E7D61030F932A25752C1A9 679C8B63 – review by the writer Ken Kalfus published in *The New York Times*
www.abc.net.au/rn/arts/bwriting/stories/s1461208.htm – interview with Ramona Koval at the 2005 Edinburgh International Book Festival published at the Australian Broadcasting Corporation's *Radio National* website
http://observer.guardian.co.uk/travel/story/0,,1484154,00.html – Andrey Kurkov's insider's guide to Kiev published in *The Guardian*
http://en.wikipedia.org/wiki/Orange_revolution –Wikipedia page on the Orange Revolution

📚 Suggested further reading

The Master and the Margarita by Mikhail Bulgakov (1967); *The Trial* by Franz Kafka (1925); *A Short History of Tractors in Ukranian* by Marina Lewycka (2005); *Babylon* by Victor Pelevin (translated by Andrew Bromfield) (1999)
OTHER BOOKS BY ANDREY KURKOV TRANSLATED INTO ENGLISH
Fiction: *The Case of the General's Thumb* (2003); *Penguin Lost* (2004); *A Matter of Death and Life* (2005); *The President's Last Love* (2007)

THE PHOTOGRAPH (2003)

Penelope Lively

📖 About the book

Kath was an exquisitely beautiful woman; carefree and spontaneous, she lit up a room when she entered it, drawing people to her and carrying them along with her enthusiasm. Or at least so it seemed. When Glyn, her husband, finds an envelope amongst his papers labelled in Kath's hand 'Don't open – destroy' he is unable to resist, but the photograph he finds inside will shake his view of both himself and Kath. By the end of this slim, elegantly constructed novel, Glyn and several of the people who had thought themselves closest to Kath, are forced to the painful conclusion that they had not the slightest idea who she was or of the unhappiness that haunted her. In characteristically cool, spare prose Penelope Lively tells Kath's story through the voices of the novel's main characters, punctuating their narratives with vivid, snapshot memories of Kath.

Background

Penelope Lively has said in interviews that although she is not an historian she can become 'obsessively interested in the past'. She is fascinated by memory: its fragmentation and its ambivalence, a theme which runs through several of her novels, in particular *Moontiger*, *Passing On* and *Treasures of Time*. She returns to this theme in *The Photograph* which vividly illustrates the way in which perceptions of the past can influence the present but which is also concerned with how well, or perhaps how little, we know each other, even those to whom we believe ourselves to be closest. Lively has also proclaimed herself 'intrigued' by the way in which physical appearance can profoundly influence a life. The gloriously beautiful Kath, whose apparent inability to settle at any kind of occupation was indulgently excused as a quirk of her spontaneous nature, is desperately unhappy, while her closest friend, the 'short compact and sturdy' Mary leads a contented and fulfilled life, happy to listen and provide a solid base of friendship but self-fulfilled and independent of others.

Written in Lively's characteristic elegant and quietly understated prose, reminiscent of Edith Wharton, one of her favourite writers, *The Photograph* is cleverly structured so that both Kath's story and the stories and characters of those who thought they knew her well gradually emerge. As each character narrates their own part, small hints are dropped and dim memories begin to surface. The characters are forced to examine their own parts in Kath's sad story, and we, too, begin to understand what has happened to her and the way in which almost everyone who thought they were close to her has failed her.

About the author

Penelope Lively was born in Cairo in 1933. She spent her early childhood in Egypt and was sent to boarding school in Sussex when she was twelve before reading Modern History at St Anne's College, Oxford. She began her career as an author writing for children, publishing her first book, *Astercote*, in 1970 and winning the Carnegie Medal with *The Ghost of Thomas Kempe* in 1973 and the Whitbread Award for best children's book with *A Stitch in Time* in 1976. Her first novel for adults, *The Road to Lichfield*, was shortlisted for the 1977 Booker Prize, followed by *According to Mark* which was shortlisted in 1984. She won the prize with

Moontiger in 1987. As well as her acclaimed novels and children's books Lively has also written for radio and television.

For discussion

○ What were your first impressions of Kath? How had those impressions changed by then end of the novel?

○ 'Fondness is overtaken by annoyance; Kath is getting in the way of his work, which was not allowed, as she well understood.' To what extent has Glyn's neglect of Kath caused her death? What kind of marriage did Glyn and Kath have? Why did Kath marry Glyn after rejecting so many others? Why did he marry her?

○ What does Glyn's reaction to the discovery of the photograph tell us about him? What kind of man is he? What is his attitude to relationships?

○ How would you describe Elaine? What kind of sister is she to Kath? If she had found the photograph when turning out Kath's papers would her reactions have differed from Glyn's and if so how? What effect does Glyn's discovery have on Elaine?

○ 'And in the last resort, Elaine loved Nick, didn't she?' How would you describe Elaine and Nick's marriage? How does it compare with Kath's to Glyn?

○ Glenda Hapgood says 'it was a problem for Kath, looking the way she did.' What does she mean? How has Kath's beauty shaped her life? How would you compare it with Mary Packard's life?

○ Oliver feels that Kath 'has become like some mythical figure, trawled up at will to fit other people's narratives.' How do the other characters adjust their own versions of events to 'fit' Kath into their lives? Does Kath emerge as a narrative voice?

○ Elaine is shaken by the Mary's revelations about Kath. How is her perception of the past and of Kath's part in it changed?

○ Of all the characters Mary seems to be the only one to have truly known and understood Kath. Why is this? Why have those closest to Kath failed to see the 'dark malaise' that haunted her despite her apparent enthusiasm for life? How well do any of the characters really know each other?

○ After Mary's revelations Glyn returns to his old life, absorbed in his work yet haunted by the day he found Kath dead: 'The sight is the same as ever it was, except that it is informed by new wisdoms, and he looks differently.' What are those 'new wisdoms'? How has Glyn been changed by what he has discovered? How have his perceptions of Kath changed?

○ The novel is narrated from several points of view. How does this narrative structure help the story unfold?

○ Polly's narrative sections are all written as monologues, often as one side of a phone conversation. How well do you think this technique worked? Why do you think Lively chose to write Polly's narrative in this way?

💻 Resources

www.barnesandnoble.com/writers/writerdetails.asp?userid=bsq13alRf6&cid= 1077316 – interview with barnesandnoble.com which details some of Lively's literary influences

www.contemporarywriters.com/authors/?p=auth61 – profile of Penelope Lively at the British Council website including a critical essay by James Proctor

http://books.guardian.co.uk/reviews/generalfiction/0,6121,872794,00.html – review by Kate Kellaway in *The Observer*

http://books.guardian.co.uk/review/story/0,12084,880840,00.html – review by Alfred Hickling in *The Guardian*

www.arts.telegraph.co.uk/arts/main.jhtml?xml=/arts/2003/02/02/boliv26.xml – review by Jane Shilling in *The Telegraph*

http://query.nytimes.com/gst/fullpage.html?res=9B04E5DD103DF933A15754C0A9 659C8B63 – review by the novelist Valerie Martin in *The New York Times*

📚 Suggested further reading

Telling Liddy by Anne Fine (1998); *Marriage: A Duet* by Anne Taylor Fleming (2003); *The Memory Box* by Margaret Forster (1999); *Charming Billy* by Alice McDermott (1997); *The Wife* by Meg Wolitzer (2003)

OTHER BOOKS BY PENELOPE LIVELY

Fiction: *The Road to Lichfield* (1977); *Treasures of Time* (1979); *Judgement Day* (1980); *Next to Nature, Art* (1982); *Perfect Happiness* (1983); *According to Mark* (1984); *Moon Tiger* (1987); *Passing On* (1989); *City of the Mind* (1991); *Cleopatra's Sister* (1993); *Heat Wave* (1996); *Spiderweb* (1998); *Making it Up* (2005); *Consequences* (2007)

Short stories: *Nothing Missing but the Samovar, and other stories* (1978); *Corruption, and other stories* (1984); *Pack of Cards, Stories 1978–86* (1986)

Non-fiction: *The Presence of the Past: An introduction to landscape history* (1976); *Oleander, Jacaranda: a Childhood Perceived* (1994); *A House Unlocked* (2001)

CHARMING BILLY (1997)

Alice McDermott

📖 About the book

When Billy Lynch's family and friends adjourn to a bar in the Bronx after his funeral it's a time for affectionate reminiscing. Billy was someone that everyone loved; a romantic and poetic figure who left an impression on all who met him. But Billy's death was far from romantic. He died an alcoholic – passed out on the street like a tramp. His life had been marked by heartbreak and many who knew him were convinced that he drank to ease the pain of the loss of his sweetheart many years ago. His devoted cousin, Dennis, came to his aid at any time of the day or night. But it is only after Billy's funeral that Dennis tells his daughter the truth behind the legend of Billy's sweetheart and the lie that was at the heart of his friendship with Billy.

Background

One critic has noted of Alice McDermott's work 'McDermott is something of a specialist in the literature of wry sorrow — she's Irish, after all,' (Ron Charles in *The Christian Science Monitor*), and it is indeed true that she was born into the kind of Irish American family of which she writes. She has said that she did not set out specifically to write Irish American fiction but that it is more a matter of convenience, that it 'saves me lots of research time, and I can spend the time instead trying to develop the things that I think are important in fiction, and that is the inner life of the characters'. In writing fiction what interests her is not so much the storytelling as capturing 'the sense of a place seen in retrospect ... the role of memory, the relation of memory to storytelling, to faith, to mythmaking'. When asked what to look for in fiction by a non-fiction reader she remarked: 'I guess I would suggest you begin reading a novel not with the question of What's this about but How does this sound – to notice language and image and voice before story and plot.'

Her use of language is often remarked upon and it is her delicate poetic style that enables her to evoke a sense of sympathy in the reader for Billy's yearning for Eva despite his degraded state and the unhappiness this longing has caused his wife Maeve. Her descriptions are wonderfully evocative. What harried woman could fail to identify with Aunt Peg from McDermott's fifth novel *Child of My Heart*, who was 'only, it seemed, a good night's sleep away from being pretty.' She has said 'I wouldn't want to spend the energy just telling a story. I've got to hear the rhythm of the sentences; I want the music of the prose', a music which sings out loud and clear in the wonderfully wistful elegiac tone of *Charming Billy*.

About the author

Alice McDermott was born in 1953 and brought up in Elmont, New York. *Charming Billy*, McDermott's fourth novel, won the American National Book Award for fiction in 1998. In addition to writing she teaches part-time at Johns Hopkins University.

For discussion

⊙ Dennis's daughter narrates the book. Why do you think McDermott chose a character from the next generation to recount Billy's story? What effect does this achieve? What impression do you get of the narrator?

⊙ 'If you knew Billy at all, then you loved him,' says a guest at Billy's funeral, a sentiment which echoes throughout the book. What was it that people loved about Billy? Do you think Billy was capable of loving other people?

⊙ Why does Dennis choose to tell Billy that Eva is dead rather than tell him the truth? How does it change the course of Billy's life? What effect does it have on Dennis and his family?

⊙ How important is faith in the book and how does it manifest itself? Why is it so important to Billy? Is faith necessarily linked with religion in the book? What problems does Dennis experience with faith and why?

⊙ How would you describe Dennis? How does his character compare to Billy's? What are the most important factors in shaping Dennis's character?

⊙ Billy's sister Rosemary describes Billy's alcoholism as 'a disease' but Dan Lynch emphatically challenges this, saying: 'Don't say it was a disease that blindsided him and wiped out everything he was.' Which of these views seems to apply to Billy? Why do both Rosemary and Dan defend their positions so passionately?

⊙ *Charming Billy* is set firmly in an Irish neighbourhood in New York. How important is their Irish identity to the characters? How does this manifest itself? Are there characters to whom it is particularly important and, equally, are there characters that distance themselves from it? Why do you think this is so?

⊙ How would you describe McDermott's writing style? What tone does it take and how is this achieved?

🖳 Resources

www.boston.com/globe/search/stories/books/alice_mcdermott.htm – review by Gail Caldwell published in *The Boston Globe*

www.salon.com/books/sneaks/1998/01/09review.html – review by Dan Cryer at *Salon* internet magazine

www.washingtonpost.com/wp-dyn/articles/A31756-2003Aug22.html – transcript of an online chat moderated by Carole Burns published at *The Washington Post*'s website

www.nytimes.com/books/98/01/11/reviews/980111.11beckert.html – review by Alida Becker published in *The New York Times*

www.pbs.org/newshour/bb/entertainment/july-dec98/mcdermott_11-20.html – transcript of an interview by Elizabeth Farnsworth broadcast by the American organization PBS

www.powells.com/authors/mcdermott.html – interview with Dave Weich published at Powell's bookshop website

☟ Suggested further reading

For Kings and Planets by Ethan Canin (1998); *Telling Liddy* by Anne Fine (1998); *Memory Box* by Margaret Forster (1999); **Empress of the Splendid Season by Oscar Hijuelos** (1999); **The Photograph by Penelope Lively** (2003); *Cal* by Bernard MacLaverty (1983); *The Folded Leaf* by William Maxwell (1945); *Last Orders* by Graham Swift (1996)

OTHER BOOKS BY ALICE MCDERMOTT

A Bigamist's Daughter (1982); *That Night* (1987); *At Weddings and Funerals* (1992); *Child of My Heart* (2002); *After This* (2006)

BRIGHTNESS FALLS (1992)

Jay McInerney

📖 About the book

Corrine and Russell are a glittering New York couple, in love with each other and pursuing successful careers in a world where anything seems possible if you are young, bright and fearless. To their friends, they epitomize the perfect marriage but when Russell becomes caught up in an audacious plan to take over the publishing company in which he is the rising editorial star, things begin to fall apart. The adrenaline-fuelled atmosphere of the deal begins to take its toll on both Russell and Corrine, just as the excesses of the 1980s have taken their toll on many others in New York City, from their close friend Jeff, now in detox, to the homeless crack addicts on every street corner. With the knowledge gained from her job as a stockbroker, Corrine begins to realize that the heady days of the rising Dow must surely come to an end. The reckoning finally comes on October 19, 1987 when the bubble bursts with the Wall Street crash.

Background

Set in New York in the months before the stockmarket crash of 1987, *Brightness Falls* captures an atmosphere of frenzied recklessness through the story of Russell and Corrine, an attractive and likeable young couple. With a cast of characters ranging from Victor Propp, who negotiates regular increases in advance payments for his twenty-year-old unfinished novel (thought to be modeled on the late Harold Brodkey who took over thirty years, and reputedly several advances, to produce his novel *The Runaway Soul*), to the homeless Corrine sees at the soup kitchen, Jay McInerney takes a swipe at the rash profligacy of the 1980s and the high price that was paid for it.

Brightness Falls is set very much in the milieu of smart 1980s New York publishing, parties and excess, a territory in which McInerney was very much at home. From the publication of his first novel, *Bright Lights, Big City*, which, together with *The Story of My Life*, inhabited the world of cool young New Yorkers, he gained something of a reputation as a playboy. *Brightness Falls* was considered to be the first of his more mature novels and he has described it as having 'a special place in my heart'. The novel has often been spoken of in the same breath as Tom Wolfe's *The Bonfire of the Vanities*, a satire which also lambasts the excesses of the eighties. While Wolfe has said that both Balzac and Thackery serve as his models in writing his fiction, writers that McInerney has also acknowledged as influencing him in writing *Brightness Falls*, the two novels are very different. While McInerney's characters are sympathetically drawn, sucked into the whirlwind of eighties avarice and ambition, unable to resist, Wolfe's Sherman McCoy suffers from a hubris with which it is difficult to identify, and becomes embroiled in an increasingly outlandish plot.

Fourteen years after the publication of *Brightness Falls*, Corrine and Russell both appear in McInerney's post 9/11 novel, *The Good Life* with Corrine as one of the main protagonists.

About the author

Jay McInerney was born in Connecticut in 1955 and has lived in London, Tokyo and New York. His writing has appeared in a number of magazines such as *Esquire* and *Atlantic*. His first novel, *Bright Lights, Big City*, published in 1984, was made into a film for which he wrote the screenplay.

For discussion

○ In Jeff's musings as he watches Russell and Corrine walk up the hill to the hospital at the beginning of the novel, he sees them as a golden couple. Is this an accurate portrayal of their relationship? How would you describe their marriage as the novel opens? How is it changed at the end? What chance do you think it would have of survival and on what basis?

○ Corrine is portrayed as a 'modern woman' with a foot on the career ladder. Would you describe her as being in charge of her life? How does her view of life differ from Trina's?

○ When Russell takes Victor Propp for lunch, Victor says to him: 'Men are the great romantics, the dreamers and fools. Women are realists.' Do you think this idea is borne out in the novel and if so, how? To what extent would you apply it to the real world?

○ What sort of friend is Russell to Jeff and vice versa? Near the end of the book Jeff says to Russell: 'I sometimes think of everything I've done since college as an inverse image of your life.' Why do you think that the two friends took such different paths? Is Jeff's suggestion, that Russell's marriage to Corrine saved him, an adequate explanation?

○ How important is money in the novel? What part does it play in the disintegration of Russell and Corrine's marriage? Is it the driving force behind the need for Trina and Melman to make deals? If not, what is?

○ How would you describe the social world in which Russell and Corrine move? How does McInerney use peripheral characters to build up a picture of New York in the 1980s?

○ Much is made of the fact that Washington, one of the colleagues who join Russell in his new venture, is black. How is the issue of race treated in the novel?

○ Corrine is a volunteer at the soup kitchen. Does McInerney offer any explanation for the gulf between Corrine's life and the life of people on the streets and, if so, what is it?

🖳 Resources

www.nytimes.com/books/98/09/27/specials/mcinerney-falls.html – review by the novelist Cathleen Schine published in *The New York Times*

http://books.guardian.co.uk/departments/generalfiction/story/0,6000,366487,00.html – interview by Lynn Barber published in *The Observer*

www.beatrice.com/interviews/mcinerney – interview by Ron Hogan published at beatrice.com

🕮 Suggested further reading

The Fall by Albert Camus (1956); *The House of Sand and Fog* by Andre Dubus III (1999); *The Great Gatsby* by F. Scott Fitzgerald (1925); *Goodbye to Berlin* by

Christopher Isherwood (1939); *Two Guys from Verona* by James Kaplan (1998); *The Emperor's Children* by Claire Messud (2006); *Martin Dressler* by Steven Millhauser (1996); *In a Land of Plenty* **by Tim Pears** (1997); *The Custom of the Country* by Edith Wharton (1913); *Bonfire of the Vanities* by Tom Wolfe (1987)

OTHER BOOKS BY JAY MCINERNEY

Novels: *Bright Lights, Big City* (1984); *Ransom* (1985); *Story of My Life* (1988); *The Last of the Savages* (1996); *Model Behaviour* (1998); *The Good Life* (2006)

Short stories: *How It Ended* (2000)

Non-fiction: *Bacchus and Me: Adventures in the Wine Cellar* (2002); *A Hedonist in the Cellar* (2006)

THE ORCHARD ON FIRE (1995)
Shena Mackay

📖 About the book

In 1953 eight-year-old April Harlency's parents escape from their gloomy Streatham pub to take over the running of the Copper Kettle tea rooms in a small village in Kent. When April meets Ruby, they become best friends, forming an exclusive alliance against the rest of the world. Ruby, a little too in love with adventure, valiantly contends with her bullying parents while fiercely protecting April against the inevitable teasing which any newcomer suffers. While her parents struggle with their new business, April tries to cope with the unwelcome and unhealthy attentions of the seemingly respectable Mr Greenidge. Seeking refuge in their camp, writing letters in invisible ink and calling to each other with their secret signal, April and Ruby cement a friendship that seems unassailable. Told through April's voice, *The Orchard on Fire* vividly evokes a rural childhood in the 1950s.

Background

Childhood is popularly portrayed as a time of carefree innocence yet children are often haunted by worries that are dismissed as trivial by adults and sometimes beset by very real terrors that they feel unable to confide. *The Orchard on Fire* is set in a small Kent village in the 1950s, but deals with aspects of childhood which are relevant anywhere and at any time. By telling the story of the friendship between April Harlency and Ruby Richards through April's fresh and often funny eight-year-old voice, Shena Mackay vividly depicts both the dark fears and the happy excitements of childhood.

Although published when Mackay was twenty her first book, the two novellas, *Dust Falls on Eugene Schlumburger* and *Toddler on the Run* was written when she was still a teenager. She had gained her first public recognition as a writer when she won a poetry competition held by *The Daily Mirror* at the age of sixteen just before she left school. She found a job in an antique shop managed by Frank Marcus whose play *The Killing of Sister George* later became a sixties classic. Marcus encouraged Mackay with her writing, introducing her to her first publisher, André Deustch. As a young attractive female writer in the sixties she found herself thrust into the literary limelight and fêted on the publishing party circuit. Now she prefers to avoid the razzmatazz of book promotion and has been described as 'a publicist's nightmare'. After a lull in her writing from the early seventies to the mid-eighties when she was bringing up her children, she has continued to publish short stories and novels, some quietly accomplished, others bitingly satirical, which have been admired by writers as diverse as Iris Murdoch and Julie Burchill. *The Orchard on Fire* is generally regarded as one of her finest novels.

About the author

Shena Mackay was born in Edinburgh in 1944. As well as serving on the London Arts Board, she has been a judge for a number of literary prizes including the Whitbread Prize and the Macmillan Silver Pen Award. In 1993 her work was the subject of a BBC Bookmark film. She won the Fawcett Society Prize for her novel *Redhill Rococo*, published in 1986. *The Orchard on Fire* was shortlisted for the 1996 Booker Prize, the Saltire Prize and the McVitie's Prize. Shena Mackay lives in London.

For discussion

❍ *The Orchard on Fire* is told through the voice of April, an eight-year-old girl. How successful do you feel Mackay is in portraying the world through a child's eyes? Are there particular things that you feel she gets right or wrong and what are they?

❍ What does the book have to say about adults' attitudes towards children? Why does April feel she can't tell her parents about Mr Greenidge? Do you think they would have believed her? What do you think their reaction would have been? How damaging to you think Mr Greenidge has been to April?

❍ Are Percy and Betty good parents to April? How do you think their upbringing of April would compare with the parents of an eight-year-old today? How different do you think today's children are from the children in the novel?

❍ How would you describe Ruby? How does she deal with her parents' bullying behaviour? Do you think that people like the Richards would be treated any differently today and, if so, how?

⭘ How would you describe the grown-up April of the first and final chapters of the novel? How has the loss of Ruby affected April?

⭘ How authentic do you think April's memories of her childhood are likely to be? How do attitudes to childhood change as people get older? How does that attitude change if people have children of their own?

⭘ How does Mackay anchor *The Orchard on Fire* so firmly in the 1950s?

⭘ April says of the 'kitchenalia' shop: 'They are trying to buy their way into the past they think we had, they want to be snug and safe down Rabbit Lane.' How much safer, if at all, do you think life was in the 1950s? How safe was life at Stonebridge?

🖥 Resources

www.contemporarywriters.com/authors/?p=auth64 – profile of Shena Mackay at the British Council website including a critical essay by Dr Jules Smith

www.richmondreview.co.uk/books/orchard.html – review by Helena Mary Smith published in *The Richmond Review* internet magazine

www.guardian.co.uk/saturday_review/story/0,,290283,00.html – profile by Ian Hamilton published in *The Guardian*

www.telegraph.co.uk/arts/main.jhtml?xml=/arts/2004/01/04/bomackay.xml&sSheet=/arts/2004/01/04/bomain.html – interview by Helen Brown published in *The Telegraph*

📚 Suggested further reading

FICTION

Behind the Scenes at the Museum **by Kate Atkinson** (1996); *Cat's Eye* by Margaret Atwood (1989); *Girl in the Garden* by Lesley Chamberlain (2003); *Eve Green* by Susan Fletcher (2004); *Hideous Kinky* by Esther Freud (1993); *The Ten O'Clock Horses* by Laurie Graham (1996); **The Kite Runner by Khaled Hosseini** (2003); *Five Boys* by Mick Jackson (2001); **So Long, See You Tomorrow by William Maxwell** (1980); **Anita and Me by Meera Syal** (1996); *The Little Friend* by Donna Tartt (2002)

NON-FICTION

Cider With Rosie by Laurie Lee (1959)

OTHER BOOKS BY SHENA MACKAY

Novels: *Music Upstairs* (1965); *Old Crow* (1967); *An Advent Calendar* (1971); *A Bowl of Cherries* (1984); *Redhill Rococo* (1986); *Dunedin* (1992); *The Artist's Widow* (1998); *Heligoland* (2002)

Novellas: *Dust Falls on Eugene Schlumburger/Toddler on the Run* (published in one volume, 1964)

Short stories: *Babies in Rhinestones* (1983); *Dreams of Dead Women's Handbags* (1987); *The Laughing Academy* (1993); *Collected Stories* (1994); *The World's Smallest Unicorn and Other Stories* (1999); *Heligoland* (2003); *The Atmospheric Railway* (2006)

Edited: *Such Devoted Sisters* (short story anthology) (1994); *Friendship* (essays) (1997)

REMEMBERING BABYLON (1993)

David Malouf

📖 About the book

On a sweltering day in the mid-nineteenth century, a strange and ragged figure dances out of the Australian bush and into the lives of a small group of white settlers. Gemmy Fairley has spent almost sixteen years living with aborigines. At first his eccentricities are greeted with the amusement of novelty but in time the settlement becomes riven with suspicion. As the settlers attempt to impose their own kind of order on an environment which they perceive as hostile, many of them find Gemmy's presence both unsettling and threatening. Where do the loyalties of this man, who is white like them but seems to have more in common with aborigines, lie? As Gemmy tries to find a place for himself in the community, friendships are strained to breaking point, brutality begins to surface but one family finds a new way to look at the world.

Background

In the mid-nineteenth century, when news of free land in Australia reached Britain many were inspired to set out in search of a prosperous future. *Remembering Babylon* is both an examination of the arrival of an outsider in a small, close-knit but barely established community and a commentary on colonialism.

Gemmy's arrival threatens the fragile identities of settlers described by David Malouf as 'a community that wouldn't otherwise have held together but for their whiteness and Europeanness'. Strangers as they are in a strange land, they are faced with a man who seems to be is neither truly British nor Australian but a disturbing amalgamation of the two, a worrying prospect of what might become of them and their children. As Malouf acknowledges in the note which follows the novel Gemmy's character was based on James (Gemmy) Morril or Morell who having been shipwrecked in 1846, spent seventeen years with the Bindal tribe in the Bowen region of Queensland. Just as the fictional Gemmy walked out of the Australian bush and announced himself as 'a British object' so did the real life Morril but Malouf points out that apart from that 'this novel has no origin in fact'.

Gemmy is a man who has lost his language, something that Malouf considers to be paramount in any civilization: 'One of my concerns is the place of language, not just as a means of communication, but as a way of apprehending and organizing our world.' He has said that there is a 'dislocation' between the English language and the Australian landscape, but that for him Australian identity lies 'in the fact that we share that language with one another and have changed that language in ways that fit us, but fit us socially rather than fit the land.' Malouf's own careful use of language is evident throughout his writing. He began his writing career as a poet rather than a novelist and it is its vividly evocative descriptions and striking images which make *Remembering Bablyon* linger in the mind long after the novel has been read.

About the author

David Malouf was born in Brisbane in 1934. His father's family emigrated to Australia from the Lebanon in the 1880s. His mother's family came from London on the eve of the First World War. After graduating from the University of Queensland, he taught in the English department for two years. In 1959 he moved to the United Kingdom, working as a teacher, first in London and later, in Birkenhead, returning to Australia in 1968 to teach at the University of Sydney. In 1977 he took up writing full time and moved to Tuscany, returning to Australia in 1985. He is internationally acclaimed both as a novelist and a poet and has also written several opera libretti. His novel *The Great World*, winner of the Miles Franklin Award in 1990, also won both the Commonwealth Writers' Prize and the Prix Femina Etranger in 1991. *Remembering Babylon* was shortlisted for the Booker Prize in 1993 and won the 1996 International IMPAC Dublin Literary Award.

For discussion

⭘ David Malouf is a poet as well as a novelist. How do you think this has influenced his writing in *Remembering Babylon*? Can you find particular examples to support your view?

⭘ How would you describe Lachlan's reaction to Gemmy when he arrives? How important is his relationship with Gemmy in shaping his life both as a child and an adult? Why do you think Gemmy made such an impression on Lachlan? How important was Gemmy to Janet?

✪ How would you describe the community's reactions to Gemmy when he arrives? Is everyone's reaction the same and, if not, how do they differ? How do people's feelings towards Gemmy change over time? Why do you think they change?

✪ How would you describe the majority of the settlers' feelings towards the landscape around them? What do they feel about the aborigines? Why do you think they feel this way? Are there characters that don't share this view? Can you explain why this might be?

✪ Why does Jock continue to protect Gemmy at the risk of antagonizing his neighbours? How does giving Gemmy a home change him? How does the relationship between Ellen and Jock change? What do you think provokes those changes?

✪ There are references to nature throughout the novel – in the descriptions of the landscape, Frazer's botanizing and Mrs Hutchence's bee-keeping. How important do you think nature is as a theme in the novel? How does the aborigines' attitude to the bush differ from the settlers'?

✪ Why does Gemmy feel at ease with Frazer? What do you think Frazer is saying about colonialism in the extracts from his field notebook quoted in chapter 14? Are these ideas illustrated elsewhere in the novel and, if so, where? What do you think of them?

✪ 'Could you lose it? Not just language but *it. It.*' Why does Gemmy make the settlers so uneasy? What do they mean by '*It*'?

✪ What is the significance of the novel's title, *Remembering Babylon*?

🖥 Resources

www.nytimes.com/books/00/08/20/specials/malouf-babylon.html – review by the novelist Suzanne Berne published in *The New York Times* together with a brief interview by Joseph A. Cincotti

www.contemporarywriters.com/authors/?p=auth66 – profile of David Malouf at the British Council website including an essay by James Proctor

www.lib.latrobe.edu.au/AHR/archive/Issue-Sept-1996/intermal.html – an interview by Helen Daniel published in the *Australian Book Review*

📖 Suggested further reading

The Songlines by Bruce Chatwin (1987); *Gould's Book of Fish* by Richard Flanagan (2001); *A Passage to India* by E.M. Forster (1924); *Rites of Passage* by William Golding (1980); *The Secret River* by Kate Grenville (2006); *Snow Falling on Cedars* by David Guterson (1995); *Promised Lands* by Jane Rogers (1995)

OTHER BOOKS BY DAVID MALOUF

Novels: *Johnno* (1975); *An Imaginary Life* (1978); *Fly Away Peter* (1982); *Child's Play* (1982); *Harland's Half Acre* (1985); *Antipodes* (1985); *The Great World* (1990); *The Conversations at Curlow Creek* (1996); *Dream Stuff* (2000)

Short stories: *Every Move You Make* (2007)

Poetry: *Bicycle and Other Poems* (1970); *Neighbours in a Thicket* (1974); *The Year of the Foxes and Other Poems* (1976); *Wild Lemons* (1980); *First Things Last* (1980); *Selected Poems 1959–1989* (1994)

Libretti: *Baa Baa Black Sheep* (1994); *Jane Eyre* (2000)

Drama: *Blood Relations* (1988)

Autobiography: *12 Edmonstone Street* (1985)

SO LONG, SEE YOU TOMORROW (1980)
William Maxwell

📖 About the book

Set in small town Illinois and written in William Maxwell's characteristically elegant understated prose, *So Long, See You Tomorrow* is narrated by an elderly man looking back over fifty years to his painful adolescence, and an incident that still torments him: his decision to ignore a friend in need. Isolated by his mother's sudden death the narrator's fleeting friendship with Cletus Smith comes to a sudden end when Cletus is caught up in a domestic tragedy which culminates in the murder of his mother's lover and the suicide of his father. When the narrator moves to Chicago, he and Cletus pass each other in the corridor of their new school, but each remains silent. Stricken with a remorse that haunts his adult life, the narrator constructs a vividly imagined story of the passion which tore two families apart, leaving Cletus in a solitary misery which echoes the narrator's own.

Background

William Maxwell's writing, with its delicately understated depictions of love, loss and betrayal in the lives of ordinary people, ranks alongside the best of his generation. For Maxwell, literature was the stuff of life. In his introduction to his collection of essays, *The Outermost Dream*, he wrote 'Reading is rapture' and it was this passion for literature that made him both a fine writer and a perceptive editor.

Maxwell took to the sometimes thorny relationship between writer and editor beautifully. His tact and delicacy together with his own experience as a writer led him to empathize with his authors, building close relationships that often developed into friendship. Such a sensitive understanding of the editorial process helped Maxwell in his approach to his own writing.

As he was happy to admit, Maxwell drew heavily upon his early life in his fiction. He spent his first ten years in Lincoln, Illinois, a small town that provided the blueprint for all the small towns in which his fiction is set. His childhood was shattered when his mother died from Spanish influenza in the epidemic that swept the world in 1918. He was only ten years old and his relationship with his mother had been particularly close. Her death, he has said, was the defining event of his life.

The influence of this sudden and terrible loss can be clearly seen in *They Came Like Swallows* published in 1937, the year that Maxwell was appointed fiction editor of the *New Yorker*, which evokes the desolation of a house now emptied of the loving attentions that so often went unacknowledged. This was a theme to which Maxwell returned many times both in his short stories and in his novels *The Folded Leaf* and *So Long, See You Tomorrow*, the narrator of which shares Maxwell's slight build, shyness and antipathy to sport.

Sadly, William Maxwell was never so well known as the authors whose work he edited, many of whom praised his writing unreservedly. Although *So Long, See You Tomorrow* brought him a little more attention when it won the American Book Award, his work has been largely under appreciated.

About the author

William Maxwell was born in 1908 in Lincoln, Illinois. He attended the University of Illinois, followed by a period of graduate study at Harvard. In 1937 he became fiction editor of *New Yorker* where he remained for forty years. The friend and editor of many literary luminaries of the time, including J.D. Salinger, Eudora Welty, Vladimir Nabokov and John Updike, Maxwell published six novels, several collections of short stories and a memoir of his family history. *So Long, See You Tomorrow* won the American Book Award in 1980, three years after he retired from the *New Yorker*. William Maxwell died in New York in 2000.

For discussion

✪ 'This memoir – if that's the right name for it – is a roundabout, futile way of making amends.' What is it that the narrator so desperately wants to make amends for? Do you feel that his guilt is justified? What does the incident in the school corridor tell us about him?

○ How would you describe the narrator? What kind of child is he? What effect does the loss of his mother have on him, and on his father? What kind of man is his father and how would you describe his relationship between father and son? How important is the narrator's father's inability to talk about the loss of his wife?

○ Are there parallels between the narrator's story and the story he reconstructs for Cletus? How important is Cletus to him and why? What effect do the tragic events in his family have upon Cletus?

○ How would you describe the relationship between Clarence and Lloyd before Lloyd begins his affair with Fern? Why does Clarence shoot Lloyd – is it simply because Lloyd has been sleeping with Fern or are the reasons more complex?

○ How would you describe the marriages of Marie and Lloyd, and Fern and Clarence? What were expectations of marriage likely to be in 1920s Lincoln? Do you think Fern's hope of happiness with Lloyd were realistic?

○ 'In the Palace at 4 a.m. you walk from one room to the next by going through the walls ... It is there that I find Cletus Smith.' What does the narrator mean by this? Does he, ultimately, find peace? How have the sad events of his adolescence affected his adult life? How different is he as an adult from the troubled child of the 1920s?

○ Why do you think that Maxwell chose to write much of the penultimate chapter from the point of view of Trixie, Cletus's dog? What effect does it have?

How would you describe the societies of both 1920s Lincoln and Chicago? Which better suits the narrator and why?

○ 'In any case, in talking about the past we lie with every breath we draw.' What do you think Maxwell means by this statement? What is its significance in the context of a novel whose narrator is recalling events which took place fifty years ago? The narrative is refracted through narrator's adult experience. How is this likely to have changed his interpretation?

○ How would you describe Maxwell's writing? What is the tone of the narrative and how does it differ throughout the book?

○ The loss of a mother is a recurrent theme in Maxwell's fiction – he lost his own mother in the 1918 influenza epidemic, as did the narrator. How useful do you find knowledge of an author's life in analysing their fiction?

🖳 Resources

http://archives.lincolndailynews.com/2000/Nov/04/features/arts.shtml – speech to Lincoln College on Maxwell by his biographer Barbara Burkhardt

📚 Suggested further reading

A Crime in the Neighbourhood by Suzanne Berne (1997); *For Kings and Planets* by Ethan Canin (1998); *The Kite Runner* by Khaled Hosseini (2003); *On the Night Plain* by J. Robert Lennon (2001); *The Orchard on Fire* by Shena Mackay (1995); *The Story of Lucy Gault* by William Trevor (2002)

OTHER BOOKS BY WILLIAM MAXWELL

Fiction: *Bright Centre of Heaven* (1934); *They Came Like Swallows* (1937); *The Folded Leaf* (1945); *Time Will Darken It* (1948); *The Chateau* (1961); *All the Days and Nights: The Collected Stories* (1995)

Non-fiction: *Ancestors* (1972); *The Outermost Dream* (1989)

FUGITIVE PIECES (1996)

Anne Michaels

📖 About the book

Athos Roussos discovers a mud-covered boy while excavating an archaeological site in Poland, and takes the child home to the Greek island of Zakynthos. Seven-year-old Jakob Beer has escaped the Nazis, forced to listen to the cries of his parents as they were murdered while he lay hidden in a closet. Athos nourishes Jakob with knowledge and words, applying balm to the wounds inflicted by such devastating loss. After the war they move to Toronto but when his beloved mentor dies and his brief marriage fails, Jakob returns to Greece to work as a translator and write poetry. When he meets Michaela, the possibility of happiness finally becomes a reality only to be snuffed out by a traffic accident. After Jakob's death Ben, the child of concentration camp survivors, sets out in search of Jakob's journals. Written in richly poetic language and studded with striking images, *Fugitive Pieces* is profound meditation upon the nature of loss, love and the healing power of words.

Background

Although *Fugitive Pieces* has a beginning, a middle and an end, plot is not its most significant element. It is more a novel of ideas, a many-layered exploration of the way in which even the deepest wounds may be healed through love. The first two parts of the novel are narrated by Jakob Beer, the young Jewish boy whom Athos Roussos saves from the Nazis. Jakob witnessed the murder of his parents but he does not know what happened to his sister Bella. Memories of her are threaded through his narrative – she is always just out of reach, on the fringes of his consciousness. The third part is narrated by Ben, the child of concentration camp survivors. Anne Michaels has said when asked about her decision to include this narrative strand that: 'The book would have been entirely different and the meaning entirely different if the story had ended after the first half. It is important that both Jakob and Ben are profoundly influenced by events they did not live through or actually experience. The book explores the effect of memory and history. The second part needed to be there. On another level Ben is, in a sense, Jakob's heir. So Jakob has one heir although he has no children. There's a kind of hope to that ... a hope that many who lost their families could experience ... a hope for those who have no one to remember them. I didn't want to leave the reader in a dark place. I wouldn't have written the book without the second part. No, I would never leave the reader in a dark place like that. It would have changed the whole meaning of the book.'

Fugitive Pieces was ten years in the writing, a long gestation period for a novel. During her researches Michaels read a multitude of books on military history, botany, biology, archaeology, Greek history and the history of the Jews; her book is firmly rooted in the physical world yet deals with questions of enormous philosophical importance. Lisa Jardine, Chair of the panel of Orange Prize judges who chose *Fugitive Pieces* as their winner in 1997, described both Michaels' personality and her writing as 'careful', a word that she noted many other critics had applied to her work. She is careful both in her choice of words and in the way that she examines the questions raised by the Holocaust. As Jardine notes: '[Jakob Beer] says, "Questions without answers should be asked very slowly." Michaels slowly tries to make sense of the permanent psychic damage done to individuals as they collided, even at one remove, with the horror of the Holocaust. She chips painstakingly away at the layers of incomprehension and loss, with the concentrated determination of an archaeologist. No authorial investment in the outcome of the excavation, she makes clear, must be allowed to damage the precious traces of memory, to obliterate the casual brutality of history.' On what had prompted her to write about such difficult, painful but wholly necessary questions Michaels has said: 'One question had to do with photographs I saw when I was very young of the "laughing Nazi." They were of ... soldiers who performed unspeakable acts, and were caught in photographs laughing. I had to ask [how they could laugh] and probe that image. The hope was, if I could enter into relationship with certain historical facts, maybe I could wring some meaning out of them.' And in *Fugitive Pieces* she has surely done that. This beautiful, profound and deeply moving novel illuminates human nature, both evil and good, honouring those who suffered so appallingly and offering a beacon of hope to grasp in even the darkest of hours.

About the author

Anne Michaels was born in Toronto in 1958. She was educated at Toronto University where she spent several years teaching creative writing. She studied music from childhood and has worked as a composer in the theatre. Her first volume of poems, *Weight of Oranges*, was published to great acclaim in 1986 when it won the Commonwealth Poetry Prize for the Americas. *Fugitive Pieces*, her first novel, won both the Orange Prize and the Guardian Fiction Award. Michaels has since published another two volumes of poetry.

For discussion

✪ Even before the book opens we learn that Jakob Beer has been killed in an accident. How did the foreknowledge of Jakob's death affect your reading of the book? Why do you think that Michaels chose this moment for Jakob to die?

✪ 'When the prisoners were forced to dig up the mass graves, the dead entered them through their pores and were carried through their bloodstreams to their brains and hearts. And through their blood into another generation.' What echoes does this graphic image have later in the book? How does the influence of the dead run through the lives of the living and of the next generation? Does this still apply today?

✪ Michaels weaves Jacob's memories through Kostas' and Daphne's stories of the German occupation of Athens and the violence orchestrated by the Communist partisans which erupted after their departure. Why do you think that Michaels chose to put across their memories in this way?

✪ Jakob writes: 'I already knew the power of language to destroy, to omit, to obliterate. But poetry, the power of language to restore: this is what Athos and Kostas were trying to teach me.' How has the destructive power of language been revealed to Jakob? How is the restorative nature of poetry illustrated in the book? What part does language play in Jakob's life?

✪ Michaels is primarily a poet and *Fugitive Pieces* is her first novel. How are her skills as a poet reflected in the language of the novel? Were there particular words, phrases or passages that you found striking and, if so, what were they? What was it that you found so arresting in your examples?

✪ Music runs through the book as vital to several of the characters – Bella, Alex and Naomi are all passionate music lovers and Jakob also finds solace in it. Why is music so important to each of these characters?

○ Jakob's narrative is threaded with memories of his sister Bella, although we learn little of his parents. Why does Bella's absence seem to haunt Jakob more than his parents' murder?

○ Jakob states: 'History is amoral: events occurred. But memory is moral; what we consciously remember is what our conscience remembers.' How is this idea illustrated in the novel? What conclusions does Jakob draw about history?

○ When Jakob reasons his way through the Nazis' justification of their treatment of the Jews, what do you make of his argument? Have you read other arguments and, if so, how do they compare?

○ Ben describes a flash of recognition when reading one of Jakob's poems. How does Ben's indirect experience of the Holocaust differ from Jakob's? How are they similar? Why do you think Michaels chose to call the first sections of both Ben's and Jakob's narratives 'The Drowned City'?

○ Towards the end of the book Ben describes the different ways in which his parents deal with loss: 'Loss is an edge; it swelled everything for my mother and drained everything from my father.' Why do they react so differently? Are there aspects of their characters that govern the way they cope with the legacy of their terrible experiences?

○ Why are both of Ben's parents able to reach out to Naomi but not to Ben? Why does this anger Ben so much?

○ The last line of Ben's narrative, and of the novel, reads: 'I see that I must give what I most need.' What is it that Ben most needs and to whom will he give it?

○ What did the title of the novel mean to you? What are the 'fugitive pieces' in the book?

💻 Resources

www.nytimes.com/books/97/04/20/reviews/970420.20dipiert.html – review by the poet and critic W.S. Di Piero published in *The New York Times*

www.geocities.com/annemichaels/OdeToMemory.html – review by Gail Caldwell published in *The Boston Globe*

www.geocities.com/annemichaels/WordsworthInterview.html – interview by Kathleen O'Neill published at WordsWorth Books website

www.geocities.com/annemichaels/OrangePrizeJudgesComments.html – includes a lengthy piece by Lisa Jardine, chair of the 1997 Orange Prize Judges, on Anne Michaels

www.geocities.com/annemichaels/Askingquestionswithoutanswers.html – piece published in the *Gazette*, the magazine of York University, Canada, on a visit by Michaels.

🍃 Suggested further reading

FICTION

Captain Corelli's Mandolin by Louis de Bernières (1994); *The Archivist* by Martha Cooley (1998); *Everything is Illuminated* by Jonathan Safran Foer (2002); *Stones From the River* by Ursula Hegi (1994); **The Kite Runner by Khaled Hosseini** (2003); *Schindler's Ark* by Thomas Keneally (1985); *Yosl Rakover Talks to God* by Zvi Kolitz (1996); *The Time of Light* by Gunnar Kopperud (1998); *The English Patient* by Michael Ondaatje (1992); **The Reader by Bernhard Schlink** (1997); *The Dark Room* by Rachel Seiffert (2001); *Music For the Third Ear* by Susan Schwartz Senstad (1999)

AUTOBIOGRAPHY

Anne Frank: The Diary of a Young Girl by Anne Frank (1947); *If This is a Man/The Truce* by Primo Levi (1960)

HISTORY

Konin by Theo Richmond (1996)

OTHER BOOKS BY ANNE MICHAELS

Poetry: *Weight of Oranges* (1986); *Miner's Pond* (1991); *Skin Divers* (1999)

INGENIOUS PAIN (1997)

Andrew Miller

📖 About the book

Conceived on an icy night in the middle of the eighteenth century, the result of an adulterous coupling with a stranger, James Dyer is a strange child whose inability to feel physical or emotional pain marks him out. When his family are all but wiped out by smallpox his adventures begin. He attaches himself to a quack show, is abducted and kept in a rich man's house as a curiosity, acts as an assistant to a ship's physician and, later, becomes a brilliant but supremely arrogant surgeon in fashionable Bath. When scandal ruins his practice he joins the race to St Petersburg to inoculate the Empress of Russia against smallpox. En route he meets his nemesis – a strange woman whose miraculous powers give him the gift of pain. From here the road to redemption leads through madness and eventually to a modicum of peace before he dies, aged thirty-three, in a small West Country village.

Background

Set in the eighteenth century, *Ingenious Pain* straddles the old world of quack shows and superstition and the new world of religious doubt and scientific enquiry. This was a time of enormous change in European thinking: the time of Hume, Rousseau, Voltaire, Kant and Goethe. Often described as the Enlightenment, it was a truly revolutionary period during which many ideas long held to be definitive were overturned, as scientific discoveries offered rational explanations for phenomena previously thought to be either the work of God or of the devil. Such thinking was, of course, confined to those who had the time, money and opportunity to explore it while the vast majority continued to clutch at the old ideas, often enthralled by the freakish and gullibly buying the quacks' wares for their ills. This is the fascinating world which Andrew Miller explores as James Dyer's strange inability to feel pain takes him on the long journey from his impoverished Somerset home to the court of the Empress of Russia, via fairgrounds, press gangs, ship's surgeons, Bath society, and, finally, to his own kind of enlightenment.

Dyer's inability to feel either physical or emotional pain allows him to pursue a career in surgery unimpeded by empathy. Although a pain-free existence may, at first, appear enviable it precludes an understanding of suffering, isolating him from the rest of humanity, and preventing him from feeling pleasure and love, until a woman as strange as his own peculiarity relieves him of it, opening a new world to him. Both an exciting adventure story and a vivid depiction of a world on the brink of modernity, *Ingenious Pain* is also an exploration of the essential nature of compassion.

About the author

Born in Bristol in 1960, Andrew Miller grew up in the west of England. He has lived in Holland, Spain, Japan, France and Ireland. He studied Creative Writing at the University of East Anglia in 199, completing his PhD in Critical and Creative Writing at Lancaster University in 1995. *Ingenious Pain*, his first novel, met with a good deal of critical acclaim and went on to win both the James Tait Black Memorial Prize in 1997 and the Dublin IMPAC Literary Award in 1999. His third novel, *Oxygen*, was shortlisted for both the Booker Prize and the Whibread Novel Award in 2001.

For discussion

✪ Why do you think Andrew Miller chose the title *Ingenious Pain* – what is ingenious about pain?

✪ Reverend Lestrade muses to himself: 'What does the world need most – a good, ordinary man, or one who is outstanding, albeit with a heart of ice, of stone?' To what extent do you feel that the novel answers this question and what answers does it provide? How would you answer the question?

❍ How does the absence of pain affect Dyer's ability as a surgeon? What leads him to make the decision to become a surgeon?

❍ Several people describe Dyer as 'dangerous'. What is it that is dangerous about him? How does this manifest itself in the book?

❍ When Dyer lives in Mr Canning's house, he is attracted to the library. The librarian seeks out books for him – 'Not poetry, of course, or stories – the boy is blind to them'. Why is Dyer blind to poetry and stories? Are there other instances of literature which leave him untouched and how does Miller use literature to illustrate the change that is brought about in him towards the end of the book?

❍ When Dyer awakes to pain, Miller writes of Mary: 'He knows that she is his only hope, the beginning and the end of the nightmare.' What is the relationship between Mary and Dyer? Would you describe her as a healer? Why do you think she smiles when Dyer dies?

❍ Miller depicts a world on the threshold of the Enlightenment. What elements do you recognize of the modern world in the book? How are the new ways beginning to change the old?

❍ What do you think of Miller's use of language in the novel? Are there images or descriptions which you find particularly striking and, if so, what are they and why?

💻 Resources

www.nytimes.com/books/97/04/13/reviews/970413.13mcgratt.html – review by the novelist Patrick McGrath published in *The New York Times*

www.contemporarywriters.com/authors/?p=auth230 – profile of Andrew Miller at the British Council website including a critical essay by Dr Jules Smith

www.andrewmiller-author.co.uk/index.htm – Andrew Miller's website

📖 Suggested further reading

FICTION

Mr Vertigo by Paul Auster (1994); *Nights at the Circus* by Angela Carter (1984); *The Rationalist* by Warwick Collins (1993); *The Vintner's Luck* by Elizabeth Knox (1998); *A Case of Curiosities* by Allen Kurzweil (1992); *Lemprière's Dictionary* by Lawrence Norfolk (1991); *Perfume* by Patrick Süskind (1985); *The Horrific Sufferings of the Mind Reading Monster Hercules Barefoot* by Carl-Johan Vallgren (translated by Paul and Veronica Britten-Austen) (2002); *The Lightning Cage* by Alan Wall (1999)

NON-FICTION
The Enlightenment by Norman Hampson (1996); *English Society in the Eighteenth Century* by Roy Porter (1982)
OTHER BOOKS BY ANDREW MILLER
Casanova (1998); *Oxygen* (2001); *The Optimists* (2005)

THE WORLD BELOW (2001)
Sue Miller

📖 About the book
Fifty-two years old, twice divorced, the mother of three grown-up children and holding down the kind of humdrum teaching job that she could do in her sleep, Catherine Hubbard has reached a stage in her life when it's time to take stock. When she learns that her aunt has bequeathed the old family home to her and her brother, she negotiates a sabbatical, rents out her San Francisco house, packs up and sets off east. After she stumbles upon her grandmother's diaries in the attic of the old Vermont house, Catherine begins to understand that the bedrock of security and love she had taken for granted in her grandparents' home was not as easily won as she had assumed. Woven through Catherine's reflections on her own life and tentative beginnings of something new, is her grandmother's story of sexual awakening, misunderstandings and the eventual negotiation of a marriage based on partnership.

Background
Sue Miller has explained that the discovery of her own grandmother's diaries written in 1869 and 1870 gave her the idea to write *The World Below*. The entries in the diary were short and mostly mundane but one, in particular, caught Miller's eye: 'I am a person due to be disappointed in the very things I most wish to take pride in.' Miller went on to say: 'People lived so differently then. There was a world below the world they showed on the surface. And when things were hard, you simply went on. You put it behind you or beneath you and you moved ahead with your life.' Interweaving Georgia's diaries with Cath's experience Miller contrasts their very different approaches to life, highlighting the enormous social change that has taken place since the nineteenth century. She has also mentioned a second source of inspiration for the novel explaining that she had begun to think about the idea of alienation and exile after an argument with a friend whose parents had emigrated to the US from Ukraine. While her friend had insisted that indigenous Americans

would be unable to truly understand the concept, Miller had claimed that her own deeply religious parents must have felt alienated when their children proclaimed their atheism. In *The World Below* Georgia and the rest of the 'san's' inmates find themselves in exile from a world which wants to keep them firmly at arm's length.

With their concerns with family life, relationships and what happens when things go awry, Miller's writing has been compared with that of Joanna Trollope in the UK and Ann Tyler in her home country. She describes her writing as 'domestic realism', a form often labelled somewhat pejoratively 'women's fiction'. Aware of this dismissive tag, Miller welcomed the controversy that surrounded the selection of Jonathan Franzen's *The Corrections* by Oprah Winfrey for her book club, saying: 'Jonathan Franzen's discomfort at being taken up by Oprah and women readers opened up some intelligent American journalism about the schisms between male/female; high art/low art – 'womens' books' as opposed to serious books written by men. There's this whole notion, dominant in the 19th century, that writing novels was a pretty low art form, created for the daughters of shopkeepers to read.' In a world where so many marriages end in divorce, her own fiction with its sharp observations on the way we try to build a life together and the fallout when that life falls apart, deserves to be taken very seriously indeed.

About the author

Sue Miller was born in Chicago in 1943. She gained a place at Radcliffe when she was only sixteen years old and married shortly after graduating from Harvard, holding a variety of jobs until her son was born in 1968. Her first short story was published in 1981 and, after teaching a number of creative writing programmes around Boston, she held a writing fellowship at Radcliffe from 1984 to 1985. Her first novel, *The Good Mother*, was published in 1986 and was later made into a film starring Liam Neeson and Diane Keaton. Her sixth novel, *While I Was Gone*, was chosen for Oprah Winfrey's Book Club in June 2000.

For discussion

○ The narrative switches back and forth from the first to the third person as Catherine reconstructs Georgia's life from her diaries and letters, occasionally quoting from them directly. How successful did you find this structure? Why do you think Miller chose this way of telling Georgia's story rather than simply using the diaries themselves?

○ 'But they'd all gotten skilled by this time at never acknowledging what they knew, at pretending they didn't see what they saw.' Fanny's family becomes adept at convincing themselves that there is nothing seriously wrong with her. Why do you think they do this? How does Miller explore the links between illness and shame in the book? Is this still a problem for us today?

⚪ When remembering the silence that surrounded her mother's schizophrenia Catherine put forward her own philosophy on hard truths with the statement: 'I explained everything to my children, long before their questions could have been framed.' Is this philosophy reflected throughout Catherine's life? How does it fit with her reflections on reading Georgia's diary when she says that she 'would never have wanted my children – or their children when they came – to know the way I made the decisions that resulted in their lives'?

⚪ Ostensibly, Catherine and Georgia have lived very different lives yet the diaries reveal many parallels. What are they? Are there character traits that the two women share? How do the two women's lives differ? How would you compare Georgia's marriage with Catherine's, first to Peter and then to Joe?

⚪ Georgia describes the sanatorium as 'a place that existed out of time'. What does she mean by this? Why do you think the atmosphere in the 'san' was so much more liberated than outside it? What are the lasting effects of her time there? To what extent does it set her apart from other women of her generation?

⚪ When Georgia hears of Seward's worsening condition in Colorado, she feels no terrible grief. Can her feelings for Seward be described as love? What might have attracted her to him? Would the relationship have formed in other circumstances?

⚪ John says to Catherine that being Georgia's doctor had given him 'Too much power in her life'. Do you think this is the case? How has he exercised that power? Are there ways in which he has balanced it? What has the overall effect been on their lives?

⚪ Catherine considers the possibility of a relationship with Samuel. Why does she choose to turn away? Why do you think Miller chose to portray Samuel as so much older than Catherine?

⚪ Catherine has mixed feelings about whether diaries should be read by anyone other than the diarist. What do you think of the debate between Catherine and Samuel on this subject? Whom do you most agree with?

⚪ Why is Catherine drawn back to Vermont? What purpose has her sojourn there served for her? How has it changed her attitude to the future? What are the factors that have brought her to the decision that she doesn't want to 'begin again' as she tells Fiona?

⚪ Why do you think Miller chose the title *The World Below*? To what do you think it refers?

○ Miller has been described as a writer with feminist sympathies. Although, perhaps, not a feminist novel in the traditional sense, would you say that there are feminist aspects to *The World Below*?

💻 Resources
www.findarticles.com/p/articles/mi_qn4158/is_20020727/ai_n12643502 – interview by Sue Fox published in *The Independent*
www.randomhouse.com/rhpg/rc/library/display.pperl?isbn=9780345440761&view =qa – interview by the novelist Michelle Huneven for Ballantine, Sue Miller's American publishers
www.beatrice.com/interviews/miller – interview by Ron Hogan published at beatrice.com

📗 Suggested further reading
Behind the Scenes at the Museum by Kate Atkinson (1995); *The Forms of Water* by Andrea Barrett (1993); *Sights Unseen* by Kaye Gibbons (1995); *A Short History of a Prince* by Jane Hamilton (1998); *Animal Dreams* by Barbara Kingsolver (1990); *Charming Billy* by Alice McDermott (1999); *The Stone Diaries* by Carol Shields (1993); *Fortune's Rocks* by Anita Shreve (2000)
OTHER BOOKS BY SUE MILLER
Novels: *The Good Mother* (1986); *Family Pictures* (1990); *For Love* (1993); *The Distinguished Guest* (1995); *While I Was Gone* (1999); *Lost in the Forest* (2005); *The Senator's Wife* (2008)
Short stories: *Inventing the Abbotts* (1997)
Non-fiction: *The Story of My Father* (2003)

THE BOY IN THE MOON (1997)
Kate O'Riordan

📖 About the book
Julia and Brian have been married for ten years. Their marriage is full of cracks, papered over and held together by the presence of their seven-year-old son, Sam. On a visit to Brian's family in Ireland, tragedy strikes when Sam is killed in an accident while playing with his father. Stunned with grief, Julia leaves Brian to try to deal with his terrible guilt, made worse by childhood memories of the accidental

death of his twin brother. When Julia decides to go to Ireland to stay with Brian's tyrannical father, Jeremiah, the decision seems perverse. At first, she finds an escape in routine and hard work, inching her way back to some sort of normality. But when she discovers a diary that unlocks the secrets of Brian's childhood fears, Julia begins to understand that Jeremiah has inflicted terrible pain on his children. When, eventually, Brian and Julia come together again, they share a new understanding and the beginnings of a hard-won peace.

Background

The Boy in the Moon is a disturbing but rewarding novel which tackles the deepest fears lurking beneath ordinary domestic lives. When Sam falls to his death while under his father's supervision, his parents' lives are struck by the very tragedy that his father constantly fears but perversely courts. Kate O'Riordan's description of the anguish of both parents is starkly vivid but Brian's and Julia's eventual acceptance of Sam's death and the beginnings of reconciliation leave us with a sense of the resilience of the human spirit.

O'Riordan's fiction varies from what can loosely be called the romantic comedy of *Angel in the House* in which a young man, desperate to fall in love, thinks he has found himself an angel only to find her family is one of comic eccentricity, to the spare, aching prose of loss which characterises *The Boy in the Moon*. Her fiction explores the conflicts that lie at the heart of families, often surrounding secrets long buried but disturbed by a returning member of the family or a new partner: she made her much-praised debut with *Involved*, a powerful novel of love and obsession in which a young woman seeks to rescue her lover from a forbidding family whose secrets are locked tight. Her characters often find themselves facing hard truths from their past. In *The Memory of Stones* Nell has made a successful, sophisticated life for herself in France but must shoulder the responsibilities she has been fleeing when she is called home to Ireland. O'Riordan's writing career extends to stage and screen where she has had notable success, including her screenplay for *The Return* starring Julie Walters as a woman just released from a 10-year sentence after killing her violent husband, a theme that could easily have been the subject of one of her novels.

Although her books are not to be found riding high in the bestseller lists, O'Riordan's novels are wonderfully perceptive in their characterization, and thought-provoking in their tackling of the dark, difficult areas of family life: *The Boy in the Moon* is a fine example of her writing

About the author

Kate O'Riordan was born and brought up in the west of Ireland. A playwright and screenwriter as well as a novelist, she has had several plays performed on the London stage. She has also won the *Sunday Tribune*/Hennessy Prize for Best Emerging Writer. *The Boy in the Moon* is her second novel.

For discussion

✪ The first chapter of the book is headed 'Is it Love?' What do you think the answer to this question is, at this point in the book? How does your view change, if at all, and at what point?

✪ What sort of mother do you think Julia is? What sort of father is Brian? What does the incident in the service station, when Sam gets lost, and its aftermath say about the way they work together as parents?

✪ Why do you think Brian takes risks with Sam? Has Brian's position as Noel's protector and Noel's subsequent fatal accident influenced his behaviour with Sam? Why has he 'always been afraid' and why is this the first time in his life that he can acknowledge it?

✪ Why do you think Julia returns to Ireland after Sam's death, despite the aversion she has to it in the opening chapters? Does she find any comfort there and, if so, what form does it take?

✪ Despite Jeremiah's cruel and bullying behaviour, people around him – Brian, Cathal and even Julia – seem to adapt themselves to his requirements. How do you explain this? Why does Edward not do this?

✪ To what extent does Julia begin to understand Brian after living under the same roof as Jeremiah? How has her own behaviour towards Brian shaped their relationship? At various points Julia compares herself to Jeremiah. Do you think this is fair and, if so, which elements of Julia's behaviour towards Brian might remind him of his father? In what ways has Julia's upbringing affected her ability to show love?

✪ When Brian visits Jennifer and Richard, they find themselves laughing hysterically. Does this reaction surprise you? How can you explain it within the context of grief?

✪ The encounter between Julia and the dog that has been bullying Jeremiah's collie is very powerfully described. What do you think O'Riordan is trying to convey in this incident and in the recurrent persecution of the collie that leads up to it?

📚 Suggested further reading

The Sweet Hereafter by Russell Banks (1991); ***Talking to the Dead* by Helen Dunmore** (1996); *Mothers' Boys* by Margaret Forster (1994); *Altered Land* by Jules

Hardy (2002); *What I Loved* by Siri Hustvedt (2003); *The Child in Time* by Ian McEwan (1987); *The Dark* by John McGahern (1965); *The Story of You* by Julie Myerson (2006); *The Lovely Bones* by Alice Sebold (2002); *The Pilot's Wife* by Anita Shreve (1996); *The Little Friend* by Donna Tartt (2002); *Thin Air* by Kate Thompson (1999)

OTHER NOVELS BY KATE O'RIORDAN

Involved (1995); *The Angel in the House* (2000); *The Memory of Stones* (2003); *Loving Him* (2005); Kate O'Riordan has also contributed to the short story anthology *Ladies' Night at Finbar's Hotel* (1999), edited by Dermot Bolger

THE ICARUS GIRL (2005)

Helen Oyeyemi

📖 About the book

Jessamy Harrison is a frightened, lonely little girl afflicted with unexplained panic attacks and screaming fits. After a particularly disturbing episode, her parents decide to take her to meet her mother's family in Nigeria. Here Jess finds herself drawn to the old servants' quarters where one day she meets the mysterious Titiola, or TillyTilly as Jess decides to call her. Emboldened by TillyTilly, Jess becomes more confident. When the family returns home Jess is bereft but TillyTilly has followed her. All sorts of strange and unexplained events occur, gradually becoming more sinister as TillyTilly 'gets' all those who threaten or hurt Jess. But TillyTilly wants something in return and Jess finds herself desperately trying to escape the strange little girl who invades her life, her dreams and even herself. Helen Oyeyemi writes vividly of alienation, the loneliness of being different, the terrors of the unexplained and the searing sadness of separation.

Background

Helen Oyeyemi attracted a good deal of media attention even before the publication of *The Icarus Girl*, written in secret in a whirlwind seven months while she was studying for her A-levels. She signed a two-book contract on the day she got her results and has since garnered a sheaf of enthusiastic reviews for her first novel. Although her sister has read *The Icarus Girl*, she has said that she doesn't want her parents to read it, concerned they may be upset by her view of Nigeria.

    The Icarus Girl takes its premise from the Yoruba belief that twins inhabit three separate worlds: the Bush, a 'wilderness for the mind', the normal world and the spirit world. Oyeyemi explains that TillyTilly is from the Bush, 'a world that doesn't have the same structure as our world'. Through Jess's loss of her twin and her isolation at school, Oyeyemi explores themes of loneliness, alienation and the difficulties – particularly for a young child – of being very obviously different. Jess's mixed race, her precocity and her tantrums set her apart from her schoolmates, marking her out and only serving to intensify the loneliness she already feels. Oyeyemi has drawn on her own experience in exploring this emotional terrain. She describes herself as 'a real mess at school', isolated from her classmates and regarded as 'the weird girl'. At the age of fifteen she took an overdose and while recovering took refuge in reading: she still proclaims herself to be 'more of a reader than a writer'. That summer her parents took her to Nigeria, a country that she had not visited since her immigration to Britain. The visit set the seal on her recovery although she doesn't feel Nigerian: 'I'm just British' she says.

About the author
Helen Oyeyemi was born in Nigeria in 1984 and moved to London when she was four. *The Icarus Girl* was written while Oyeyemi was studying for her A-levels and she is also the author of two plays, *Juniper's Whitening* and *Victimese*.

For discussion
❍ How successful is Helen Oyeyemi at capturing the voice, thoughts and fears of a disturbed eight-year-old?

❍ Jess has a black Nigerian-born mother and a white English father. How important is her mixed race? How important are these two very different cultures to her? How does Sarah feel about Nigerian beliefs and culture and how do her feelings affect Jess?

❍ Jess is a disturbed, lonely and frightened little girl before TillyTilly arrives. Why do you think this is?

❍ 'Jessamy, are you scared of your Mum?' asks Colin Mackenzie. Is this part of Jess's problem? How does Sarah feel about her daughter?

❍ '... Jess's expression of remorse shifted into an empty reflex expression, the corners of her mouth tugging up into a smile.' What is happening to Jess? How does TillyTilly change her life? Is her presence entirely bad?

❍ What is the significance of the 'long-armed woman' who appears in Jess's dreams? What does she mean when she says 'We are the same'?

❍ When Jess begs TillyTilly to 'show me how to be like you' what is it that she wants?

❍ What is the meaning of the poem that Jess and TillyTilly write? What is Sarah's reaction to it? How does the discovery of Fern's existence affect Jess?

❍ '"What are you?" Jess cried out from her safe place. TillyTilly's reply: I don't know! You know! *You* know!' What does TillyTilly mean? What is TillyTilly – a ghost, a demon, Jess's *alter ego* as Colin Mackenzie suggests, or something else?

❍ Jess's grandfather tells her 'Two hungry people should never make friends.' What does he mean? How important is Jess's grandfather to her?

❍ How appropriate is the book's title?

❍ What do you make of the book's ending?

❍ When reviewing *The Icarus Girl* the novelist Lesley Glaister wrote: 'I was actually trembling when I put it down and had to keep the light on all night. I think it's the most haunting and disturbing novel I've ever read.' What was your own reaction to the book? Do you agree with Glaister? How does Oyeyemi achieve the dark, sinister atmosphere that pervades the second half of book?

🖥 Resources

http://portal.telegraph.co.uk/arts/main.jhtml?xml=/arts/2005/01/09/boyeyemi.xml – Interview with Helen Brown in *The Telegraph*

http://books.guardian.co.uk/departments/generalfiction/story/0,6000,1386619,00.html – interview with Anita Sethi in *The Guardian*

http://scotlandonsunday.scotsman.com/opinion.cfm?id=25272005 – interview with *Scotland on Sunday*

http://www.timesonline.co.uk/article/0,,2102-1446057,00.html – review by Peter Parker in *The Sunday Times*

http://www.telegraph.co.uk/arts/main.jhtml?xml=/arts/2005/01/30/boye30.xml&sSheet=/arts/2005/01/30/bomain.html – review by Patrick Ness in *The Telegraph*

http://books.guardian.co.uk/reviews/generalfiction/0,6121,1395774,00.html – review by Ali Smith in *The Guardian*

📚 Suggested further reading

26a by Diane Evans (2005); *The Yellow Wallpaper* by Charlotte Perkins Gilman (1892); *I Know This Much is True* by Wally Lamb (1998); *The Fifth Child* by Doris Lessing (1998); *Sleepwalking* by Julie Myerson (1994); *Puttermesser Papers* by Cynthia Ozick (1997)

OTHER BOOKS BY HELEN OYEYEMI

Fiction: *The Opposite House* (2007)

Drama: *Juniper's Whitening/Victimese* (2005)

THE MAGICIAN'S ASSISTANT (1998)

Ann Patchett

📖 About the book

Sabine has loved her husband for over twenty years but this is no ordinary love story, for Parsifal is gay and Sabine has always known it. When Parsifal dies suddenly, she is devastated. Swaddling herself in her duvet in an attempt to hide from her grief, she is shocked out of it by her lawyer, who tells her that Parsifal's family want to get in touch with her. This would hardly be surprising except that he had long ago told Sabine that they had been killed in a car crash. Her suspicions are aroused but when she meets Dot and Bertie Fetters, they want nothing more than to envelop her in love and affection. At first unwillingly and then wholeheartedly, she is drawn into their world agreeing to leave her beloved Los Angeles for the snowy wastes of Nebraska. There she learns the shocking truth behind Parsifal's break with his family and finds love where she least expects it.

Background

Although already a successful novelist in the States, it was *The Magician's Assistant* that first brought Ann Patchett to British readers' attention. The book earned her a place on the short list for the 1998 Orange Prize which she later went on to win with her next novel, *Bel Canto* in 2002. Her novels often question conventional perceptions of family and relationships, exploring the nature of love with a warmth and generosity that awakens a keen sympathy for her characters. They all share the common ground of a drama played out upon a small stage: *The Patron Saint of Liars* is set in a house for unmarried mothers, *Taft* takes place in a bar and *The Magician's Assistant* is set largely in Sabine's apartment and in the Fetters' small Nebraska home. *Bel Canto*, inspired by the four-month long Peruvian hostage-taking in 1996, occupies the smallest space, as Patchett has remarked 'in this one, you're totally enclosed. Nobody gets out.' She counts *The Magic Mountain* by Thomas Mann as an important influence on her: 'It's a book that had a huge impact on me. I loved that as a shape for a novel: put a bunch of people in a beautiful place, give them all tuberculosis, make them all stay in a fur sleeping bag for several years and see what happens.' However, Elizabeth McCracken, herself an acclaimed novelist, is perhaps the most important influence on Patchett's writing. McCracken is the first person to see her work and although she is a rigorous critic Patchett gladly acknowledges her debt to her friend saying: 'I have often thought, if anything, God forbid, were to happen to Elizabeth, I don't know that I would write anymore. I don't write for an audience, I don't think whether my book will sell, I don't sell it before I finish writing it. I write it for myself, and I write it for her.' Long may such a productive relationship prosper.

About the author

Originally from Los Angeles, Ann Patchett took her first degree at Sarah Lawrence College in 1984 and her masters from Iowa University in 1987where she was taught but writers such as Russell Banks, Grace Paley and Alan Gurganus. Before taking up writing full time, she worked as a waitress and as a college professor. Her first novel, *The Patron Saint of Liars*, was published to critical acclaim in 1992. *The Magician's Assistant* was shortlisted for the 1998 Orange Prize for Fiction. Her fourth novel, *Bel Canto*, won the prize in 2002. She has since published a memoir of her close friendship with Lucy Grealey, author of *Autobiography of a Face*, who died in 2002.

For discussion

❍ Why does Patchett start the novel 'PARSIFAL IS DEAD. That is the end of the story'? A few pages on she writes: 'It was, in a way, the end of Sabine.' What is it that ends for Sabine with Parsifal's death? What is it that begins for her?

❍ How would you describe the relationship between Parsifal and Sabine? Is their marriage simply one of convenience? What effect has their rather unorthodox arrangement had on Sabine's life?

❍ Sabine seems to take a slightly condescending view of Dot and Bertie when she first meets them, but which of them proves to be more capable of dealing with loss and grief? What is it that changes her attitude towards the Fetters?

❍ Sabine must deal not only with the loss of the man she loved but also with the revelation that he was not what he seemed. Does Parsifal become Guy for Sabine and, if so, at what point and why? How different is Parsifal from Guy? Does Guy ever become Parsifal for any of the Fetters?

❍ Why does Patchett choose to make Parsifal a magician? How important is the theme of illusion in the novel?

❍ Sabine goes to Nebraska to find out what she can about Parsifal. What else does she find there?

❍ What part does violence play in the Fetters' lives? Kitty is a strong and capable woman. Why do you think she endures Howard's behaviour for so long? What makes her finally leave?

❍ Early in the novel Patchett writes: 'But Sabine never remembered her dreams, or maybe she didn't have them', yet Sabine's dreams of Phan and Parsifal are extra-ordinarily vivid. What are we to make of them? In particular, what is the significance of her final dream at the Magic Castle?

Resources

www.nytimes.com/books/97/11/16/reviews/971116.16bernet.html?_r=1&oref=slogin – review by the novelist Suzanne Berne published in *The New York Times*
www.powells.com/authors/patchett.html – interview with Dave Weich at Powell's bookshop website
www.orangeprize.co.uk/opf/author_interview.php4?bookid=118 – interview by Lisa Gee on winning the Orange Prize published at Orange's website
www.barnesandnoble.com/writers/writerdetails.asp?userid=hP568YgCLy&cid=102 0421#interview – interview at the American bookseller barnesandnoble.com
www.annpatchett.com/index.html – Ann Patchett's website

Suggested further reading

Mr Vertigo by Paul Auster (1994); *Love Invents Us* by Amy Bloom (1997); **A Home at the End of the World by Michael Cunningham** (1990); *Carter Beats the Devil* by Glen David Gould (2001); *The Idea of Perfection* by Kate Grenville (1999); *The Giant's House* by Elizabeth McCracken (1997); **Charming Billy by Alice McDermott** (1999); *The Pilot's Wife* by Anita Shreve (1998); *Ladder of Years* by Anne Tyler (1995)

OTHER BOOKS BY ANN PATCHETT
Fiction: *The Patron Saint of Liars* (1992); *Taft* (1995); *Bel Canto* (2001); *Run* (2007)
Non-fiction: *Truth & Beauty: A Friendship* (2004)

IN A LAND OF PLENTY (1997)

Tim Pears

About the book

Charles Freeman is an ebullient, ambitious industrialist who knows exactly what he wants and generally achieves it. It's the early 1950s and although Britain is still experiencing post-war austerity, Charles's optimism is in tune with the times. He buys a mansion overlooking the small middle England town where he was born, marries his beautiful fiancée and transforms the family firm into a thriving business empire, fathering four children and acquiring an extended family along the way. But life is far from easy. He becomes estranged from one of his sons, his wife dies tragically, industrial relations are strained to breaking point and finally, out of step with the modern technological world, he is overtaken by a son-in-law whose ambition equals his own. From the early 1950s to the early 1990s, *In a Land of Plenty* documents a period of enormous social upheaval through the changing fortunes of the Freeman family and the small town they overlook.

Background

Seen through the eyes of the inhabitants of Northtown, somewhere in middle England, and focusing on the fortunes of one family, *In a Land of Plenty* explores the ways in which Britain adapted to the slow, quiet social and economic revolution which spanned the optimistic 1950s to the well-worn cynicism of the 1990s and changed the country irrevocably. In the manner of George Eliot's *Middlemarch*, which also portrays a small community as a microcosm of a world in the midst of enormous change, it is an intensely political novel reflecting Tim Pears' own passionate belief that 'A novel can't change the world. But a great novel opens the mind like nothing else. And when the mind opens, so too does the future'. Pears continued this theme of the novel as a chronicle of social change with his next book, *A Revolution of the Sun*, which follows a disparate collection of young people through the year of 1997, a year of enormous political upheaval. Something of a departure from his previous fiction his fourth novel, examined a more overtly political theme on a much smaller stage. *Wake Up* follows John Sharpe, co-owner of Spudnik, champion of a genetically modified future and a man of distinctly dubious morality, through one day as he repeatedly drives around the ring road of his small town trying to face the consequences of an experiment gone badly wrong.

A second hallmark of Pears' fiction is its cinematic quality, a quality which reflects his interest in television and cinema (an interest shared by both James and Zoe) and which is particularly evident in his first novel, *In the Place of Fallen Leaves* set in a lyrically described Devon against the backdrop of the long hot summer of 1984. In 2001 *In a Land of Plenty* was dramatized for BBC2. The four-part series met with a good deal of critical acclaim, an acclaim that must have been particularly satisfying to Pears, a graduate of the National Film and Television School.

About the author

Tim Pears was born on November 15th 1956. He grew up in Crewe and Devon, and left school at sixteen. He has worked in a variety of jobs and has published both poetry and travel writing as well as fiction. His first novel, *In the Place of Fallen Leaves*, was published to great acclaim in 1993 and won both the Hawthornden Prize for Literature and the Ruth Hadden Memorial Award.

For discussion

⊙ The novel documents many social changes that have occurred since the early 1950s. Which would you say were the most important changes and how do they affect individual characters in the book? Have comparable changes happened since the close of the novel in 1993?

⊙ James identifies two conditions of loneliness and freedom that seem to be both inseparable and inescapable in his life. How have these two conditions come to be so important for him and how do they influence the way he lives his life? To what extent does he want to escape them?

⊙ Charles Freeman builds up an industrial empire and becomes the 'man in charge'. By the end of the book, Harry could be said to have taken over that position. What are the different approaches the two men take to their businesses and to their private lives? How are those approaches shaped by the times they live in? How do they affect other characters?

⊙ From the outset we know that James is in a coma. How does this colour your reading of the book? Pears uses a technique of prefiguring events throughout the book. Why do you think he chose to do this? What effect does it achieve?

⊙ Why do you think Pears chose to bring the book to such a tragic climax?

⊙ To what extent do you recognize the world that Pears depicts in the novel? Are there particular aspects that strike a chord for you and, if so, what are they? How successful is Pears in recreating the atmosphere of the period? How does he attempt to do this?

⊙ Pears has been to film school and his encyclopaedic knowledge of film is evident in Zoe. Are there other ways in which cinema influences the book and, if so, what are they?

🖳 Resources

http://books.guardian.co.uk/top10s/top10/0,6109,1012819,00.html – Tim Pears' Top 10 20th-century Political Novels published in *The Guardian*
www.contemporarywriters.com/authors/?p=auth245 – short profile of Pears at the British Council website

🕮 Suggested further reading

Winesburg, Ohio by Sherwood Anderson (1919); *Anthem* by Tim Binding (2003); *Short Cuts* by Raymond Carver (1993); *What a Carve Up!* by Jonathan Coe (1994); *Flesh and Blood* by Michael Cunningham (1995); *Middlemarch* by George Eliot (1872); *The Facts of Life* by Patrick Gale (1995); *The Hotel New Hampshire* by John Irving (1981); ***Brightness Falls* by Jay McInerney** (1992); *We Were the Mulvaneys* by Joyce Carol Oates (1996); *White Teeth* by Zadie Smith (2000)

OTHER BOOKS BY TIM PEARS

In the Place of Fallen Leaves (1993); *A Revolution of the Sun* (2000); *Wake Up* (2002); *Blenheim Orchard* (2007)

THE SHIPPING NEWS (1993)

Annie Proulx

📖 About the book

Quoyle loses his wife in the most dreadful circumstances. For one thing she has already left him, having spent much of their married life in the arms of other men. She has also 'sold' their two daughters to a man whose intentions are all too clear. When the wreckage of her car is discovered, the address of their 'purchaser' is found on a receipt in her bag. Yet Quoyle continues to love her. When his long-lost aunt turns up, he finds himself accompanying her back to Newfoundland with his rescued daughters. Together they begin a new life back in the old family home, rubbing along as best they can. Battling with dreadful weather, his own demons and the eccentricities of the people around him, Quoyle manages to turn his life around until he has a new home, a new love and a measure of unexpected happiness.

Background

The Shipping News is the story of a man whose life seems doomed to misfortune. Shambling and clumsy from boyhood, mocked by his father and his brother, a failure at most things he puts his hand to, Quoyle seems destined for unhappiness. But when his aunt arrives after a series of crises, Quoyle takes a step along a path that ends in a worthwhile and happy life. Annie Proulx's novel is a classic redemption story that encompasses family, friendship, love, tragedy and murder, leavened with her own brand of humour.

Proulx wrote magazine articles for many years on a multitude of subjects from cider making (co-authoring a book on the subject with Lew Nichols) to canoe making, but her first collection of short stories, *Heart Songs*, was not published until she was fifty-three. Asked if she regretted coming to fiction late she replied: 'I certainly don't regret doing it later because I know a lot more about life than I did 20 years ago, 10 years ago, and I think that's important, to know how the water's gone over the dam before you start to describe it. It helps to have been over the dam yourself.' She does not, however, confine herself to writing about what she knows. For Proulx, research is a very enjoyable part of the process of writing. She studied history at university and it was during this time that her love of research began as she explained to one interviewer 'It became second nature to me to explore how and where things were done'. Her writing reflects the result of 'serious academic hours in libraries and archives and an inborn curiosity about life'. As part of her research for *The Shipping News* she made eight or nine trips to Newfoundland, listening to people talk and soaking up the atmosphere of the island, a process crucial to instilling the strong sense of place that, together with a sense of history, is the hallmark of all her fiction. *The Shipping News* captures an island on the brink of momentous change. The cod fishing industry was on the point of collapse, the North Atlantic cod stocks woefully depleted, when Proulx began her research for the novel. 'That's all anyone talked about' she has said 'It was clear that something was very, very wrong.'

But if Proulx's research is meticulous she is careful to remind her readers that her novels are works of fiction, including a disclaimer in *The Shipping News* explaining that 'The Newfoundland in this book though salted with grains of truth, is an island of invention.' And what a glorious invention it is.

About the author

Annie Proulx was born in 1935 to a French-Canadian father and an American mother. In 1993, Proulx became the first woman to win the prestigious PEN/Faulkner Award for her first novel, *Postcards*. *The Shipping News* won the Pulitzer Prize for Fiction, the American National Book Award and the *Irish Times* International Fiction Prize. Something of a modern classic, the novel has remained a consistent bestseller since its publication in 1993. In 2001 it was made into a film starring Kevin Spacey as Quoyle. After many years in Vermont, Annie Proulx moved to Wyoming and quietly dropped the 'E.' from E. Annie Proulx, the name under which *The Shipping News* was originally published.

For discussion

○ How does Proulx use language to evoke the landscape and weather of Newfoundland? What makes her use of language so distinctive? Are there particular examples that appealed to you or that you felt were particularly effective?

○ How important are the landscape and the weather to the people who live in Newfoundland? What effect does it have on their lives? What sort of community has grown out of it?

○ Proulx prefaces many of her chapters with quotations from *The Ashley Book of Knots*. What did this add to the narrative for you? Were there particular quotations that struck you and, if so, what were they?

○ Most of the characters in *The Shipping News* have suffered unhappiness, even tragedy, in their lives and yet the book is suffused with humour. How would you describe Proulx's humour? What amused you in the book?

○ Proulx writes of Quoyle: 'It came to him he knew nearly nothing of the aunt's life. And hadn't missed the knowledge.' The narrative explicitly concentrates on Quoyle's life but what is the aunt's story? Why has she been drawn back to Newfoundland? What makes her dispense with her brother's ashes in the way that she does?

○ When Quoyle picks up his daughters from Dennis and Beety's house he thinks that at this time of the day 'his part in life seemed richer, he became more of a father, at the same time could expose true feelings which were often of yearning'. What is it about Dennis and Beety that makes him feel this? What is it that he is yearning for and does he find it?

○ When Dennis tells Quoyle about Wavey and Beety setting up the Saving Grace group, Quoyle finds himself thinking of Petal, 'my lovely girl'. Why does Petal continue to have such a hold over Quoyle despite the six years of hell that he spent with her? How does his relationship with Petal influence the way he approaches Wavey?

○ Quoyle muses that in Newfoundland 'it was as though he had found a polarised lens that deepened and intensified all seen through it'. What are the changes that have brought about this new clarity and intensity in his life?

○ Jack Buggit says to Quoyle: 'There's two ways of living here now. There's the old way ... Then there's the new way ...' What other old ways and new ways have been illustrated in the book? Where does Quoyle fit in to this?

○ Why does Quoyle turn his back on Nolan, his elderly relative, even though he finds out about him soon after he arrives in Killick-Claw? Have Quoyle's attitudes to his family and where he comes from changed by the time the novel ends and, if so, how?

🖥 Resources

www.litencyc.com/php/speople.php?rec=true&UID=3654&PHPSESSID=6750dbff9
7a7905b46c10b1ac37871f3 – profile of Annie Proulx by Aliki Varvogli at the *Literary Encyclopedia* website

www.nytimes.com/books/99/05/23/specials/proulx-shipping.html – review by the novelist Howard Norman published in *The New York Times*

www.nytimes.com/books/99/05/23/specials/proulx-home.html – interview with Sara Rimer published in *The New York Times*

🌱 Suggested further reading

The Width of the Sea by Michelle Chalfoun (2001); *The Short History of a Prince* by Jane Hamilton (1998); *The Colony of Unrequited Dreams* by Wayne Johnston (1999); *Animal Dreams* **by Barbara Kingsolver** (1990); *Fall On Your Knees* by Ann-Marie MacDonald (1996); *Goodnight, Nebraska* by Tom McNeal (1998); *The Bird Artist* by Howard Norman (1994)

OTHER BOOKS BY ANNIE PROULX

Novels: *Postcards* (1992); *Accordion Crimes* (1996); *That Old Ace in the Hole* (2002)

Short stories: *Heart Songs and Other Stories* (1988); *Broke Back Mountain* (1998); *Close Range* (1999) includes the novella, *Broke Back Mountain*; *Bad Dirt* (2004)

BLACK AND BLUE (1997)

Ian Rankin

📖 About the book

The sadistic murder of a young oil worker, the fallout from a long ago possible miscarriage of justice, a Glasgow drug-dealing ring and Johnny Bible whose serial murders echo those of Bible John in the sixties: these are the cases with which DI John Rebus must contend in this, the ninth in Ian Rankin's bestselling crime series. The unorthodox detective Rebus finds himself facing a host of demons from his past, from the struggle of his colleague Brian Holmes in balancing his marriage with his job, a painful reminder of Rebus's own failed marriage to the demon drink and its attendant nightmares. *Black and Blue* is a tightly plotted, highly complex detective novel with all the elements associated with the genre yet the psychology of John Rebus takes centre stage and is every bit as gripping as the novel's four closely interwoven cases.

Background

Black and Blue marked the beginning of Ian Rankin's rise to become Britain's most widely-read British crime writer. In it the complicated psychology of DI Rebus comes to the fore as he finds himself facing painful truths. Forced to deal with the shortcomings of his much respected mentor Lawson Geddes, from whom Rebus's own unorthodox methods spring, and tormented by appalling nightmares induced by his alcoholism, Rebus finds his own failed marriage brought sharply into focus by the marital difficulties of his colleague. Rebus's obsessive streak is given full rein through his dogged out-of-hours investigation of Johnny Bible who appears bent on a disturbing *homage* to Bible John, the real-life serial killer whose crimes shocked 1960s Glasgow and still remain unsolved

Aside from his tightly controlled plots and adroitly managed denouements, traditional skills that would surely have earned him a place in at the top of the crime writers' pantheon, Rankin's astute characterization of his recalcitrant, hard-drinking, rock music-loving DI and his portrayal of Edinburgh which is so vivid that it almost becomes a character in itself, mark him out as a writer who would be acclaimed in any genre. Rankin's novels explore many issues that trouble modern society, from sectarianism to internet crime, paedophilia to asylum seekers. He has been credited with establishing the 'literary crime novel' and has won a large following outside the usual crime writing readership which may seem fitting for a man who did not come naturally to the genre. Rebus' first outing *Knots and Crosses*, published in the mid-eighties shortly after he had completed his PhD, was planned as a Gothic novel about a detective and his alter ego, drawing on the tradition of Robert Louis Stevenson's *Jekyll and Hyde*. Its reception as an accomplished crime novel left Rankin somewhat surprised. Fortunately for his many fans he took to the genre to the extent that he was awarded the Crime Writers' Association 2005 Diamond Dagger Award, a life-time achievement award which he said he felt should have gone to Rebus rather than himself, but that he was happy to accept on his creation's behalf. DI Rebus's long career came to an end in 2007 when Ian Rankin had him retired from the force in *Exit Music*.

About the author

Born in 1960 in the mining village of Cardenden, Fife, Ian Rankin graduated from the University of Edinburgh. He has been employed as a grape-picker, swineherd, taxman, alcohol researcher, hi-fi journalist and punk musician, and spent several years working towards a PhD on modern Scottish fiction before becoming distracted by his own writing. As well as writing under his own name, Rankin has written a number of novels under the pseudonym Jack Harvey. *Black and Blue* was published in 1997. It won the Crime Writers' Association Macallan Gold Dagger Award and secured Rankin a place as one of Britain's top crime writers. His work now appears on a number of university syllabuses. Ian Rankin has regularly contributed to BBC2's *Newsnight Review*.

For discussion

○ 'I'd say it was a straight assassination, with a bit of malicious cruelty thrown in.' Does this prove to be the case with Allan Mitchison's murder? What was the motive behind the killing?

○ Why is it so important for Rebus to avoid the fallout from the Spaven case? Is it simply his dislike of the media or are there more deep-seated reasons? How is the case resolved and how does Rebus feel about it?

○ 'Spinning in a narrowing gyre: Allan Mitchison ... Johnny Bible ... Uncle Joe ... Fergus McLure's drug deal.' Are there connections between these four, and if so what are they?

○ Why is Rebus so fascinated with the Bible John and Johnny Bible cases? At what point did you realize Bible John's identity and why?

○ How would you describe Rebus's character? If you have read any of the pre-ceding novels in the Rebus series how would you say his character has developed?

○ What kind of detective is Rebus? How does he compare with the other police characters in the novel? How does he get on with other detectives?

○ There are few female characters in the novel. How does Rebus relate to women? How does his work affect his relationships?

○ 'Work had a way of wrapping itself around you, so you were cut off from the rest of the world.' How does Rankin depict the life of a detective?

○ What did you make of the book's ending? Did the Afterword make you think differently about the novel, and if so how?

○ *Black and Blue* ranges from Edinburgh to Glasgow to Aberdeen and the oilfields beyond. How important is a sense of place in the novel, and how does Rankin evoke that sense?

○ How does Rankin build suspense in the novel?

○ *Black and Blue* is a crime novel but Rankin spends as much time on the psychology of his characters as on the resolution of the crimes. Which element in the novel did you find most satisfying and why?

💻 Resources

http://books.guardian.co.uk/departments/crime/story/0,6000,1493837,00.html – profile by novelist Nicholas Wroe in *The Guardian*

www.contemporarywriters.com/authors/?p=autho2A17M435212626443 – profile of
Ian Rankin at the British Council website including a critical essay by Dr Jules Smith
www.ianrankin.net – Ian Rankin's website detailing musical influences
www.geocities.com/verbal_plainfield/coldcases/biblejohn.html – web page on
Bible John

🐬 Suggested further reading
***The Crow Road* by Iain Banks** (1992); *The Black Echo* by Michael Connelly (1992);
Survival of the Fittest by Jonathan Kellerman (1997); *Faceless Killers* by Henning
Mankell (1991)
OTHER BOOKS BY IAN RANKIN

The Inspector Rebus series: *Knots and Crosses* (1987); *Hide and Seek* (1990);
Tooth and Nail (1992); *Strip Jack* (1992); *The Black Book* (1993); *Mortal Causes*
(1994); *Let it Bleed* (1995); *The Hanging Garden* (1998); *Dead Souls* (1999); *Set in
Darkness* (2000); *The Falls* (2001); *Resurrection Men* (2001); *A Question of Blood*
(2003); *Fleshmarket Close* (2004); *The Naming of the Dead* (2006); *Exit Music*
(2007)
Other novels: *The Flood* (1986); *Watchman* (1988); *Westwind* (1989)
Short stories: *A Good Hanging and Other Stories* (1992); *Beggars Banquet*
(2002)
Writing as Jack Harvey: *Witch Hunt* (1993); *Bleeding Hearts* (1994); *Blood Hunt*
(1995)
Non-fiction: *Rebus's Scotland* (2005)

PROMISED LANDS (1995)
Jane Rogers

📖 About the book
On 2 January 1788 those aboard the *First Fleet*, laden with a cargo of convicts,
catch their first glimpse of Australia. On board the *Supply*, William Dawes has the
astronomical instruments with which he has been entrusted by the Board of
Longitude to observe the Australian sky. This is the story of the settling of Sydney,
built with the blood, sweat and tears of convicts. As Governor Phillip struggles to
keep his unruly labour force under control, the seeds of a tragedy that will
reverberate through the centuries are sown. Woven through this account are two
twentieth-century narratives. Stephen is an idealist but his attempts to build an

egalitarian school have ended in disaster and his marriage is in tatters. His wife, Olla, is convinced that their severely brain-damaged son has messianic powers, which he will reveal to the world when the time is right. These three narratives loop in and out of each other, reflecting and refracting history as each story unfolds.

Background

Promised Lands is a complex and ambitious novel that focuses on characters fired by their own particular mission. The main narrative concerns William Dawes, a young marine lieutenant charged with setting up an astronomical observatory in the new colony of Australia, whose Christian conscience sometimes clouds his judgement of human nature. Stephen Beech is a teacher in our own times; his idealistic efforts to revolutionize education have ended in failure and he has dedicated himself to telling William's story. Olla, Stephen's wife, has fled her drunken and abusive father in Poland. Her marriage to Stephen seems ill matched: he is fired with idealistic liberal fervour while she is resigned to the vagaries of human nature and determined to limit her role to being a housewife. After several miscarriages and the death of an infant son, Olla is determined that their severely handicapped son Daniel will survive, convinced that he will reveal his messianic powers to the world.

These three highly accomplished narrative strands, written in very different voices, touch on several of the themes which run through Jane Rogers' work: the idealistic search for a form of Utopia, which preoccupies William and has been thwarted in Stephen, education, and the intense bond between mothers and their children. Rogers has recognized the common threads running through her fiction explaining 'There seem to be recurring themes, although I'm not always conscious of them when starting a new book, because each book feels to me to be completely different. But these themes do seem to have cropped up more than once: an exploration of idealism and its effects, of people trying to create new and better ways of living (*Mr Wroe's Virgins*, *Promised Lands*); an interest in people whose way of experiencing the world lies outside the norm (Orph in *Separate Tracks*, Martha in *Mr Wroe's Virgins*, Daniel and Olla in *Promised Lands*, Calum in *Island*); and in women's lives and roles, with particular reference to motherhood (*The Ice is Singing*, *Her Living Image*, *Mr Wroe's Virgins*, *Promised Lands*, *Island*).'

Perhaps of all Rogers' fiction the novel with which *Promised Lands* has most in common is *Mr Wroe's Virgins* which also has its roots in historical fact and explores the antics of an extreme religious zealot, based on John Wroe, a nineteenth century self-styled prophet bent on forging a Christian Utiopia. Both books are extraordinarily powerful novels which challenge their readers but both more than repay that challenge.

About the author

Jane Rogers was born in London in 1952 and grew up in Birmingham, Oxford and New York state. She read English at Cambridge and went on to take a post-graduate teaching certificate at Leicester University. She has taught in comprehensive schools and further education, and has been a writing fellow at Northern College, at Cambridge and at Sheffield Hallam University. She has also held a variety of jobs in children's homes, in a mental hospital and at a London housing association. In addition to her novels, she has written several TV dramas including the BBC adaptation of her book *Mr Wroe's Virgins*. *Promised Lands*, her fifth novel, won the Writers Guild Fiction Book Award when it was published in 1995.

For discussion

○ What is the significance of the title *Promised Lands*? What were the 'promised lands' of the book? To whom was the promise extended and was it fulfilled?

○ William reflects on the idea of a land without people and concludes that 'the land was man's backdrop, his setting. Land without man would be as futile as a stage with no actors; it would have no meaning.' What are the consequences of this conclusion for the aborigines? Do you agree with it? What do you think of Stephen's reactions to the idea?

○ The King's commission to Governor Phillip clearly states that no harm must come to the original inhabitants of the land, yet they suffer terribly because of the colonizers. Their food is depleted, their belongings stolen and smallpox wipes many of them out. Can their suffering and the invasion of their land be justified? What do you think of the exchange between William and Phillip about Phillip's part in the smallpox epidemic in chapter 16? Would the fate of the aborigines have been any different if Governor Phillip had been more like William?

○ William finally accompanies Watkin Tench on the expedition to take six aborigines prisoner after McEntire has been mortally wounded. To what extent do you think he was right to refuse in the first place? Is he guilty of the 'sin of pride' or simply idealistic?

○ William learns several hard lessons about himself. What are they and how do they change him? How would you describe the William Dawes who first arrived in Australia? What sort of man is he when he leaves?

○ The structure of the book is very complex. Stephen tells us William's story, frequently interrupting it to reflect on his own life. Olla gives us her version of her marriage to Stephen. To what extent did you feel the narratives meshed together? Were there parts of the structure that did not work for you and, if so, what were they?

○ Are there parallels between William's story and Stephen's and Olla's narratives and, if so, what are they? How similar are William and Stephen? In what ways do their characters overlap? In what ways do they differ? How have these characteristics shaped their lives?

○ Stephen and Olla both have very different views of humanity. How would you describe Olla's view of the world? What does Stephen think? How have these two very different attitudes affected their marriage?

💻 Resources

www.nytimes.com/books/97/09/21/reviews/970921.21mccollt.html?_r=1&oref=slogin – review by the novelist and writer David Willis McCullough published in *The New York Times*

www.contemporarywriters.com/authors/?p=auth217 – profile of Jane Rogers at the British Council website including a critical essay by Dr Jules Smith

www.litencyc.com/php/speople.php?rec=true&UID=5036 – profile of Jane Rogers by Rob Spence at the *Literary Encyclopedia* website

www.janerogers.org/index.html – Jane Rogers' website

📚 Suggested further reading

FICTION

The Voyage of the Narwhal by Andrea Barrett (1998); *Water Music* by T. Coraghessan Boyle (1981); *Oscar and Lucinda* by Peter Carey (1988); *The Songlines* by Bruce Chatwin (1987); *The River Thieves* by Michael Crummey (2001); *Gould's Book of Fish* by Richard Flanagan (2001); *Strandloper* by Alan Garner (1996); *The Secret River* by Kate Grenville (2006); *The Seal Wife* by Kathryn Harrison (2002); *English Passengers* by Matthew Kneale (2000); *Remembering Babylon* by David Malouf (1993); *The Last Time I Saw Jane* by Kate Pullinger (1996)

NON-FICTION

The Fatal Shore by Robert Hughes (1986)

OTHER BOOKS BY JANE ROGERS

Fiction: *Separate Tracks* (1983); *Her Living Image* (1984); *The Ice is Singing* (1987); *Mr Wroe's Virgins* (1991); *Island* (1999); *The Voyage Home* (2004)

·Edited: *The Good Fiction Guide* (2005), 2nd edition

THE READER (1997)

Bernhard Schlink (translated by Carol Brown Janeway)

📖 About the book

At the age of fifteen, Michael Berg begins a passionate affair with Hanna, a thirty-six-year-old woman. At first the affair is purely physical but when Michael starts to read to his lover, it becomes an essential part of their lovemaking ritual. One day Hanna disappears from Michael's life. When he next sees her, he is a law student and she is on trial as an SS camp guard. Michael becomes obsessed by the trial, convinced that in loving Hanna he is also guilty. When she is convicted, he remains haunted by the unanswered questions that the trial has posed for him. His marriage fails after five years and he struggles to find some sort of meaning in his work. Eventually, he begins to record his favourite books for Hanna. When the prison governor writes to tell him that Hanna will soon be leaving prison, he visits her for the first, and last, time.

Background

Set in post-war Germany, *The Reader* begins as an erotic love story between a fifteen-year-old boy and a thirty-six-year-old woman. But what begins as a love story becomes a philosophical enquiry into the effects of the Holocaust on a generation whose parents are perceived as either its perpetrators or complicit in its perpetration. Central to this difficult but rewarding and sharply intelligent novel is the question: what is to be done with the knowledge and guilt of the Holocaust?

Born in 1944, Bernhard Schlink is a member of the 'second generation', the generation that found itself asking difficult questions about what its parents had done during the Second World War. In Schlink's case his parents had, to a degree, been the victims of Nazi persecution rather than its perpetrators. His father lost his job as professor of theology for being a member of the *Bekennende Kirche* which had called for a break from the Protestant church for its support of the Nazi régime. Although his parents had taken no part in the Holocaust Schlink had to deal with the knowledge that its perpetrators were all around him; some openly confronting their participation, like the teacher who 'taught us gymnastics and we could see his SS tattoo' while others such as one of his favourite professors who Schlink discovered had written an anti-Semitic book in the thirties, were more covert. Schlink acknowledges that the problem of how to live with the legacy of guilt is an insoluble one: 'We solved the problem of hiding things, but not how to cope with what we found and how to integrate it into our collective biography. There is the problem of loving and admiring these people yet knowing what they have done. Can one do this? I thought that professor was a wonderful man, and at the same time I couldn't accept it. We had to live with all these tensions. The '68 movement had the ambition to deal with all this, but even then I didn't know what to do about it and now I still don't know what to do. What we have to live with is that there is no solution.' He denies, however, that *The Reader* is autobiographical saying 'because I have experienced some of these things I use them. We can only write about what we know on some topics'.

The Reader was one of the first novels to step outside the conventions of Holocaust literature, which mainly dealt with its events, and examine the dilemma of the 'second generation'. It was enormously successful on both sides of the Atlantic and met with a great deal of critical acclaim but its publication was not without criticism. Schlink has said that such criticism came from within his own generation for not unambiguously condemning Hanna: 'It was very interesting that in Israel and New York the older generation liked the book, but among my generation I was more than once told it shouldn't have been a problem for Michael, or for me, to condemn. I've heard that criticism several times but never from the older generation, people who have lived through it.'

The Reader remains Schlink's best-known work. His previous crime novels which also tackled Germany's post-war history and its attendant problems through Dr Gerhard Selb, a former Nazi prosecutor who saw the error of his ways and turned private detective, have been translated since the publication of *The Reader*. He continues to write but also to teach explaining: 'When friends encourage me to give up the university and the courts completely to write because they know that I enjoy it so much, I wonder if perhaps I will have too much fun. I'll be doing something just for myself. Doing something that other people can benefit from was an important part of the way I was brought up. And no matter what else has happened to me, that is still important in the way I want to live my life.'

About the author

Bernhard Schlink was born in the small town of Bethel in Germany on July 6th 1944, the son of a German father and a Swiss mother and the youngest of four children. He grew up in Heidelberg and studied law in both Heidelberg and Berlin. He is a professor of law at the University of Berlin and the author of several prize-winning crime novels. He divides his time between Bonn and Berlin.

For discussion

❂ Who do you think 'the reader' of the title is, or can it be applied to more than one character? At what point was it apparent to you that Hanna was illiterate? What is the importance of literacy in the book?

⭗ How would you describe the tone and style of Schlink's writing in part one of the book? How does it differ from the second and third part? What effect does this difference achieve, if any?

⭗ The relationship between Hanna and Michael begins with an act of kindness on her part but we later learn of her involvement in the concentration camps. Do you find that Hanna engages your sympathy at any point after you found out that she was a camp guard? How convincing are Michael's arguments why Hanna became a guard and for her selection of girls to read to her? How can we explain why ordinary people commit atrocities without resorting to calling them monsters?

⭗ Why does Michael find it so difficult to make a relationship with other women work? How does the affair with Hanna affect him as an adolescent?

⭗ Michael says: 'And if I was not guilty because one cannot be guilty of betraying a criminal, then I was guilty of loving one.' Michael did not know of Hanna's crime during their affair so why does he feel guilty? How do other characters of his generation seem to feel about the Holocaust? What about his father's generation?

⭗ Michael refers to the many images that have been produced of the camps, particularly in films. Is there a danger that continued exposure of Holocaust images lessens their impact until they become frozen into clichés as Michael suggests? How do you feel about the images of war recorded in the newspapers and on television?

⭗ Is Hanna just a scapegoat for her co-defendants or in a more general way? When she turns to the judge and asks him what he would have done in her position, what does his answer imply? Could the judge be considered as guilty as Hanna if he knew about the camps but did nothing?

⭗ Why do you think Hanna does what she does at the end of the novel? How do you think learning to read might have changed her view of what she had done in the camps?

⭗ The novel poses the question: 'What should our second generation have done, what should it do with the knowledge of the horrors of the extermination of the Jews?' Does it answer this question? What do you think the answer might be or is it an unanswerable question?

⭗ Does the novel give any grounds for hope of forgiveness, and, if so, what are they?

🖳 Resources

www.oprah.com/obc/pastbooks/bernhard_schlink/obc_pb_19990226.jhtml – entry for *The Reader* at Oprah Winfrey's Book Club site

www.beatrice.com/interviews/schlink – interview by Ron Hogan published at beatrice.com

http://books.guardian.co.uk/departments/generalfiction/story/0,,647221,00.html
– profile by the writer and novelist Nicholas Wroe published in *The Guardian*

⮂ Suggested further reading

FICTION

My Father's Country by Wibke Bruhns (translated by Shaun Whiteside) (2007); *The Archivist* by Martha Cooley (1998); *Crime and Punishment* by Fyodor Dostoevsky (1866); *War Story* by Gwen Edelman (2001); *Everything is Illuminated* by Jonathan Safran Foer (2002); *The Tin Drum* by Günter Grass (1959); **Stones From the River by Ursula Hegi** (1997); *Schindler's Ark* by Thomas Keneally (1982); *The Time of Light* by Gunnar Kopperud (1998); *The Twins* by Tessa de Loo (1993); **Fugitive Pieces by Anne Michaels** (1997); *The Dark Room* by Rachel Seiffert (2001); *Music For the Third Ear* by Susan Schwartz Senstad (1999); *Sophie's Choice* by William Styron (1979); *A Model Childhood* by Christa Wolf (1976)

NON-FICTION

Eichmann in Jerusalem by Hannah Arendt (1963); *If This is a Man/The Truce* by Primo Levi (1966); *The Holocaust and Collective Memory* by Peter Novick (1999); *Night* by Elie Weisel (1960)

OTHER BOOKS BY BERNHARD SCHLINK

Self's Punishment with Walter Popp (1987); *Self's Deception* (1994); *Flights of Love* (2002); *Homecoming* (2008)

THE MINOTAUR TAKES A CIGARETTE BREAK
(2000)

Steven Sherrill

📖 About the book

Doomed to immortality the mythical Minotaur has fetched up at a restaurant in North Carolina where he's found an uneasy acceptance, working as a short-order cook. Desperate to avoid embarrassment he watches his co-workers carefully, trying not to offend but waiting for the inevitable as their tolerance wears thin. He lives in a trailer park and tinkers with cars, a bit-player in his neighbours' lives. When a new waitress joins Grub's Rib, M's interest is piqued. He finds himself drawn to her and, miraculously, she to him. In this wonderfully imaginative novel, Steven Sherrill weaves a bright thread of wry humour through his descriptions of M's daily life: the all-too familiar misunderstandings, his fears, his hopes and his resignation in the face of an eternity spent observing but never belonging. Sherrill's characters embody all the traits of frail humanity: both frightened and repelled by difference, and generous and accepting of it.

Background

When reading *The Minotaur Takes a Cigarette Break* it is easy to forget that it is a first novel. It is a confident assured work; its author unafraid to take the fantastical, transpose it to a prosaic situation and expose raw but deeply-felt human emotions in the process. Perhaps it's hardly surprising that Steven Sherrill found it difficult to get his novel published, resorting to Blair Publishing, a small Carolina publisher specialising in cookery, travel and local stories, who took the brave step of publishing it. So successful was the book that it was picked up by a mainstream publisher and Sherrill was able not only to publish a second novel but also to sell the idea of his third. Sherrill had previously published poetry and the germ of the idea for *The Minotaur Takes a Cigarette Break* first came to him as a poem about the Minotaur some eight years before he decided to turn it into a novel.

Sherrill's main protagonist is a creature taken from Greek mythology. Half-man, half-bull, the Minotaur was the progeny of Pasiphae, wife of Minos king of Crete, and a beautiful, snow-white bull given to Minos by Posiedon as a sign of the gods' approval. Minos found himself incapable of sacrificing the bull in the expected tribute of gratitude to Posiedon but Posiedon took his revenge by making Pasiphae lose her heart to it. Their monstrous offspring terrorized the island. Minos called upon the inventor Daedalus to design the labyrinth, an intricate maze into which Minos locked the Minotaur, and into which seven young men and seven young women were sent each year to be devoured. Determined to end this slaughter Theseus volunteered to enter the labyrinth and with the help of Ariadne, Minos's daughter, found his way to the centre of the maze and slew the sleeping Minotaur.

About the author

Steven Sherrill was born in the small town of Mooresville, North Carolina in 1961. He is a graduate of the University of North Carolina and holds an MFA in poetry from the prestigious Iowa Writers' Workshop as well as a welding diploma from Mitchell Community College. His poems and stories have appeared in such publications as *Best American Poetry*, *Kenyon Review* and *Georgia Review*. *The Minotaur Takes a Cigarette Break* was nominated for both the Pulitzer Prize and the National Book Award. Sherrill lives in Pennsylvania and is assistant professor of English and Integrative studies at Penn State Altoona. As well as writing fiction and poetry he is also a talented artist.

For discussion

⚫ *The Minotaur Takes a Cigarette Break* requires its readers to suspend their disbelief from the first page. How difficult did you find this? How does Steven Sherrill engage our sympathy for M?

⚫ Why do you think Sherrill chose the Minotaur as his main protagonist and the American South as his location?

⚫ What are the reactions of the various characters to M? What do their reactions tell you about them? Who does M get along with best and why? What did you think of M? How did you feel about him by the close of the novel?

⚫ What draws M to Kelly and she to him?

⚫ M describes Grub as 'a man with heart and compassion'. Does this prove to be the case? Are there any other characters in the novel who would fit this description?

⚫ 'The Minotaur wants to say something. He wants to defend Kelly in some way ... almost as much as he wants to join in Mike and Shane's repartee.' M frequently finds himself pulled in different directions. What is his predominant trait?

⚫ 'In the Minotaur's mind the allegiance of men is mainly pathetic. Is terrifying. Is seductive. Is unattainable.' How are men portrayed in the novel? How do male reactions to M differ from the reactions of female characters?

⚫ At the store in Florida, Laurel comes to serve Sweeny and M, Sweeny says 'She's one of yours, ain't she?' Do you think Sweeny recognizes M as the Minotaur of Greek myth? Who are the other mythological characters that M encounters and what is their significance for him?

⚫ 'He hopes that the man with the kind face tells his son something like the truth – that the Minotaur exists out of necessity, his own and the world's.' What do you think Sherrill means by this?

⚫ What are the motives of Shane, Mike and Adrienne when they come to the Lucky-U estate in the early hours of the morning? Were you surprised by Hank and Sweeny's actions?

⚫ What did you make of the novel's ending?

⚫ What does the novel have to say about difference and our reactions to it?

⚫ How would you describe the novel's style?

🖥 Resources

www.southernlitreview.com/authors/steven_sherrill_interview.htm – interview by J.C. Robertson in the *Southern Literary Review*

www.bookmuse.com/pages/resources/int_sherrill.asp – interview by Kenneth Brewer at bookmuse.com, and American book discussion website

www.blairpub.com/outdoortitles/readinggroupguides/minotaurguide.htm – page at Blair Publishing's website devoted to the novel with a note from Steven Sherrill
http://books.guardian.co.uk/review/story/0,12084,981402,00.html – review by Colin Greenland in *The Guardian*

🕮 Suggested further reading
FICTION
American Gods by Neil Gaiman (2001); *Metamorphosis* by Franz Kafka (1915); **The Vintner's Luck by Elizabeth Knox** (1998); *Ingenious Pain* **by Andrew Miller** (1997); *Frankenstein* by Mary Shelley (1831)
NON-FICTION
The Greek Myths by Robert Graves (1955)
OTHER BOOKS BY STEVEN SHERRILL
Visits From the Drowned Girl (2004)

LARRY'S PARTY (1997)
Carol Shields

📖 About the book
Larry Weller's story unfolds year by year, starting in 1977 when he is twenty-seven and culminating twenty years later at the eponymous party. Larry is an average kind of guy; the only thing that really marks him out is his passion for mazes, a passion conceived at Hampton Court on honeymoon with his first wife, Dorrie. But despite his ordinariness he is never dull. As each year is recounted we are privy to the shifts in Larry's relationships with his family and friends, the amazed joyfulness of his love for both his wives, the pain of divorce and the changes in his work from florist to acclaimed maze maker. The centrepiece of the concluding year is the dinner party at which the many threads of Larry's life are satisfyingly pulled together.

Background
This is the story of an ordinary guy who leads a reasonably uneventful life, told with a lingering and playful delight in everyday detail. Spanning twenty years in the life of Larry Weller, from the evening when he mistakenly picks up an altogether smarter version of his own Harris tweed jacket, to the dinner party at which his two ex-wives first meet, *Larry's Party* is a subtle and many-layered narrative of a life that many of us might recognize.

In its quiet but sharp observations of everyday life – its small tragedies, its occasional heady triumphs and its ebb and flow – Carol Shields' writing is comparable to that of Jane Austen, one of her favourite authors and the subject of her only biographical work. Shields' fiction is concerned with 'Birth, life, love, work, death' or the 'arc of life' as she also described it. Such a concern inevitably saw her dubbed as a women's writer, a label about which she eventually ceased to care saying to one interviewer "I used to get very irritated being described as a women's writer. But I don't anymore. Why should I? Women read the most books!', and later remarking 'When men write about "ordinary people", they are thought to be subtle and sensitive. When women do, their novels are classified as domestic.' To many critics, then, Larry seemed an unusual choice as the central character for a Shields novel. When asked why she had chosen a male protagonist Shields replied: 'Men are portrayed as buffoons these days and I was trying not to do that, but men are the ultimate mystery to me. I wanted to talk about this business of men in the world.' She set about her research for the novel by interviewing her husband and male friends about their lives, aspirations and friendships. Talking about such things proved to be something of a novelty for her subjects: 'Some were all jocular and I could tell they weren't ready to talk about it. Some were touchingly grateful to be having this conversation. My women friends, we talk about everything, but men are deprived of these kinds of conversations. They need them, though.' She emerged from the process 'very glad to be a woman. Maybe women struggle more with this sense of who am I, but we have a greater reality base, a sense of where we really are.'

About the author

Carol Shields was born in Oak Park, Illinois, in 1935. She was educated at Hanover College, Exeter University and the University of Ottawa where she took her MA. In 1957 she married and moved from the United States to Canada. In between bringing up five children, she taught at the universities of Ottawa, British Columbia and Manitoba, and was Chancellor of the University of Winnipeg. Her first novel, *Small Ceremonies*, was published in 1976. She won many prizes for her fiction, including the 1995 Pulitzer Prize for *The Stone Diaries*, which was also shortlisted for the Booker Prize in the same year. In 1997, *Larry's Party* was awarded the Orange Prize for Fiction.

Shields was diagnosed with breast cancer in 1998. Lovingly supported by her husband and their five children, she continued to work throughout her illness writing her biography of Jane Austen, a collection of short stories and her last novel, *Unless*, before she died in July 2003. She is a great loss to literature.

For discussion

⚙ Why do you think Shields chose the unusual occupation of maze maker for Larry? What is it that so attracts Larry to mazes?

⚙ Each of the chapters has a theme – 'Larry's Folks', 'Larry's Friends' – culminating in 'Larry's Party'. Why do you think Shields chose to structure the novel in this way and how does it shape the narrative?

⚙ There is much reiteration of the detail of Larry's life as he moves through the years, each retelling subtly different from the last. Why do you think Shields chose to do this and what effect does it achieve?

⚙ Shields writes of the Wellers: 'Nothing real will ever get said out loud in this house, though Midge will bleat and blast, and Larry will prod and suggest.' Why is this the case and what effect has it had on Larry? Are the Wellers any different from the average family in their lack of communication?

⚙ 'The day will arrive in his life when work ... will be all that stands between himself and the bankruptcy of his soul.' How important is work to Larry and how is this illustrated in the book? How important is work to the other principal characters and how does it affect their lives?

⚙ How does Larry's second marriage to Beth differ from his first to Dorrie and why? How does each marriage change Larry?

⚙ When Larry remembers taking his son around his first maze in Winnipeg, Shields writes: 'It may be that Larry has romanticised this particular memory.' Do you think he has and, if so, why? How does Larry's memory change the way he looks back over the years?

⚙ Larry remembers Eric Eisner telling him that: 'Forty is the end of the party ... What's left for us oldies is a freefall into hoary age and the thinning of imagination.' Does this prove to be the case for Larry? Does the fact that mid-life crisis is a cliché of our times make it any less painful? How does it affect Larry?

⚙ What role do the women in the novel play in shaping Larry's life? How do his relationships with women change as time moves on and what prompts those changes?

⚙ How much of Larry's life is shaped by accident? Can he be said to be a man in control of his life?

⚙ How well do you feel you know Larry by the end of the book? Do you think Shields succeeds in conveying his character and the changes it has undergone during the twenty-year span of the book? How different is the Larry who picked up the wrong jacket in chapter 1 from the Larry who holds a dinner party for his two ex-wives?

⚙ At the party the guests debate what it is to be a man in the late twentieth century. Do you agree with Ian's assessment – have men been 'walking on egg-shells since about 1980' and, if so, why? What about the women's assessment of their position? How have these ideas been illustrated in the novel?

○ Were you surprised by the way the novel ended? Were you convinced by the ending?

▣ Resources

www.nytimes.com/books/97/09/07/reviews/970907.07klinket.html?_r=1&oref= slogin – review by the writer and novelist Verlyn Klinkenborg published in *The New York Times*

www.bookpage.com/9709bp/firstperson2.html – interview by Ellen Kanner about the writing of *Larry's Party* published in *BookPage*

http://us.penguingroup.com/static/rguides/us/larrys_party.html – interview about the themes of *Larry's Party* published at the Penguin website, Shields' American publishers

http://observer.guardian.co.uk/magazine/story/0,11913,706289,00.html – interview by Barbara Ellen published in *The Observer*

www.litencyc.com/php/speople.php?rec=true&UID=4058&PHPSESSID=ce6980d6 8e92089d91560475c7dd2be4 – profile by Wendy Roy at *The Literary Encyclopedia* website

http://books.guardian.co.uk/obituaries/story/0,11617,1000873,00.html – obituary by the critic Alex Clark published in *The Guardian*

▤ Suggested further reading

Preston Falls by David Gates (1998); *Mrs Kimble* by Jennifer Haigh (2003); **Empress of the Splendid Season by Oscar Hijuelos** (1999); *A Widow For One Year* by John Irving (1998); *The Namesake* by Jhumpa Lahiri (2003); *Ladder of Years* by Anne Tyler (1996)

OTHER BOOKS BY CAROL SHIELDS

Novels: *Small Ceremonies* (1976); *The Box Garden* (1977); *Happenstance* (1980); *Mary Swann* (1987); *The Republic of Love* (1992); *The Stone Diaries* (1993); *A Celibate Season* (with Blanche Howard) (2000); *Unless* (2002)

Short stories: *Various Miracles* (1994); *Dressing Up For the Carnival* (2000); *Collected Stories* (2004)

Biography: *Jane Austen* (2001)

THE LAST TIME THEY MET (2001)

Anita Shreve

About the book

When Linda Fallon and Thomas Janes meet at a literary festival in Toronto, it is the first time they have seen each other since the end of their affair in Nairobi, twenty-six years ago. Each had been in the kind of marriage that, although companionable enough, lacked the irresistible passion that drove Linda and Thomas to deception, betrayal and the brink of tragedy. But even this had not been the beginning. They had first met when they were seventeen-year-old students at a Massachusetts high school, their tentative relationship blown apart by a car crash. Using the unusual structure of telling their story in reverse chronological order, Anita Shreve peels back the layers of Linda's and Thomas's lives. Beginning in their fifties, the novel traces the intervening years, marked by the tragic loss of Thomas's child and the early death of Linda's husband, back to their heady days in Kenya and then to their high school years in the 1960s, edging towards a startling finale which turns the story upon its head.

Background

The Last Time They Met addresses themes of betrayal, forgiveness and passion, themes familiar to readers of Anita Shreve's quietly understated and elegant novels, while exploring the possibilities of a life unlived. The novel's reverse chronological structure is unusual and challenging, both to the reader and to the author, a challenge that Shreve has acknowledged while discussing the process of writing the book explaining that in leading her readers towards the novel's surprising conclusion she needed to plant clues along the way, 'clues that are not meant to register too much at the time of the first reading, but that might click in once the book had been read and the ending digested.' Shreve has said that the novel's ending was its *'raison d'être'*, that 'the conceit for the novel is contained within a description of Thomas's life's work in *The Weight of Water*.' Readers of *The Weight of Water* may recognize Thomas Janes as the husband of Jean, a photographer whose assignment to document the site of a nineteenth-century murder just off the New England coast ended in the drowning of their young daughter

The middle section of *The Last Time They Met* is set in Kenya where Shreve lived for three years in the late 1970s. Although this is not an autobiographical novel Shreve drew upon her journals to evoke the atmosphere in Nairobi at that time. An unaccustomed diarist (her time in Africa is the only time when she has kept a diary)

Shreve found her journals 'incredibly valuable' saying that 'They lent an impression-istic immediacy to the book that I might not otherwise have been able to tap into.'

The selection by Oprah Winfrey of *The Pilot's Life* for her book club inevitably resulted in bestseller status for Shreve's novels. Critics have described her work as occupying the difficult middle ground between literary fiction and romance, an antidote to 'grim-lit' as the novelist Amanda Craig describes them. Her delicately wrought, absorbing novels inhabit that territory with a fine grace.

About the author

Anita Shreve is American. She began writing fiction while working as a high school teacher. Although one of her early short stories was awarded the O. Henry Prize in 1975, she felt that she could not earn a living writing fiction and turned to journalism. She worked in Kenya for three years writing articles for a number of US magazines including *Newsweek*. When her first novel, *Eden Close*, was published in 1989 she took up writing fiction full time. In 1998 *The Weight of Water*, which can be read as a companion volume to *The Last Time They Met*, was shortlisted for the Orange Prize. *The Pilot's Wife*, published in 1998, became an Oprah Winfrey book club choice, ensuring Shreve a place on the US bestsellers list. She teaches writing at Amherst College and divides her time between Massachusetts and New Hampshire.

For discussion

☉ Anita Shreve has chosen an unusual structure for *The Last Time They Met*. What effect does reversing the conventional chronological order of the narrative achieve? How does Shreve trace the threads of Linda's and Thomas's stories backwards through the years? What do you think might be the pitfalls of such a structure? How successful did you find it?

☉ At the literary festival, when Linda is quizzed about why she writes about love, she says: 'I believe it to be the central drama of our lives.' To what extent does this prove to be the case for her? When she suggests that marriage cannot be accurately described in fiction the Australian novelist agrees, saying: 'A marriage doesn't lend itself to art. Certainly not to satisfying structure or to dialogue worth reading.' To what extent do you agree with this? Are there literary examples that you feel disprove this idea?

☉ Although the three narratives that make up the novel are not written in the first person, they are clearly written from either Linda's or Thomas's point of view. What differentiates the two in style? How does Shreve convey their characters through the narratives? To what extent did you have to reassess your ideas about the characters when you finished the book?

○ The name Magdalene runs through the novel like a motif. What is its significance for Linda and Thomas?

○ Thomas says of living in Kenya: 'Living here is like watching an endless documentary.' This sentiment is echoed when he says: 'it is as though I watch an exotic, imagistic movie. It does not include me. I am in the audience. I suppose that allows me to critique the movie, but I don't feel capable of even that.' What do you think he means by these statements? How does his response to Africa differ from Linda's? Can you think of reasons why this might be the case?

○ Linda is a Catholic but Thomas is not. How important is Linda's Catholicism in the novel – in particular, the concept of confession?

○ The book ends in a particularly startling fashion. What did you think of the ending? How did it change your interpretation of the rest of the novel? To what extent did you feel that the ending was a success?

💻 Resources

www.bookreporter.com/authors/au-shreve-anita.asp – page on Anita Shrve published at bookreporter.com containing an interview by Rachel Kempster about the writing of *The Last Time They Met*

📖 Suggested further reading

Out of Africa by Karen Blixen (1937); *Cause Celeb* by Helen Fielding (1995); *Sin* by Josephine Hart (1992); *Making it Up* by Penelope Lively (2005); *Rules of the Wild* by Francesca Marciano (1998); *Evening* by Susan Minot (1999); *The Story of You* by Julie Myerson (2006); *Loving Him* by Kate O'Riordan (2005); *Anna Karenina* by Leo Tolstoy (1874–6)

OTHER BOOKS BY ANITA SHREVE

Eden Close (1989); *Strange Fits of Passion* (1991); *Where or When?* (1993); *Resistance* (1995); *The Weight of Water* (1997); *The Pilot's Wife* (1998); *Fortune's Rocks* (2000); *Sea Glass* (2002); *All He Ever Wanted* (2003); *Light on Snow* (2004); *A Wedding in December* (2005); *Body Surfing* (2007)

BALZAC AND THE LITTLE CHINESE SEAMSTRESS (2000)

Dai Sijie (translated by Ina Rilke)

About the book

In 1971, their parents designated 'enemies of the people', two young men are sent to a remote Chinese village as part of Mao Zedong's 're-education' programme. Luo and his friend, the book's unnamed narrator, find themselves assigned the worst jobs in the village, with little hope of returning to the city where they grew up. Luo's storytelling skills prove the boys' salvation holding the villagers in thrall but the discovery of their friend Four-Eyes's collection of forbidden books kindles a fascination and delight in Western literature which will prove to be dangerous, seductive and liberating, in equal measure. When both boys fall in love with the local seamstress, it is Luo's reading of Balzac's novels that wins her heart but the narrator who saves her. Written with wit and humanity, Dai Sijie's lyrical novel tells of a dark time in Chinese history and the transforming power of literature.

Background

The son of doctors condemned as 'enemies of the people' Dai Sijie found himself in a similar situation to Luo and the narrator of his elegant novella when he was sent to a remote region of China as part of a four-year 're-education' programme. He acknowledges that there is an autobiographical thread running through the novel: 'There was a real love story ... but not as romantic. The stealing books part is true and the experience of reading stories to farmers is also true.' During Mao Zedong's draconian Cultural Revolution all books were forbidden: stealing and hiding then was commonplace if dangerous.

In writing his novel Sijie explains, ' I wanted to show how much impact culture could have on an isolated mountain village, and especially for [the seamstress]. It was a revelation of freedom, of self-consciousness. The little seamstress had seen more in Balzac ... learned that men could flirt with women, that it is natural ... This is what she had never learned during her days of being indoctrinated ... that life could be filled with many nice things.' It is this part of his novel which was most criticized by the Chinese government when the book was published in Sijie's adopted country, France, and was one of the reasons why the book was not published in his native China. When asked how such a young woman could be transformed through reading the literature of a culture so very different from her own Sijie says: 'The influence of literature is universal. [The story] was not only an ode to the literature we had read, but also simply to show that in a difficult situation, we, at that young age, had a yearning to learn, to see new things and nice things.'

About the author

Dai Sijie was born in the Fujian province of China in 1954 and was 're-educated' in the years between 1971 and 1974, the height of Mao Zedong's Cultural Revolution. In 1984 he won a scholarship from the University of Arts to study abroad and moved to France where he still lives and works as a filmmaker. *Balzac and the Little Chinese Seamstress* became an international bestseller and was made into a film in 2002, adapted and directed by Sijie himself.

For discussion

⊙ Dai Sijie's novel is set in Mao Zedong's China. How different is the China of today from the China of the 1970s?

⊙ When Luo asks the narrator what he knows about Western literature he replies: 'Not much. You know my parents were only interested in their work. Aside from medicine they didn't know very much.' Luo replies 'It was the same with mine'. Why have their parents been labelled 'enemies of the people'? Why has Four-Eyes's mother escaped this designation? Why did Mao Zedong and his régime want to discredit and humiliate 'intellectuals'?

⊙ Why does Luo punch the narrator when he sees that he is crying when Luo's father is publicly humiliated? What does this incident tell us about the narrator and about Luo? How would you describe each of the boys?

⊙ What does the two boys' 're-education' to consist of? How is Four-Eyes changed by his 're-education'? What do the peasants make of Mao Zedong's vision of their world? What has been the effect of Mao's regime on their lives?

⊙ 'Whatever his reasons, his choice was to have a profound effect on our lives.' How does the discovery of Western literature, and Balzac in particular, change the boys? What effect does it have on their lives? Why is it forbidden? How important is literature as a force for change in people's lives?

⊙ Early in the novel the narrator calls Luo's storytelling 'a pleasing talent to be sure, but a marginal one, with little future in it.' Does this prove to be the case? How important is storytelling in helping us form a view of the world? What does it enable us to do? What does it tell us about ourselves?

⊙ How important is humour in the novel? How would you describe that humour?

⊙ Has the seamstress undergone her own 're-education', and if so what part has Luo played in it? What do you make of the book's ending?

○ Dai Sijie is a filmmaker – *Balzac and the Little Chinese Seamstress* is his first novel. Would you describe the novel as cinematic and if so why?

○ Sijie was himself the subject of 're-education'. Why do you think he chose fiction rather than autobiography to give an account of that time? Which form do you consider to be more effective? Sijie has lived in France since 1984. How do you think his understanding of, and exposure to Western culture has influenced his writing of the novel?

Resources
www.taipeitimes.com/News/feat/archives/2002/05/20/136866 – interview with Yu-Sen-lun in *The Taipei Times*

http://query.nytimes.com/gst/fullpage.html?res=9F05E2DC1339F935A2575AC0A9 679C8B63 – review by Brooke Allen in *The New York Times*

www.sfgate.com/cgi-bin/article.cgi?file=/chronicle/archive/2001/10/28/RV236755. DTL – review by David Wiegand in *The San Francisco Chronicle*

http://film.guardian.co.uk/News_Story/Critic_Review/Observer_Film_of_the_week /0,4267,953386,00.html#article_continue – review of Dai Sijie's film of *Balzac and the Little Chinese Seamstress* by Philip French, published in *The Observer*

Suggested further reading
FICTION

Ursule Mirouët by Honore de Balzac (1842); *Fahrenheit 451* by Ray Bradbury (1953); *The Drink and Dream Teahouse* by Justin Hill (2000); **The Reader by Bernhard Schlink** (1997); *Waiting by Ha Jin* (1999); *The Kitchen God's Wife* by Amy Tan (1991)

NON-FICTION

Wild Swans by Jung Chang (1991); *Red Dust* by Ma Jian (2001); *Red Azalea: Life and Love in China* by Anchee Min (1995)

OTHER BOOKS BY DAI SIJIE

Mr Muo's Travelling Couch (2005)

THE DEATH OF VISHNU (2000)

Manil Suri

About the book

Vishnu, the odd-job man in a Bombay apartment block, lies dying on the stairs of the building where he both lives and works. Tenants tiptoe around him, wondering whether he still needs his daily cup of tea and arguing about who should pay for the ambulance to take him to hospital, swatting away the nagging buzz of conscience as if it were an especially irritating fly. Meanwhile, life goes on. Food is prepared, card parties are disrupted amid accusations of cheating, elopements planned and a terrible violence ignited. Manil Suri weaves a bright thread of Hindu mythology through this tale of life in Bombay, as Vishnu's soul begins its ascent of the stairs, observing the lives of the tenants while sights, sounds and smells vividly evoke memories of his own life.

Background

In *The Death of Vishnu*, Manil Suri turns a single Bombay apartment block into a vibrant portrait of India in microcosm, with all its aspirations, intricate social structures and religious divisions. While Vishnu lies dying on the stairway where he has lived for almost eleven years, slipping in and out of consciousness, the dramas of the tenants' lives are played out around him. Social rivalries, strained marriages, the search for spiritual truth, romantic love and grief are all explored, as Vishnu's soul begins its ascent of the building's stairs. Suri underpins this tale of all too human desires and preoccupations with a rich blend of Hindu mythology and an observation of human folly which is both humorous and astute

The Death of Vishnu was begun as a short story in 1995, inspired by the true story of a man who lived and died on the landing of the Mumbai apartment block where Suri grew up, but as the short story evolved into a novel Suri became stuck. He had attended a course taught by the author Vikram Chandra who liked the outline for the novel very much, describing it as 'trenchant'. Perhaps a little intimidated Suri ground to a halt but made a bargain with himself that if he was accepted for the novelist Michael Cunningham's writing workshop he would continue writing. Not only was he accepted but he found Cunningham to be extraordinarily enthusiastic about his work, spurring him on to finish the book.

While writing the novel Suri read both the Bhagavad Gita and the Koran for the first time but explains that 'Vishnu is the preserver, the preserver of the Universe. That's the only thing you really need to know to understand the story'. The thread of Hindu mythology which runs through the book 'was more to tantalize people —

this is what Hindu mythology is like, here's a little taste of it, there's a whole world out there if you want to explore it.' Suri was born a Hindu but describes himself as an agnostic, although he has said that 'having written this book I have started thinking more about various spiritual aspects. Which you have to, I can't imagine not having done that. I have stated questioning a lot of things that I wouldn't have before. The whole idea of ego, of materialism and so on.'

The Death of Vishnu changed his life in other unexpected ways. It was first published in India and Suri was immensely gratified by its reception in his homeland saying that his Indian readers 'welcomed it as an Indian book, "a Bombay book"'. He has said that writing the novel has put him back in touch with his roots – he left India in the early eighties – that 'this man Vishnu who died on my steps five years ago pulled me back into the country in some ways. Exploring all this, thinking back on my life in Bombay, trying to extract things out of that ... there's a real connection there. Life here will never change. Every time I go back I feel that even more.'

About the author

Manil Suri was born in Mumbai (Bombay) in 1959. After taking his doctorate at the Carnegie-Mellon University, he took his first job as an assistant professor of mathematics at the University of Baltimore, Maryland, where he became a full professor. He finished his first short story, *The Tyranny of Vegetables* in 1985. It was published in 1995, the year he began *The Death of Vishnu*, in a Bulgarian-language journal, but was only able to identify it by the author photograph printed next to the piece. *The Death of Vishnu* was published to great acclaim in 2000. It is the first of a planned trilogy, the second volume of which, *The Age of Shiva*, is based on the Hindu god Shiva, the destroyer, while the third will be about Brahma, the creator.

For discussion

✪ The book is prefaced by a quotation from *The Bhagavad-Gita* in which the god Vishnu is described as 'sustaining the entire world with a fragment of my being'. Why do you think Suri chose this quotation? Are there ways in which it can be applied to Vishnu, the odd-job man, as well as Vishnu the god, and, if so, what are they?

✪ How does Suri use the senses to evoke memory and atmosphere? Are there particular examples that struck you and, if so, what are they? To what extent does the style of writing differ between Vishnu's narrative and the rest of the book?

✪ How important is religion to the book's main characters such as the Asranis, the Pathaks, the Jalals and Vishnu himself? How does this demonstrate itself in the tenants' attitude and behaviour towards Vishnu, both when he is well and while he is dying?

○ The Jalals are the only Muslim family in the building. To what extent does this set them apart from the others? Were you surprised when the lathi-bearing mob was sparked off by Mr Jalal's description of his vision? Why do you think they were so brutal?

○ The tenants' treatment of Vishnu while he lies dying is shocking, yet Suri infuses the situation with humour. Why do you think he decided to do this? What effect does it have and how does Suri achieve it?

○ What impression do you gain from the novel of life in Bombay? What kind of social divides are apparent from the way people live their lives in the apartment block? What are the aspirations of the various characters?

○ Bombay is the centre of the burgeoning Bollywood film industry and cinema is never far away in the novel. Some characters seem to visualize their actions as if they are acting a part in a movie. How does this affect their lives? Are there particular situations where the cinema comes into play? If so, what are they and why do you think Suri chose to do this? Could the book be described as 'cinematic', and, if so, why?

○ Were there any characters in the book who engaged your sympathy? If so, who were they and what was it about them that attracted you? Which characters did you most dislike and why?

○ At the screening of *The Death of Vishnu*, Vishnu watches himself as he climbs the stairs of the apartment block and 'wishes the movie would be more clear about what he is climbing towards. Whether he is the god Vishnu, or just an ordinary man'. Which do you think he is meant to be, and why?

○ 'Who are you?' Vishnu asks the flute-playing boy on the final page of the book. The boy replies, 'You know who I am.' Who do you think he is and why?

○ There has been something of a vogue in the West for fiction by Indian writers over the past decade. How does *The Death of Vishnu* compare with other novels such as Arundhati Roy's *The God of Small Things* or Vikram Seth's *A Suitable Boy*? Are there similarities in style or subject with books by these and other Indian authors such as Salman Rushdie or do you think they are simply lumped together because of their race?

💻 Resources

www.powells.com/authors/suri.html – interview by Dave Weich published at Powell's bookshop website

www.identitytheory.com/people/birnbaum4.html – interview with Robert Birnbaum published at *Identity Theory* website

www.sfgate.com/cgi-bin/article.cgi?file=/chronicle/archive/2001/01/07/RV8822.DTL
– review by Elizabeth Kadetsky originally published in the *San Francisco Chronicle*
http://books.guardian.co.uk/reviews/generalfiction/0,6121,432980,00.html –
review by the author and critic Adam Mars-Jones published in *The Guardian*
http://eawc.evansville.edu/anthology/gita.htm – translation of *The Bhagavad Gita*
by Ramanand Prasad published at the Exploring Ancient World Cultures website
www.manilsuri.com/welcome.htm – Manil Suri's *Death of Vishnu* website which
includes an interview by the author Michael Cunnningham, notes on Suri's sources
and a glossary

🥢 Suggested further reading
FICTION
The Yacoubian Building by Ala Al Aswany (translated by Humphrey Davis) (2007);
Love and Longing in Bombay by Vikram Chandra (1997); *If Nobody Speaks of
Remarkable Things* by Jon McGregor (2002); *A Fine Balance* by Rohinton Mistry
(1996); *Gods, Demons and Others* by R.K. Narayan (1965); *Life, A User's Manual* by
Georges Perec (1970); *The God of Small Things* by Arundhati Roy (1997); *Midnight's
Children* by Salman Rushdie (1981); *A Suitable Boy* by Vikram Seth (1993)
NON-FICTION
The Bhagavad Gita; *India: A Million Mutinies Now* by V.S. Naipaul (1990);
Hinduism by K.M. Sen (1961)
OTHER BOOKS BY MANIL SURI
The Age of Shiva (2008)

ANITA AND ME (1996)
Meera Syal

📖 About the book
When the local bad girl, Anita, suggests that she and nine-year-old Meena get
together and form their own gang, Meena can hardly believe her luck. Daughter of
the only Sikh family in the village of Tollington, she is more used to living in her own
imagined world than being part of a gang. Soon she is adopting a Wolverhampton
accent and doing everything else she can to fit in, while her parents and her legions
of aunties fret over her misdemeanours. But Anita blows hot and cold, playing one
friend off against another, flexing her popularity by manipulating others. When her

mother gives birth to a little boy, Meena's grandmother comes over from India to help and Meena's view of her Punjabi roots begins to change. When the racism bubbling away below the community's surface boils over, Meena finally realizes that her friendship with Anita is not what she had hoped.

Background
Born in 1962, Meera Syal was brought up in the Midlands mining village of Essington close to Wolverhampton. Hers was the only Asian family in the village and it would be easy to assume that *Anita and Me* is a purely autobiographical novel, particularly as it is her first. When asked about the autobiographical content of the novel she has explained that while it is semi-autobiographical; what happens to Meena in the book did not happen to her although 'emotionally it's very reflective'. There was no single Anita she explains. Her character 'was an amalgamation of two or three older girls in my village who I used to follow around'.

The multi-talented Syal is perhaps better known as an actor, and particularly as a comic actor, appearing both in her own work and that of others. She has a multitude of scriptwriting credits to her name for radio, television and film. During the eighties, she wrote scripts for the comedy series *Tandoori Nights* and was commissioned by the BBC in 1992 to write a three-part drama, *My Sister Wife*. She went on to write the screenplay for the critically acclaimed film, *Bhaji on the Beach* and has written regularly for radio, including *Masala FM* and two series of *Goodness Gracious Me*, later adapted for television. Her television successes also include the satirical *The Kumars at No. 42* and her comedy the BAFTA-winning short film *It's Not Unusual*, in which she played a Tom Jones-obsessed cabbie. Just as in her novels *Anita and Me* and *Life Isn't All Ha Ha Hee Hee*, much of her other writing takes a gently swipe at the aspirations of British Asians while retaining a warm affection and sympathy for them.

With so many scriptwriting and acting success to her name it's hardly surprising that *Anita and Me* was made into a film in 2002 for which Syal wrote the screenplay and in which she played the part of Auntie Shaila.

About the author
Meera Syal studied English and drama at Manchester University, where she gained a first class hinours degree in Drama and English. She worked as an actress at the Royal Court Theatre after graduation. *Anita and Me*, Syal's first novel, won the Betty Trask Award and was shortlisted for *The Guardian* Fiction Prize.

For discussion

⊙ 'I'm not really a liar, I just learned very early on that those of us deprived of history sometimes need to turn to mythology to feel complete, to belong.' What does Syal mean by this and what bearing does it have on the rest of the novel? Are there other reasons why Meena tells so many stories? If so, what do you think they are?

⊙ The novel is set in the 1960s and narrated by nine-year-old Meena. How successful do you think Syal is at capturing a nine-year-old's voice and at conveying the period?

⊙ The book is infused with a good deal of humour – how amusing did you find it and what made you laugh?

⊙ How different are Meena's feelings about Britain and the British from those of her parents and their friends? Do Meena's feelings about being Indian change in the book, and if so what triggers this change and how does it alter her view of life? How well does the family fit into the village and how does their effort to adapt affect them?

⊙ There are instances of overt racism in the book but, on the whole, instances of prejudice are covert or unconscious. How does Syal convey this to her readers? To what extent do you think attitudes about race have changed since the 1960s? Would the Kumars have an easier time in Tollington today?

⊙ What impression did you form of Anita? Why do you think she sought Meena out? How does her 'friendship' with Anita change Meena?

⊙ What effect does Nanima's arrival have on Meena, her family and the rest of the village?

⊙ How does Tollington change over the course of the novel and what triggers those changes?

🖳 Resources

www.contemporarywriters.com/authors/?p=auth94 – profile of Meera Syal at the British Council website including a critical essay by Dr James Sproctor

www.bbc.co.uk/nottingham/features/2002/11/anita_and_me_interview.shtml – short interview with Meera Syal on the making of the film *Anita and Me* published on the BBC Nottingham webpage

www.salon.com/april97/sneaks/sneak970414.html – review by Christine Muhlke published at *Salon* internet magazine

www.nytimes.com/books/97/08/10/reviews/970810.10wilcoxt.html?_r=1&oref=slogin – review by the novelist James Wilcox published in *The New York Times*

🎋 Suggested further reading

The Romance Reader by Pearl Abraham (1995); *Cat's Eye* by Margaret Atwood (1988); *Venus Flaring* by Suzannah Dunn (1996); *Fruit of the Lemon* by Andrea Levy (1999); *The Orchard on Fire* by Shena Mackay (1995); *The God of Small Things* by Arundhati Roy (1997); *Staying On* by Paul Scott (1977); *White Teeth* by Zadie Smith (2000); *The Sopranos* by Alan Warner (1998)

OTHER BOOKS BY MEERA SYAL

Life Isn't All Ha Ha Hee Hee (1999)

THE HUNDRED SECRET SENSES (1995)

Amy Tan

📖 About the book

Just before Olivia Yee's father dies in a San Francisco hospital he drops a bombshell. He asks his American wife to send for the daughter he left behind in China many years ago. True to her fondness for lost causes, Olivia's mother does just that and five-year-old Olivia finds herself sharing her room with her adoring new sister, Kwan. Olivia grows up with Kwan's stories of ghosts, past lives, missionaries and mercenaries, which intrigue yet irritate her with their strangeness. Thirty years later, when Olivia's marriage falters, Kwan does all she can to get the couple back together again. When the three of them agree to visit China together, Olivia finds her mind opened to all sorts of Kwan's ideas to which she had kept it firmly closed for so many years.

Background

The Hundred Secret Senses explores the gap between two very different cultures. Kwan has grown up in a Chinese village and refuses to abandon her 'hundred secret senses' in the face of American scepticism. Determinedly rational, Olivia finds her sister's forays into the spirit world irritating and embarrassing. Kwan's stories of her previous life, caught up in the tumult of the nineteenth-century Taiping rebellion, punctuate Olivia's narrative as she charts their uneasy relationship and the break-up of her marriage.

With the tremendous success of both *The Joy Luck Club* and *The Kitchen God's Wife* Amy Tan gained something of a reputation as an 'interpreter' of Chinese culture, a label that she has eschewed, preferring instead that critics treat her fiction 'as literature – as a story, language, memory'. Both her previous books explored the mother–daughter bond, drawing on her own mother's harrowing experience in

1940s war-torn China in *The Kitchen God's Wife*. In contrast *The Hundred Secret Senses* explores the relationship between sisters and ventures into the spirit world. When asked about this aspect of her novel Tan has said that having lost several people close to her she has 'long thought about how life is influenced by death, how it influences what you believe in and what you look for,' and agrees that 'Yes, I think I was pushed in a way to write this book by certain spirits – the yin people – in my life.' 'Yin' which means invisible or shadow was a word that she chose herself to describe Kwan's spirits. It's a term she prefers to the, as she puts it, 'politically incorrect' word ghost. Just as the phrase 'yin people' came from her own imagination so did Kwan although she says 'I feel Kwan-like characters all round me'. As for the character of Olivia, Tan 'took my own skepticism and embedded it into Olivia. Some of her – or the questions that trouble her – are drawn from friends who have the usual existential questions about life and relationships and work and success, and "Why are we here?" and "Why are we with this person?"' She has previously said that *The Joy Luck Club* was written for her mother but when asked about *The Hundred Secret Senses* she replied 'I wrote this book with the idea that it was for all of my friends who had died, actually. So it was originally dedicated to all of my yin friends.' When she finished the book she decided to dedicate it to her friend Faith who she had helped through a long illness 'because it was about having faith'.

Tan ascribes her wonderfully accomplished storytelling skills to both her father, a Baptist minister who read his sermons aloud to her, and her mother who sat with her aunts for hours talking around the kitchen table. She also says: 'I think that the other reason that I've become a storyteller is that I was raised with so many different conflicting ideas that it posed many questions for me in life, and those questions became a filter for looking at all my experiences and seeing them from different angles. That's what I think that a storyteller does, and underneath the surface of the story is a question or a perspective or a nagging little emotion, and then it grows'.

About the author

Amy Tan was born in 1952 in Oakland, California to Chinese immigrants, one of three children. She graduated from high school in Montreux, Switzerland, and took a masters degree in linguistics at San Jose State University. After graduation she took a job as a language development consultant and later directed a training project for developmentally disabled children. She went on to become a successful freelance writer providing speeches for salesmen and executives for large corporations. In 1985 Tan attended a writing workshop for which she wrote a story which later became part of her first work of fiction, *The Joy Luck Club* published in 1989, when it won the American National Book Award. It was later made into a film.

For discussion

○ How does Olivia feel about Kwan when the book opens? What are her feelings towards her when it ends? Why do you think this change has come about?

○ How would you describe Kwan? What are her feelings for Olivia? Why is Kwan so forgiving when Olivia is so obviously irritated by her? Why does she so often ask Olivia what she thinks and tell her to keep things to herself?

○ Nunumu says of Miss Banner: 'I wondered whether foreigners had feelings that were entirely different from those of Chinese people.' How important is this idea in the novel? How is it illustrated in the relationship between Kwan and Olivia?

○ What do you think of the missionaries' attitude towards the Chinese? How would you describe the Chinese reactions to them?

○ The idea of the 'loyal friend' is very important to Kwan, both in her present life and her past as Nunumu. What does Kwan/Nunumu mean by a 'loyal friend'? What does Miss Banner mean by it?

○ Why does Olivia leave Simon? What effect does Elza's death have on their relationship? What does Olivia expect of her marriage and how realistic do you think her expectations are?

○ What are the 'hundred secret senses'? Does Olivia understand what they are by the end of the book?

○ What do Olivia and Simon learn from their visit to China? How different is it from their expectations? How do the Chinese view American culture? Are there any similarities between the way that Americans and Chinese view each other in the nineteenth-century narrative and the twentieth century? If so, what are they?

○ How satisfactory did you find the ending of the book? What do you think happened to Kwan?

🖳 Resources

www.nytimes.com/books/01/02/18/specials/tan-hundred.html?_r=1&oref=slogin – review by the novelist Claire Messud published in *The New York Times*

www.nytimes.com/books/01/02/18/specials/tan-home.html – interview with Sarah Lyall published in *The New York Times*

www.salon.com/12nov1995/feature/tan.html – interview at *Salon* internet magazine

www.metroactive.com/papers/sonoma/12.14.95/tan-9550.html – interview with Gretchen Giles published at metrocative.com website

www.achievement.org/autodoc/page/tanobio-1 – entry for Amy Tan on the Academy of Achievement website

📚 Suggested further reading

The House of Spirits by Isabel Allende (1985); *The Binding Chair* by Kathryn Harrison (2000); *Fruit of the Lemon* by Andrea Levy (1999); *Eating Chinese Food Naked* by Mei Ng (1998); *Pears on a Willow Tree* by Leslie Pietrzyk (1998); *The Last Time I Saw Jane* by Kate Pullinger (1996)

OTHER BOOKS BY AMY TAN

Novels: *The Joy Luck Club* (1989); *The Kitchen God's Wife* (1991); *The Bonesetter's Daughter* (2001); *Saving Fish From Drowning* (2005)

Non-fiction: *The Opposite of Fate* (2003)

Edited: *The Best American Short Stories* 1999

THE STORY OF LUCY GAULT (2002)

William Trevor

📖 About the book

One night in the troubled year of 1921, three men appear in the grounds of Lahardane to set fire to the house. Springing to the defence of his English wife and their daughter, Lahardane's Protestant owner Everard Gault fires his shotgun meaning only to frighten the trespassers but wounding one of them. The young man's family will have nothing of Everard's pleas for forgiveness, remaining obdurate in their refusal. For their own safety the Gaults must leave Ireland, an idea that eight-year-old Lucy finds unbearable. She runs away, determined to make her parents stay. Believing Lucy to be dead, her heartbroken parents turn their backs on their beloved home. When Lucy is found alive, her parents cannot be traced and her life becomes one of atonement for the wrong she feels she has done them. Written in quietly elegant, graceful prose and permeated with an aching sadness, *The Story of Lucy Gault* is a novel about chance, forgiveness and redemption.

Background

The Story of Lucy Gault begins in 1921, the year which saw the Partition of Ireland into the Protestant dominated North and the Catholic Republic of Ireland. It was a time in which many Protestant landowners fled their estates, their houses and those of their neighbours set on fire by Catholic militants. William Trevor was born in the Republic in 1928 to Protestant parents for whom the Troubles must have been an all too vivid memory although he has said that politics played no part in his upbringing. He lives in England and has done so for many years, moving there in 1954, but he frequently turns to Ireland in his fiction: 'I feel a sense of freshness when I come back [to Ireland],' he said in a 2000 Irish radio interview. 'If I lived in, say, Dungarvan or Skibbereen, I think I wouldn't notice things.' As one critic has noted; 'his writing frequently registers this [Protestant] minority's difficult co-existence with the prevailing Irish Catholic majority. But the scope of his work is inclusive, and he is just as like to delineate the plight of a rural Catholic farming family as the downfall of the Anglo-Irish Protestant aristocracy.'

Trevor is one of the most prolific of contemporary Irish writers. He is an acclaimed short storywriter and has been compared to both Chekov and de Maupassant but has said that he is equally at home with the novel, often unsure when he begins to write which form the result will take but happy to move between the two finding it: 'a great pleasure. A novel can be a wearying form. But after a few stories, it's a relief to turn back to something larger.' *The Story of Lucy Gault* typifies Trevor's novels: slim, elegant, often spare, each word carefully chosen. His writing is so marvellously crafted that it will have readers re-reading the novel for the sheer pleasure of his language.

About the author

William Trevor was born in Mitchelstown, County Cork, in the Republic of Ireland on May 24th 1928. He was educated at St Columba's College, County Dublin, and Trinity College, Dublin. He worked briefly as a teacher, and later as an advertising copywriter before taking up writing full time in 1965. He has also been a sculptor and has exhibited frequently in Dublin and London. As well as being a novelist, he is the acclaimed author of several collections of short stories, and has adapted a number of his own stories for the stage, television and radio. *The Children of Dynmouth* and *Fools of Fortune* both won the Whitbread Novel Award, and *Felicia's Journey* won the 1994 Whitbread Book of the Year Award. *The Story of Lucy Gault* won the 2002 James Tait Black Memorial Prize for fiction and was shortlisted for both the Man Booker prize and the Whitbread Novel of the Year. William Trevor lives in Devon.

For discussion

✪ Why do the Gaults feel that they must leave Lahardane? What makes them a target?

✪ 'Disobedience had been a child's defiance, deception the coinage that they had offered her themselves.' Have Lucy's parents brought her disappearance upon themselves? What does Lucy feel about what she has done? How do others judge the situation?

○ 'In his dream the curtains of the house had blown out from the windows, blazing in the dark. There was the lifeless body of a child.' What are the repercussions of that night for Horahan?

○ 'She was not lonely; sometimes she could hardly remember loneliness.' What has Lucy's life become?

○ How does the loss of Lucy shape the lives of Heloise and Everard? How is their marriage altered by it?

○ 'I'm not someone to love' Lucy tells Ralph. Why does she believe this? Why does she continue to reject his proposals despite telling him 'Of course, I love you too'? How would you describe the connection between them?

○ 'Her tranquillity is their astonishment. For that they come, to be amazed again that such peace is there: all they have heard, and still hear now, does not record it.' How has Lucy arrived at this state of forgiveness? What are her feelings towards Horahan?

○ 'Calamity shaped a life when, long ago, chance was so cruel.' What part does chance play in the novel?

○ How would you describe William Trevor's writing? How does he evoke the atmosphere of wistful melancholy that pervades the novel? Were there particular passages that struck you and if so what were they and why?

🖥 Resources

http://books.guardian.co.uk/bookerprize2002/story/0,12350,800890,00.html – review by Tim Adams published in *The Observer*

http://books.guardian.co.uk/reviews/generalfiction/0,6121,782946,00.html – review by Hermione Lee published in *The Guardian*

www.telegraph.co.uk/arts/main.jhtml?xml=/arts/2002/08/25/botre25.xml – review by Francis King published in *The Telegraph*

http://query.nytimes.com/gst/fullpage.html?res=9907EFDE1030F93AA1575AC0A9 649C8B63 – review by the novelist Thomas Mallon published in *The New York Times*

www.contemporarywriters.com/authors/?p=auth122 – profile of William Trevor at the British Council website including a critical essay by Eve Patten

www.nytimes.com/books/98/09/06/specials/trevor-stories.html – article published in *The New York Times* written by Reynolds Price on William Trevor's short story writing which contains a brief interview with Trevor

http://btob.barnesandnoble.com/writers/writerdetails.asp?r=1&btob=Y&cid=9749 52 – interview by barnesandnoble.com which includes a short profile by Gloria Mitchell

🐛 Suggested further reading

The Last September by Elizabeth Bowen (1929); *The Good Soldier* by Ford Maddox Ford (1915); *The Remains of the Day* by Kashuo Ishiguro (1989); *Charming Billy* **by Alice McDermott** (1997); *Amongst Women* by John McGahern (1990); *The Boy in the Moon* **by Kate O'Riordan** (1997)

OTHER BOOKS BY WILLIAM TREVOR

A Standard of Behaviour (1956); *The Old Boys* (1964); *The Boarding-House* (1965); *The Love Department* (1966); *Mrs Eckdorf in O'Neill's Hotel* (1969); *Miss Gomez and the Brethren* (1971); *Last Lunch of the Season* (1973); *Elizabeth Alone* (1973); *The Children of Dynmouth* (1976); *The Distant Past* (1977); *Other People's Worlds* (1980); *Fools of Fortune* (1983); *Nights at the Alexandra* (1987); *The Silence in the Garden* (1988); *Two Lives* (1991); *Juliet's Story* (1991); *Felicia's Journey* (1994); *Marrying Damian* (1995); *Death in Summer* (1998)

Short stories: *The Day We Got Drunk on Cake and Other Stories* (1967); *The Ballroom of Romance and Other Stories* (1972); *Angels at the Ritz and Other Stories* (1975); *Lovers of Their Time: and Other Stories* (1978); *Beyond the Pale and Other Stories* (1981); *Ireland: Selected Stories* (1984); *The News from Ireland and Other Stories* (1986); *Family Sins and Other Stories* (1989); *Outside Ireland: Selected Stories* (1995); *After Rain* (1996); *The Hill Bachelors* (2000); *A Bit on the Side* (2004); *Cheating at Canasta* (2007)

Drama: *Going Home* (1972); *Night with Mrs Da Tanka* (1972); *Marriages* (1974)

Edited: *The Oxford Book of Irish Short Stories* (1989)

Non-fiction: *A Writer's Ireland: Landscape in Literature* (1984); *Excursions in the Real World: Memoirs* (1993); *Personal Essays* (1999)

MORALITY PLAY (1995)

Barry Unsworth

📖 About the book

In the late fourteenth century, the country stricken with plague, famine and the consequences of war with France, a priest joins a group of impoverished travelling players as they take the body of their dear friend to the nearest town for burial. To pay the burial fees they decide to put on a play. On hearing that a young woman is to be hanged for the murder of a twelve-year-old boy the company leader, desperate to augment their depleted funds, persuades the players to re-enact the murder. But as the players investigate the circumstances of the boy's death doubt is thrown on the young woman's guilt. Over the two days that they perform their play, digging deeper into the murky circumstances that surround the murder, they come close to revealing a shocking truth that puts them all in mortal danger.

Background

Morality Play is set in the late fourteenth century, a time marked by terrible calamity; plague and famine stalked the land while the century-long wars with France still raged. The long-established feudal system had begun to crumble. Millenarian sects prophesying the Last Days sprang up in protest against the corruption of the clergy. This is the turbulent backdrop against which Martin and his players set the story of the murder of Thomas Wells, using the structure of the allegorical dramas known as morality plays or 'moralities'.

The immense changes wrenching the medieval world apart brought about a society on the brink of re-inventing itself with the rise of the merchant classes and the increasing mobility of a labour force in great demand thanks to the ravages wreaked by the plague. Drama was also in a transitional state. The Mystery Play with its depictions of biblical scenes had taken the liturgy to the streets becoming much more elaborate in the fourteenth and fifteenth centuries with cycles of plays funded by the guilds, including the renowned York Mysteries, providing a huge draw. Poorer troupes such as the one Nicolas Barber falls in with continued to travel the country with their own modest productions. Alongside the Mysteries a new form of drama, the Morality Play told the story of an individual Christian (the best-known of which was Everyman) travelling through a life beset with temptation, falling from grace and eventually attaining redemption. Allegorical figures such as Greed, Pride, Vanity and Good Will personified human vices and virtues, while God and the Devil also played their parts as the weary Christian struggled along his path. Both forms were performed alongside each other for several centuries but it was the Morality Play which was to survive, giving way, in turn, to the secular drama of the Renaissance. It is this form that Unsworth takes and crafts with enormous skill into a gripping detective story, vividly portraying an anarchic world on the cusp of enormous change.

About the author

Barry Unsworth was born in a mining village near Durham in 1930. He was educated at Stockton-on-Tees Grammar School and Manchester University. He lived for some time in the eastern Mediterranean, taught English in Athens and Istanbul and has more recently lived in Italy. His first novel. *The Partnership*, was published in 1966. *Pascali's Island*, later made into a film, was shortlisted for the Booker Prize in

1980. In 1992 Unsworth was joint winner of the Booker Prize for *Sacred Hunger*, which tied with Michael Ondaatje's *The English Patient*. *Morality Play* was also shortlisted for the Booker.

For discussion

❍ When Martin announces that the players are to play the murder they are all shocked. What is it about the idea that particularly upsets them? How is it different from the plays they usually perform? How do Nicholas's reactions differ from those of the others, and why? What is he afraid of when he says: 'if we make our own meanings, God will oblige us to answer our own questions'? Are his fears fulfilled?

❍ What are Martin's motives in staging such a provocative play? How do they change? What makes him give such a brave and dangerous performance in de Guise's castle?

❍ What risks is the company courting by staging *The Murder of Thomas Wells*? As the players improvise their parts on stage, it is as if they are impelled to reveal the truth. Why do you think they do this?

❍ How does Unsworth evoke the atmosphere of fear and foreboding which pervades the book?

❍ To what extent do you think justice was done at the end of the book? What are the implications of the conversation that Nicholas has with the Justice? Why does Nicholas decide to remain as a player rather than rejoin the clergy?

❍ What does Nicholas mean when he says, 'the player is always trapped in his own play but he must never allow the spectators to suspect this, they must always think that he is free'? How can this idea be applied in the rest of the novel?

❍ How do you interpret the meaning of the novel's title? Are there several meanings and, if so, what are they?

❍ We now accept the idea of using drama, fiction or art as a means of holding up a mirror to society in order to discover the truth. Are there particular examples that you believe to have been effective and, if so, what are they and what was the effect?

💻 Resources

www.wwnorton.com/rgguides/moralityrgg.htm – reading guide at Barry Unsworth's American publisher W.W. Norton's website which includes a short essay on drama and the fourteenth century by Unsworth

www.imagi-nation.com/moonstruck/spectop006.html – entry on medieval drama by Martha Fletcher Bellinger published at the Moonstruck Drama Bookstore website

www.historicalnovelsociety.org/solander%20files/warningvoice.htm – interview by Barry Podmore published at the Historical Novel Society website

🐢 Suggested further reading
FICTION
Hawksmoor by Peter Ackroyd (1985); *A Perfect Execution* by Tim Binding (1996); *The Leper's Companions* **by Julia Blackburn** (1999); *The Alienist* by Caleb Carr (1994); *A Maggot* by John Fowles (1985)
NON-FICTION
English Mystery Plays edited by Peter Happe (1975); *A Distant Mirror* by Barbara Tuchman (1978)
OTHER BOOKS BY BARRY UNSWORTH
The Partnership (1966); *The Greeks Have a Word For It* (1967); *Pascali's Island* (1980); *The Rage of the Vulture* (1982); *Stone Virgin* (1985); *Sugar and Rum* (1988); *Sacred Hunger* (1992); *After Hannibal* (1996); *Losing Nelson* (1999); *The Songs of Kings* (2002); *The Ruby in Her Navel* (2006)

THE CUTTING ROOM (2002)
Louise Welsh

📖 About the book
Bowery Auctions is close to bankruptcy when its expert but jaded auctioneer is offered an opportunity that will pull it back from the brink, clearing a house packed with precious objects. Rilke agrees to do the job despite the owner's insistence that it must be completed within a week and that only he must deal with the attic which he finds full of rare pornographic books. Rilke is not a squeamish man – his own habits are somewhat promiscuous – but the discovery of photographs depicting sexual torture and what may be a murder committed many years ago appals him. Despite the urgency of the job he begins an investigation that takes him into the murkiest areas of Glasgow in search of the truth. In this remarkably assured first novel, set in a colourful Glasgow peopled with eccentrics and narrated by the quick-witted Rilke, Louise Welsh explores the depths of human depravity drawing her novel towards a shocking and sobering denouement.

Background
Before writing *The Cutting Room*, Louise Welsh had honed her skills writing short stories and plays while running her second-hand and antiquarian bookshop, an experience which helped provide some of the background for her novel. She had long had an ambition to write a novel and Strathclyde and Glasgow University's

MLit in Creative Writing course finally gave her the confidence to begin.

In this unconventional crime novel, Welsh succeeds in summoning up a sordid, dark side of Glasgow which, as several critics have noted, has an almost gothic quality in keeping with the dark nature of the book's subject – the examination of extreme depravity. Welsh has described writing from a male point-of view as 'liberating' because she felt that a man 'could go anywhere' and Rilke, her narrator, a hard-drinking gay auctioneer with a wonderful knowledge of even the most esoteric antiquities, is indeed comfortably at home in the seedier side of the city. His is a par-ticularly complex character for a first novel with his dry wit, hard-drinking, promiscuity and the moral dilemmas that trouble him more than his outward persona might suggest. Welsh has said that he emerged as 'a fully formed character' who 'dictated his own terms' but that he was influenced 'by a long line of literary antiheros from Caleb Williams to Philip Marlowe', Raymond Chandler being a particular influence.

With its graphic portrayal of promiscuity, inevitably sex proved to be the most controversial aspect of the novel when it was published, provoking both strong criticism and praise for the novel's honesty. Welsh has been dismissive of the criticism explaining that: 'At the core of the book is a selection of horrifying photographs, which may depict the sexual murder of a young girl. The close description of these photographs is at least as detailed as Rilke's sexual encounters. No one has expressed shock or disgust over them. I think sex is important in novels as in life. Rilke is an out and about gay man who has consensual safe sex with men over the age of twenty-one. It's hard for me to see any great controversy there. If people don't like it they can skip a paragraph or two.'

Welsh has said that her ambition is to write a novel 'that will make people turn the pages and forget to do things – "I'll just miss work today and finish this book".' Although *The Cutting Room* may not have the pace of an Ian Rankin novel, with its unsettling atmosphere, its cast of colourful characters and its idiosyncratic but likeable narrator it takes a more than respectable swipe at that ambition.

About the author

Louise Welsh was born in 1965. She graduated from Glasgow University with a degree in history and worked for many years as a second-hand and antiquarian book dealer. *The Cutting Room* is her first novel. It won the 2002 Crime Writers' Association John Creasey Memorial Dagger Award and was jointly awarded the 2002 Saltire Society Scottish First Book of the Year Award in the same year. She is a regular radio broadcaster and has contributed both articles and reviews to most of the British broadsheets. She has published many short stories and has also written for the stage. Louise Welsh lives in Glasgow.

For discussion

⚙ What do you make of the quotations that preface each chapter of the novel? Did you find any particularly appropriate and if so, what were they and why?

⚙ 'You, you're always so moral' Rose says to Rilke when he expresses doubts about their plans to keep the sale proceeds. Would you agree? How would you describe Rilke? How does Louise Welsh convey his character? How would you describe the tone of his narrative?

⚙ Why does Rilke investigate the photographs himself rather than turn them over to the police? What drives him to continue with the investigation?

⚙ 'If this is real then it's a horrible thing, but it's a long time ago. Who did it doesn't matter.' To what extent do you share Les's view?

⚙ Rilke uses the word 'erotic' to describe the netsuke before he fully comprehends what it is depicting but later chronicles the development of 'pornography' through the ages. What do you think distinguishes one from the other?

⚙ *The Cutting Room* is, in essence, a crime novel, albeit an unconventional one. There are many asides and vignettes of Rilke's colourful life. How does Welsh maintain suspense in the novel?

⚙ Sex is graphically described in the book. How shocking did you find the descriptions? What purpose do you think they served within the context of the novel?

⚙ One critic has described the Glasgow of Welsh's novel as 'a character in itself'. How does Welsh succeed in evoking Glasgow so vividly? What kind of city does Rilke inhabit?

⚙ What did you think of the novel's denouement?

💻 Resources

http://books.guardian.co.uk/firstbook2002/story/0,,783541,00.html – review by the writer Paul Magrs published in *The Guardian*

http://query.nytimes.com/gst/fullpage.html?res=9C07E6D61031F933A05750C0A9 659C8B63 – review by Sophie Harrison published in *The New York Times*

http://books.guardian.co.uk/departments/generalfiction/story/0,,671618,00.html – piece on *The Guardian* 2002 First Book Award for which *The Cutting Room* was shortlisted

www.margaretmurphy.co.uk/pages/about_margaret/in_discussion.htm – interview by the crime novelist Margaret Murphy for *Crime Time* magazine

📖 Suggested further reading

The Big Sleep by Raymond Chandler (1939); *Something Leather* by Alistair Gray (1990); *A Case of Curiosities* by Allen Kurzweil (1992); *Bless the Thief* by Alan Wall

(1997); *The Shadow of the Wind* by Carlos Ruiz Zafón (translated by Lucia Graves) (2001)
OTHER BOOKS BY LOUISE WELSH
Tamburlaine Must Die (2004); *The Bullet Trick* (2006)

THE SHADOW OF THE WIND (2001)

Carlos Ruiz Zafón (translated by Lucia Graves)

📖 About the book

One early summer day in 1945, trying to distract his ten-year-old son from the loss of his mother, Daniel Sempere's father takes him to the Cemetery of Forgotten Books. There, Daniel finds the book that will intrigue him, bedevil him and ultimately shape his young life: *The Shadow of the Wind* by Julián Carfax. When, on his sixteenth birthday, Daniel sees a stranger smoking a cigarette from his balcony he instantly recognizes a scene from Carfax's novel and the seeds of an obsession, first sown six years earlier, take firm root. Carlos Ruiz Zafón's novel glories in the joys of storytelling with several narratives unfolding, spilling clues to the mystery of Julián Carfax as Daniel slowly pieces together Carfax's story. Set in Barcelona, a city deeply wounded by the terrible divisions and cruelties of the Civil War, *The Shadow of the Wind* vividly evokes the dark days of Franco's Spain with all its fear, repression and brutality.

Background

Straddling a multitude of genres, from gothic mystery to romance to comedy, *The Shadow of the Wind* combines many of the elements of the nineteenth century novels to which Carlos Ruiz Zafón has paid tribute in interviews, arguing that modern fiction should 'try to recapture the great scope and ambition of the nineteenth century classics but infusing it with all the narrative tools the twentieth century has left us'. A voracious reader, Zafón's own favourite authors range from Tolstoy and Dostoyevsky to Hardy and Balzac. For some time, Zafón was a scriptwriter and, although he has said that he has no particular wish to see his book made into a film, he acknowledges the influence of cinema on his work. That influence is particularly clear in his descriptions of Barcelona: its atmospheric, labyrinthine streets are so vividly evoked that they seem, at times, to be images projected upon a screen. Barcelona is Zafón's hometown, a city he describes as a 'great enchantress'. He grew up close to Gaudi's wonderfully extravagant but unfinished cathedral, the Sagrada Familia, and attended a Jesuit school housed in a fantastically Gothic building on the other side of the city.

At the heart of *The Shadow of the Wind* is a love of books: it is a hymn of praise both to storytelling and to reading. The novel is set against the background of Franco's repressive regime, a time when it was highly dangerous to possess 'subversive' books. Daniel's father declares that every book has a soul; his creator believes that 'every book is worth saving from either bigotry or oblivion', certainly not something that his own book has needed. Extraordinarily successful in Zafón's native Spain, *The Shadow of the Wind* became a bestseller across Europe and the United States, something of a feat for a novel in translation.

About the author

Born in 1964, Carlos Ruiz Zafón grew up in Barcelona, attended its university and began a successful career in advertising. In his late twenties he moved to Los Angeles where he worked as a screenwriter. Before the publication of *The Shadow of the Wind* in 2001, Zafón had already published four successful novels for young adults. He now works full time as a novelist, regularly contributing to *El Pais*, *El Mundo* and *La Vanguardia*. Chosen by Richard and Judy as one of their notable books of 2004, *The Shadow of the Wind* is the first in a planned series of four novels based in Barcelona.

The novel's translator, Lucia Graves, is the daughter of the poet Robert Graves.

For discussion

○ Carlos Ruiz Zafón's book shares the same name as his character Julián Carax's novel. What is the significance of the title *The Shadow in the Wind*? To what does it refer?

○ Who is the stranger who wants to burn Daniel's copy of *The Shadow in the Wind*? At what point did you guess his identity and why?

○ '"Not evil," Fermín objected. "Moronic, which isn't quite the same thing. Evil presupposes a moral decision, intention, and some forethought"'. Fermín determinedly distinguishes evil from thuggery when speaking of Don Federico's beating during his night in prison. What instances of evil are there in the book and who are the perpetrators?

○ 'The man who used to live within these bones died, Daniel. Sometimes he comes back, in nightmares'. What do we learn of Fermín's past life? How would you describe him? How important is he to Daniel, and Daniel to him?

○ *The Shadow of the Wind* begins just six years after the Civil War. What impression did you gain of Franco's Spain from the book? How important is the novel's setting? Why do you think Zafón chose to set it at this point in Spanish history?

✪ 'This boy reminds me of myself' Julián tells Nuria. In what ways does Daniel's life echo Julián's? How do they differ?

✪ 'Books are mirrors: you only see in them what you already have inside you' Julián tells Jorge when he declares 'Books are boring'. To what extent does this idea explain Daniel's fascination with *The Shadow of the Wind*? Do you agree with Julián?

✪ Humour plays an important part in the book. How would you describe that humour? Were there particular passages or characters that you found amusing?

✪ Zafón maintains an atmosphere of suspense throughout his novel, a suspense that becomes more intense in the last half. How does he do this?

✪ What did you think of the way the book ends?

✪ *The Shadow of the Wind* has been described as '... thriller, historical fiction, occasional farce, existential mystery and passionate love story'. How would you describe it?

✪ 'Once, in my father's bookshop, I heard a regular customer say that few things leave a deeper mark on a reader than the first book that finds its way into his heart'. What was the first book that found its way into your heart?

🖥 Resources

www.arts.telegraph.co.uk/arts/main.jhtml;?xml=/arts/2004/05/16/bozaf16.xml – review by Christopher Taylor in *The Telegraph*

http://books.guardian.co.uk/departments/generalfiction/story/0,6000,1233107,00. html – review by Robert Colvile in *The Observer*

http://books.guardian.co.uk/reviews/generalfiction/0,,1247408,00.html –review by Michael Kerrigan in *The Guardian*

http://query.nytimes.com/gst/fullpage.html?res=9F04E2D9143BF936A15757C0A9 629C8B63 – review by Richard Eder in *The New York Times*

📚 Suggested further reading

The Blind Assassin by Margaret Atwood (2000); ***Eucalyptus* by Murray Bail** (1998); *Possession* by A.S. Byatt (1990); *The Conjuror's Bird* by Martin Davies (2005); *Great Expectations* by Charles Dickens (1861); *The Name of the Rose* by Umberto Eco (1980); *The Dumas Club* by Arturo Perez-Reverte (1993); *The Carpenter's Pencil* by Manuel Rivas (1998); ***Balzac and the Little Chinese Seamstress* by Dai Sijie** (2000)

NON-FICTION

PAULA (1995)

Isabel Allende

📖 About the book

In December 1991 Isabel Allende's daughter collapsed with an attack of porphyria, an inherited metabolic disorder. Shortly after her collapse, Paula fell into a coma from which she was to emerge, after many months, severely brain damaged. *Paula* is Isabel Allende's long, moving letter to her daughter, in which she sets out to tell her the story of their extraordinary family, starting with Paula's great-grandparents. In the telling, the book becomes a meditation on life and death, the chronicle of a mother's pain and her eventual acceptance of the death of her child, and a memorial to a beloved daughter. It also offers those who are already acquainted with Allende's fiction an insight into the events which both inspire and inform her novels.

Background

Written during snatched moments, in hospital corridors and later at Paula's bedside in California, *Paula* began as a family history for Allende's daughter to read when she woke from the coma into which she had fallen after an attack of porphyria. Interspersed with the family's story are Allende's loving reflections on Paula and the slow, sad awareness that this was not an illness from which she would recover. Allende's language and storytelling mirrors that of her novels; it is warm, vivid and moving. Such an intimate book could, in less skilful hands, have descended into mawkishness, something that Allende wanted to avoid at all costs because, as she has explained, 'Paula had a horror of sentimentality.' She has described it as her most important book; the book which saved her from suicide.

Paula collapsed in her Madrid flat during her mother's visit to promote *The Infinite Plan*. Over the the next year Allende rarely left her side. Often accompanied by her mother or by Paula's husband, she remained doggedly determined that her daughter would recover until it became clear that this was impossible. Allende weaves her memories of Paula and the anguish of that year through the history of her own maternal family. Her father disappeared from her life when she was three and her early childhood was spent in Santiago de Chile with her grandparents. Her clairvoyant grandmother Meme continued to be both enormously influential and a comfort to Allende long after her death. It was to her grandfather that her first novel, *The House of Spirits*, was addressed but Meme was its inspiration.

When her mother began a lifelong involvement with a Chilean diplomat, Allende found herself moving first to Bolivia and then to the Lebanon, returning to Chile when she was fifteen. At nineteen she married Michael Frias. After hoodwinking her way into a job with the United Nations, she managed to secure work as a television presenter and later became a journalist. She cut a distinctive figure in her flamboyant clothes, both romantic and a little naïve.

In 1970 Salvador Allende, Isabel's uncle, was elected president. Thanks to the undermining activities of the right wing and an economic blockade imposed by the United States, resulting in rampant inflation and food shortages, the new government's popularity began to wane. In 1973 the president was overthrown by Augusto Pinochet's violent coup which marked the beginning of seventeen years of military rule, oppression and terror. At first Isabel was unaware of the 'disappearances' and torture that were the tools of the new régime. Almost unwittingly, she became drawn into helping those who sought asylum until the safety of her own family was at risk. They fled their beloved Chile for Venezuela. It was as if Isabel had been awakened from a cosy, if occasionally adventurous, domesticity. The strain began to tell on their marriage and eventually Isabel and Michael separated.

During this period Isabel began to write fiction. When she heard that her grandfather was dying in Chile, still in fear for her safety, she started a letter to him which became *The House of Spirits*. Her experiences of the horrors of the Pinochet régime together with the tales of other witnesses were put to good use in *Of Love and Shadows*. As *Paula* draws to its poignant conclusion, the influence of Allende's often extraordinary life on her work becomes clear and the roots of the magical realism, which forms an integral part of her fiction, can be traced.

As a memorial to her beloved daughter who worked as a volunteer in the poor communities of Venezuela and Spain, Allende created the Isabel Allende Foundation on December 9th, 1996. The Foundation's primary aim is to support 'organizations that help women and children in need, by providing education, healthcare, protection and the means to empowerment', a cause dear to Paula's heart.

About the author

Isabel Allende was born in Lima, Peru, in 1942. Her father, Tomás Allende, was the cousin of Salvador Allende, a Marxist who was democratically elected as leader of his country in 1970 but overthrown by a right-wing military coup in 1973. She married Miguel (anglicized to Michael in the book) Frias when she was nineteen and soon became involved in writing – first for a woman's magazine then writing plays and children's stories. The couple had two children, Paula and Nicolas. Isabel and Miguel separated in 1986. Isabel Allende has since remarried and lives in California. Her daughter, Paula, died in 1992. Although fluent in English, Isabel Allende writes only in Spanish. Her novels have been translated into many languages and have met with both critical and popular acclaim. *Paula* was her first venture into non-fiction.

For discussion

✪ The book opens with Isabel Allende explaining to Paula that she is going to tell her a story so that when she wakes up she won't feel so lost. What other reasons do you think there might have been for writing the book? How do you think these reasons may have changed over the course of writing *Paula*?

✪ It can be argued that since memory is not only imperfect but also subjective, autobiography can be classified as fiction. Do you think *Paula* reads like fiction? Is this the style in which it is written? Do you think that Allende believes that the book is factual from start to finish?

✪ What impression do you have of Paula from the book? To what extent do you think that this book is likely to be an accurate portrait of her?

✪ What impression do you have of Isabel Allende? What sort of mother do you think she is? What effect does Paula's condition have on Isabel Allende over the year that she is ill?

✪ What do you think Isabel Allende's attitude is to feminism? How is this illustrated? What is her view of women in Chile?

✪ How do you think the military coup and the resultant régime affected Isabel Allende? How do you think her attitude to politics changed?

✪ Magic is a strong presence in all Isabel Allende's novels. How does it manifest itself in *Paula*? What do you think of her beliefs in the spirit world?

🖳 Resources

www.metroactive.com/papers/metro/12.14.95/allende-9550.html – review by the author and academic Victor Perera published at the metroactive website
www.isabelallende.com – Isabel Allende's website
www.januarymagazine.com/profiles/allende.html – interview with Linda Richards published at the *January Magazine* website
http://archive.salon.com/people/conv/2001/03/05/allende/index.html – interview with Kaitlin Quistgaard published at *Salon* internet magazine

📖 **Suggested further reading**

FICTION

The War of Don Emmanuel's Nether Parts by Louis de Bernières (1990)

NON-FICTION

Family Life by Elizabeth Luard (1995); ***And When Did You Last See Your Father?***
by Blake Morrison (1993); ***The Hacienda* by Lisa St Aubin De Terán** (1998);
Travels in a Thin Country by Sara Wheeler (1995)

OTHER BOOKS BY ISABEL ALLENDE

Novels: *The House of Spirits* (1982); *Of Love and Shadows* (1984); *Eva Luna*
(1985); *The Infinite Plan* (1991); *Daughter of Fortune* (2000); *Portrait in Sepia*
(2001); *City of Beasts* (2002); *Kingdom of the Golden Dragon* (2004); *Forest of
the Pygmies* (2005); *Zorro* (2005); *Ines of My Soul* (2007)

Short stories: *The Stories of Eva Luna* (1992)

Non-fiction: *Aphrodite* (1999); *The Sum of Our Days* (2008)

MIDNIGHT IN THE GARDEN OF GOOD AND EVIL
(1994)

John Berendt

📖 **About the book**

John Berendt began taking regular weekend trips when he discovered that for the
price of a good meal in New York he could spend three days exploring a new city.
In 1982 he visited Savannah, Georgia, and was so taken with it that he spent the
next eight years dividing his time between Savannah and New York. *Midnight in
the Garden of Good and Evil* began as an account of a beautiful city, with a cast of
characters ranging from mildly eccentric to downright bizarre, packed with amusing
and interesting anecdotes. It took a rather different turn when, in May 1981, Jim
Williams, a prominent figure in Savannah society, was accused of murdering his
homosexual lover. Williams stood trial for murder four times, a record in the state
of Georgia.

Background

Largely restored to its pre-Civil War architectural glory, downtown Savannah is
portrayed by John Berendt as a beautiful place, inhabited by people who love to
party, proud of their reputation for eccentricity and deeply resistant to change. But
Midnight in the Garden of Good and Evil is also a murder mystery whose details

are as convoluted and baroque as any novel. Over a period of eight years, Berendt developed an intimacy with many of the people who appear in his book, including Jim Williams, later accused of murdering his lover.

In the first part of the book Berendt introduces a set of characters that would seem highly improbable even in a novel. The Lady Chablis, a stunningly beautiful black drag queen, affectionately teases and taunts him. Luther Driggers, accompanied by a set of flies on coloured thread, reputedly carries a vial of poison in his pocket. Joe Odom, a tax lawyer who prefers to party rather than practise law, moves his piano from house to house as his landlords' tolerance runs out. A retired porter walks his dead employer's dog every morning although no dog is attached to the collar and lead. This entertaining portrait of a colourful city ends on a serious note with the news that Jim Williams, an eminently successful antiques dealer, has shot his lover Danny Hansford in the early hours of a May morning in 1981.

Williams was a respected and prominent member of the Savannah elite, as knowledgeable about the scandal and foibles of his fellow Savannahians as he was about the city's architecture, but covert about his own homosexuality. He was both an initiator and an important source of financial support for Savannah's restoration programme and lived in Mercer House, one of the city's finest houses. While living like an aristocrat, Williams was open about his blue-collar origins. Such social ascent is not achieved without making enemies and for Williams these included Lee Adler, whom he had thrown off the board of a local museum committee. It was Adler that took the decision to take Williams's case to trial, despite his pleas of self defence, beginning a period of eight years in which Williams was tried for murder an unprecedented four times and launched three successful appeals.

Midnight in the Garden of Good and Evil was enormously successful when it was first published, putting Savannah firmly on the tourist map. In 1997, Clint Eastwood made the book into a film starring Kevin Spacey as Jim Williams and John Cusack as John Kelso, the character based on Berendt. John Berendt became so associated with Savannah that the city presented him with its key.

About the author

John Berendt grew up in Syracuse, New York. He studied English at Harvard where he worked on the staff of *The Harvard Lampoon*. After his graduation in 1961, he moved to New York City where he worked in publishing. From 1977 to 1979, he edited *New York* magazine. He became a freelance writer and editor for a variety of magazines, including *Esquire*, for which he wrote a monthly column from 1982 to 1994. *Midnight in the Garden of Good and Evil* was his first book.

For discussion

○ *Midnight in the Garden of Good and Evil* has been described as a non-fiction novel. What do you think is meant by this description? How accurately do you think it fits the book?

○ Berendt becomes very much involved in Savannah's social life. How objective a commentator do you think he is? What factors do you think might influence his objectivity? Do you get a sense of Berendt from his narrative? What sort of person do you think he is?

○ Savannah society seems to be divided along several lines. How would you describe each section? How do the different sections seem to get along together?

○ Berendt quotes Martin Luther King as describing Savannah as 'the most desegregated city in the South' in 1964. How do you think Savannah stands on race by today's standards?

○ As a result of the shooting, Williams's homosexuality becomes evident. What kind of reaction does this provoke, if any? What attitudes to homosexuality run through Savannah society? Would you say these attitudes are fairly typical of most modern cities? What do you think of the way Chablis handles her sexuality?

○ Williams enjoyed the trappings of aristocracy while being open about his blue-collar background. How important is class as an issue in the book? How does the importance of money compare to class?

○ What are the different attitudes to Lee Adler's involvement with the low-income housing in the Victorian district? Why do you think the project seems to provoke a mixture of scorn and suspicion? How do these views fit in with other social opinions in the book?

○ How would you describe Jim Williams? Does your view of him change through the book and, if so, at what point and why? Do you think he was guilty or not? What evidence do you have for your verdict?

○ What do you think Berendt means when he says: 'Yes, I did get Minerva's point. I got her point very clearly' after the visit to the Garden of Good and Evil? Do you think Williams did get her point? What did you make of Minerva? How does Williams consulting with her fit in with the rest of his personality?

○ What sort of role do women seem to play in Savannah society? How typical is this role in modern society?

🖳 Resources

www.geocities.com/midnightinsavannah/NYT.html – review by Glenna Whitley published in *The New York Times*

www.georgiaencyclopedia.org/nge/Article.jsp?id=h-504 – assessment of the impact of Berendt's book on Savannah by Carl Solana Weeks published at the Georgia Encyclopedia website

🗐 Suggested further reading
FICTION
Madeleine's Ghost by Robert Girardi (1995)
NON-FICTION
In Cold Blood by Truman Capote (1996); *Hiding My Candy: the Autobiography of the Grand Empress of Savannah* by Lady Chablis, introduced by John Berendt (1997); *The Shark Net* by Robert Drewe (2000)
ALSO BY JOHN BERENDT
The City of Falling Angels (2005)

SKATING TO ANTARCTICA (1997)
Jenny Diski

📖 About the book
Skating to Antarctica is Jenny Diski's account of her journey into the landscape of those legendary explorers Shackleton and Scott. It is coupled with her own exploration, perhaps equally brave, of a childhood which hardly bears contemplation, littered as it is with suicide attempts by both parents, sudden departures, the arrival of the bailiffs and the threat of eviction – all set against a continuous soundtrack of almost melodramatic histrionics. Diski sets off to Antarctica in search of oblivion, a pristine whiteout, but she finds a landscape which is often bleak, sometimes luminously beautiful, but rarely, if ever, monochrome. Leavened with a wry humour and astute observation, *Skating to Antarctica* is the story of two adventures – one into the Antarctic and one into a troubled past.

Background
Part travelogue, part searching autobiography, *Skating to Antarctica* is Jenny Diski's first full-length work of non-fiction. The description of her journey from London to Cabin 232, her refuge aboard the cruise ship *Akademik Vavilov*, and her experiences in Antarctica are interspersed with an examination of her deeply disturbed childhood and its effect on her adult life. The result is a raw, very personal book, infused with dry wit and a sense of adventure.

Diski decided to go to Antarctica to 'satisfy her hunger for blankness', a need for oblivion which she hoped to find in the whiteness of the landscape although once there it's clear that the landscape is anything but blank. The only way that she could travel to Antarctica alone was to take a cruise, something of anathema to someone who dislikes having her time organized for her and for someone who has a great need to put distance between herself and others. Thrust into intimacy with a group of strangers would seem to be the ultimate form of torture for someone who claims that: 'what I experience with most people is my estrangement from them, the distance of mutually unique separation that words or touch never quite bridge. Unlike cats, people interfere with my apprehension of reality, they muddy how I can know myself, confuse my understanding of how I am, which is centred around the notion that solitude is a state of perfection'. She finds the solace she craves in Cabin 232 the simple, white-painted 'monk's cell' that she had longed for, and in inventing nicknames for her fellow voyagers.

Such a chronic need for distance may seem difficult to understand until the details of Diski's extraordinarily dysfunctional childhood and young adulthood become clear. She spent much of her childhood yearning for the love of her feckless father while trying to cope with the histrionics of her excitable mother. It is something that she has often written about, perhaps as much to explain herself to herself as to her readers. She has spent many years in therapy, having first entered a mental institution at the age of fifteen after a suicide attempt, but has said that she has given it up and that it has 'given up on her'. She has learnt to accept the way she is. Perhaps this is what has allowed her to enter into a relationship and, after living on her own for many years, move in with Ian Patterson, whom she refers to as 'The Poet'.

Despite her confession that her 'ideal method of writing a travel book' would be 'to stay at home with the phone off the hook, the doorbell disconnected and the blinds drawn' the second volume of what is in effect her autobiography also takes the form of a travel book, the award-winning *Stranger on a Train*, in which she takes two rail journeys around the USA. Both this and *Skating to Antarctica* are searingly, almost uncomfortably, honest, and both are testaments to Diski's courage, humour and wonderfully acerbic writing.

About the author

Jenny Diski was born in 1947 in London, where she has spent most of her life. In addition to being a novelist, she has been the *Mail on Sunday*'s radio critic and regularly contributed to both *The Observer* and the *London Review of Books*. *Skating to Antarctica*, her first non-fiction book, met with a good deal of critical acclaim and the second volume of her autobiography, *Stranger on a Train*, won the 2003 Thomas Cook Award. Jenny Diski now lives in Cambridge.

For discussion

○ Why do you think Diski chose to call her book *Skating to Antarctica*? What do you think she means by it?

○ Why do you think Diski is searching for oblivion? To what extent does she find what she wants in Antarctica?

○ Why do you think that Diski is so reluctant to find out about her mother? How do you think she feels about Chloe's research and its results?

○ When she visits her ex-neighbours at Paramount Court, Diski finds she has to reassess her father. Why do you think she has been able to see her mother fairly accurately but not her father?

○ Diski has adopted a strategy of distancing herself from the child 'Jennifer'. Why do you think she did this? Has it helped her and, if so, in what way?

○ Diski describes at some length her reactions to people taking photographs and using camcorders around the bull elephant seals. What did you think about this?

○ What do you think of Diski's attitude to the rest of the people on the cruise? How do you think she feels about people in general?

○ How did you feel about the way Diski wove her childhood experiences into her description of the journey to Antarctica?

🖥 Resources

www.richmondreview.co.uk/books/skating.html – review by Jessica Woollard published at *The Richmond Review* website

www.jennydiski.co.uk/index.htm – Jenny Diski's website which includes interviews by Helen Brown and Ajay Close

📚 Suggested further reading

FICTION

Frost in May by Antonia White (1933)

NON-FICTION

The Worst Journey in the World by Apsley Cherry-Garrard (1922); *Seeking Rapture* by Kathryn Harrison (2003); *An Unquiet Mind* by Kay Redfield Jamison (1995); *South* by Ernest Shackleton (1919); *Terra Incognita* by Sara Wheeler (1996)

OTHER BOOKS BY JENNY DISKI

Novels: *Nothing Natural* (1986); *Rainforest* (1987); *Like Mother* (1988); *Then*

Again (1990); *Happily Ever After* (1991); *Monkey's Uncle* (1994); *Only Human: A Divine Comedy* (2000); *After These Things* (2004)
Short stories: *The Dream Mistress* (1996)
Essays: *Don't* (1999); *A View From the Bed and Other Observations* (2003)
Non-fiction: *Stranger on a Train* (2002); *On trying to Keep Still* (2006)

GHOSTING (2004)

Jennie Erdal

About the book

Ghosting begins with a moving, erudite letter celebrating the profound love of a husband for his wife on her birthday, written from the heart. Except that it isn't. Jennie Erdal swiftly punctures any such romantic ideas by revealing that she had written the letter on behalf of her magnificently flamboyant boss, who she nicknames Tiger, along with many other letters, newspaper articles, speeches and a dozen books, including two novels, all attributed to him. Erdal adroitly weaves scenes from her own life – her childhood spent trying to please a mother whose own disappointment could never be assuaged, the shock and grief of the breakup of her first marriage and the happiness of her new love – through the account of her fifteen years struggling to meet the ever more improbable demands of Tiger. Written with a playful and, at times, affectionate wit, in elegant, graceful prose *Ghosting* examines a unique and intriguing relationship with unflinching honesty.

Background

Although Jennie Erdal refers to her boss only as Tiger throughout her memoir, for those who had any acquaintance with the book trade during the 1980s and '90s his identity was unmistakable and was bound to be announced to the world by *Ghosting*'s reviewers. Naim Attallah is the Palestinian-born enormously flamboyant owner of The Women's Press and Quartet publishing houses, and of *The Literary Review*. He was well known for his colourful eccentricity and for employing well connected, usually very beautiful young women, collectively known by certain members of the somewhat unenlightened press as 'Naim's Harem', of whom Nigella Lawson was one. Erdal had let Attallah know that she was writing *Ghosting*: 'I showed him the first four chapters and he loved it ... He loved being Tiger, said he would help with the promotion and even offered to publish it. Except he wanted to control what I said. It all changed when I told him I'd be looking at our "creative partnership" – he wasn't happy and that was the first time we'd acknowledged between us that anything had gone on.' She contacted him after the publication of the book but received no reply.

For Atallah's part, he has described himself as 'horrified' when he saw an extract of *Ghosting* in a magazine, claiming that Erdal had said it was to be a 'fictional memoir' and describing their unusual arrangement as a 'genuine collaboration'. Determined to prove himself capable of writing a novel for himself, Attallah swiftly produced a slim novella, ***The Old Ladies of Nazereth***, based on the lives of his grandmother and her sister: 'All my life I've wanted to celebrate them, immortalise them. I started writing and the more I wrote, the more it flowed. At the back of my mind there was Jennie Erdal saying I cannot express myself, that she did everything for me. And I said to myself, "Well, let me have a go".' The novel met with a few lukewarm reviews and was greatly overshadowed by *Ghosting*.

When reviewing *Ghosting*, many critics commented on the excellence of Erdal's writing, comments that were not only well deserved but that must have been extremely gratifying after so long spent keeping her talent under wraps.

About the author

Born in Fife, Jennie Erdal studied Russian and philosophy at the University of St Andrews. She worked as an editor and translator for many years. *Ghosting* was the first book to be published under her own name. She lives in St Andrews.

For discussion

❂ In her acknowledgements Jennie Erdal mentions Tiger 'who inspired this story and allowed it to be told'. Given what we learn of Tiger why do you think he 'allowed' the story to be told?

❂ What was your reaction when you discovered who had written the love letter which opens the book? Why do you think Erdal chose 'the most intimate form of communication any of us makes' to begin her story?

❂ Although Erdal uses a nickname for her subject, he is instantly recognizable and his identity was revealed by several reviewers as she must have known it would have been. Why do you think she chose to write a book which effectively unmasked Tiger to the world? How do you think she feels about him?

❂ Erdal describes her relationship with Tiger as 'part symbiotic, part parasitic'. Does it seem to be more one than the other to you? How would you describe it?

❂ What kind of childhood did Erdal have? What sort of child was she? How would you describe her relationship with her parents?

❍ How important is language to Erdal? How important is it to her parents, and in particular, to her mother?

❍ How does Erdal's world differ from the one Tiger inhabits? How does she find a way to fit into his world?

❍ 'There were at least two Tigers: one was the exotic, flamboyant, Quixotic, love-able character defined by his generosity, compassion and energy; the other was a vainglorious dictator.' Which description do you feel best fits Tiger? How would you describe him?

❍ When reviewing a volume of Tiger's interviews, the novelist Allan Massie described him as 'masterly and sympathetic, the most self-effacing of interviewers and yet able to speak as an equal'. Erdal had written the interview questions yet Tiger put the questions to the interviewees: who do you think deserves the credit? Could one have done it without the other?

❍ 'I wonder how I have arrived at this point without actually meaning to' muses Erdal on the challenges of ghostwriting a novel. How has she? What problems do ghostwriting a novel present? Why does she find herself particularly troubled at the idea of ghostwriting fiction? What did you think of the extracts of both novels printed in the book?

❍ Why does Erdal resolve to give up her ghostwriting relationship with Tiger? Why does it take her so long to make the break?

❍ Erdal weaves recollections and reflections on her personal life through the story of her relationship with Tiger. How effective did you find this? Does the tone and style of each of these two narrative strands differ and if so how?

❍ How would you describe Erdal's writing? Where there particular passages you enjoyed and if so, what were they and why?

💻 Resources

http://books.guardian.co.uk/reviews/biography/0,6121,1376157,00.html – review by the writer and poet Blake Morrison of *Ghosting* and Naim Attallah's *The Old Ladies of Nazareth* published in *The Guardian*

www.sfgate.com/cgi-bin/article.cgi?f=/c/a/2005/04/10/RVG82C1HNT1.DTL&type =books – review of *Ghosting* by Carlo Wolf published in the *San Francisco Chronicle*

www.telegraph.co.uk/arts/main.jhtml;?xml=/arts/2004/10/31/boerd31.xml – review of *Ghosting* by Lloyd Evans published in *The Telegraph*

www.timesonline.co.uk/article/0,,7-1405443,00.html – interview with Jennie Erdal by Valerie Grove published in *The Times*

📚 Suggested further reading

Stet by Diana Athill (2000); ***Bad Blood* by Lorna Sage** (2000)

HIDDEN LIVES: A FAMILY MEMOIR (1995)

Margaret Forster

📖 About the book

Shortly after the death of Margaret Forster's grandmother, a mysterious woman knocked at the door claiming to be her daughter. No one in the family had ever heard of such a person. The woman was sent on her way and a discreet veil was drawn over the incident. When Forster's mother died it was as if a taboo had been lifted and Forster set about investigating who the unknown woman might be. She found a common enough answer; the woman was her grandmother's illegitimate child, a secret successfully hidden to preserve the family's respectability. But while *Hidden Lives* begins as an account of Forster's investigations, it soon becomes a searching portrait of a family during a period of great social change and, in particular, an account of Forster's relationship with her mother.

Background

When a mysterious visitor arrives asking for her mother in 1936, Lily is reluctant to let her in. Margaret Ann is not well and Lily does not want her upset. Although her mother never refers to the visit, she becomes withdrawn and, within three months, she is dead. On the day of her funeral, another stranger appears, claiming to be a fourth daughter of Margaret Ann. The door is firmly closed in her face. Many years later, Margaret Forster's curiosity is aroused by this mysterious family story about her grandmother but she feels unable to investigate until after her own mother's death. *Hidden Lives* begins as a family history, the result of Forster's investigation into the long buried secret of her grandmother's illegitimate child, but broadens into a fascinating slice of social history, a vivid portrait of working-class women across three generations at a time when class barriers were being eroded and women were finding their own place in the world.

In the twenty-first century it is far from unusual for children to be born openly out of wedlock but in the nineteenth century and far into the twentieth the stigma of illegitimacy was enough to ruin the lives of both the mother and the child. It was a shameful but far from uncommon secret hidden at all costs, even from close family. What begins for Foster as an exploration of this painful secret, becomes an examination of the lives of the women in her family, uncovering the sheer hard grind of life as a respectable working class housewife for her grandparents' generation and the difficult choices her own mother faced at a time when marriage and a career were an impossible combination for women. Although the examination is an intensely personal one, this is familiar territory for Foster. In both her fiction and her non-fiction she has frequently focused on the obligations placed upon women, the family duties so often assumed to be a woman's domain and the domestic servitude endured by women in the past. In the final pages of *Hidden Lives* she compares the ease of her own life with the drudgery of her grandmother's and the circumscribed nature of her mother's in a moving testament to the progress which women have made, celebrating the choices that women now enjoy, difficult as they sometimes are.

About the author

Margaret Forster was born in Carlisle in 1938. She has published both fiction and non-fiction and is the author of two award-winning biographies: *Elizabeth Barrett Browning*, which won the Royal Society of Literature's Award in 1988, and *Daphne du Maurier*, which was awarded the 1994 Fawcett Book Prize. Her first novel, *Georgy Girl*, was made into a film starring Lynn Redgrave and Charlotte Rampling. *Hidden Lives* was published in 1995 and was followed by a companion volume, *Precious Lives*, about the deaths of her father and sister-in-law. Margaret Forster is married to the writer Hunter Davies and divides her time between London and the Lake District.

For discussion

✪ What was Forster's motivation in investigating her 'hidden' family history? Given that her grandmother had gone to such great pains to hide her past, do you think her secret should have died with her or do people have a right to know their history?

✪ Forster keeps herself out of the first part of the book as much as possible, but given that she is writing about her own family, how objective is she likely to be? What do you learn about Forster, besides what she writes about herself? How does the book change when Forster begins to write in the first person?

✪ How accurate a view do you have of your own family history and how important is it to you? Does the book strike any chords for you?

✪ How would you describe the relationship between Forster and her mother? What are the main differences between them? How have their lives been shaped by their different circumstances? Forster says to her mother: 'There's no real difference in what we've achieved.' What do you think of this statement?

⊙ What impression do you have of Lily? Why is she so hard to please? What does her attitude to other people seem to be? Why is she so different from her sisters?

⊙ The book looks at three generations of women – Margaret Ann, Lily and the author. What are the significant changes between the generations? What are the opportunities available to each of the women? What factors contribute to the broadening of opportunities between each generation? What do you think has changed since Forster was a girl?

⊙ The book covers a time of great social change. What do you think were the most significant changes for the Forsters? What were Forster's parents' attitudes towards class? How important a factor was it in their lives? Were there other factors that shaped the way they lived and, if so, what were they?

⊙ Forster's marriage seems very different from her parents' relationship. What expectations do the women in the book have of marriage? Are these expectations fulfilled? How different are they from present-day expectations?

🖥 Resources

www.contemporarywriters.com/authors/?p=auth118 – profile of Margaret Forster at the British Council website including a critical essay by Cora Lindsay

🍃 Suggested further reading

Shadow Man by Mary Gordon (1996); *Family Life* by Elizabeth Luard (1995); *Angela's Ashes* by Frank McCourt (1996); ***Giving Up the Ghost* by Hilary Mantel** (2003); *British Society since 1945* by Arthur Marwick (1987); *Hons and Rebels* by Jessica Mitford (1960); ***Bad Blood* by Lorna Sage** (2000)

OTHER BOOKS BY MARGARET FORSTER

Novels: *Georgy Girl* (1966); *The Seduction of Mrs Pendlebury* (1974); *Mother Can You Hear Me?* (1979); *Private Papers* (1986); *Have the Men Had Enough?* (1987); *Lady's Maid* (1990); *The Battle for Christabel* (1991); *Mother's Boys* (1994); *Shadow Baby* (1996); *The Memory Box* (1999); *Diary of an Ordinary Woman* (2003); *Is There Anything You Want* (2005); *Keeping the World Away* (2006); *Over* (2007)

Biography: *The Rash Adventurer: The Rise and Fall of Charles Edward Stuart* (1975); *William Makepeace Thackeray: Memoirs of a Victorian Gentleman* (1978); *Significant Sisters – The Grassroots of Active Feminism 1838–1939* (1986); *Elizabeth Barrett Browning* (1988) ; *Daphne du Maurier* (1993); *Rich Desserts and Captain's Thins* (biography of the Carr biscuit manufacturing family) (1987)

Autobiography: *Precious Lives* (1998); *Good Wives* (2001)

STASILAND (2004)

Anna Funder

📖 About the book

Working at a German TV station during the mid-1990s Anna Funder receives a suggestion for a programme about the lives of ordinary people in the former GDR. Meeting with a cool response from her boss and moved by her corespondent's impassioned reply stressing the importance of remembering past injustice Funder begins her own investigation. She finds people whose lives have been blighted by the notorious Stasi in the most appalling ways: Miriam's husband died in prison, passed off as a suicide but clearly nothing of the kind; Julia's refusal to spy on her Italian boyfriend resulted in a painful violation of her privacy; Frau Paul's separation from her sick baby in the West was used in an attempt to inveigle her into betrayal. Funder also seeks out members of the GDR's old terror machine, trying to understand how they have dealt with their nefarious past. Written with a clear-sighted empathy that makes these stories all the more moving, *Stasiland* offers an eloquent and important testament to the dreadful consequences of totalitarianism.

Background

Anna Funder's interest in what went on behind the Berlin Wall was first kindled when she was a student in West Berlin. Several day trips to the East heightened her curiosity and after the Wall fell she began to collect the stories which would eventually become *Stasiland*, a very personal, carefully researched account which captures the quiet agony of the industrious Stasi's many victims through the stories of ordinary people. Her interviewees are strikingly sometimes painfully candid, speaking with an honesty made possible partly by Funder's sensitivity but also by her status as an outsider. The latter was particularly important when speaking to the ex-Stasi members who were surprisingly forthcoming in response to her advertisement in a Potsdam paper. She puts this response down to a loss of their position in the world: 'To be stripped of authority so suddenly was a very big shock to them. I think they wanted to talk to someone who found them important.'

She set out with the aim of collecting the stories of ordinary people rather than documenting the already well known or infamous. She was interested in exploring why and how informers were persuaded into betraying others, often their neighbours, friends or even lovers, but instead found people who had resisted the Stasi and became fascinated by their extraordinary courage. Her sympathy is clearly with the victims of the Stasi but rather than simply writing their persecutors off as monsters she has tried to understand them explaining that 'it's a slippery slope people face all the time. If your boss takes you out to lunch and asks you to criticize someone in the office, or a friend wants you to rat on another friend – those things happen frequently, and you can do it or not. The fact that this nation ran on such betrayals is a terrible exploitation of a very human trait.'

She applauds the Germans' decision to open the Stasi files to the public. It was considered to be very controversial at the time and continues to be so as Funder explains: 'It was assumed that blood would run in the streets, that people would seek private revenge on their informers. That didn't happen, and I don't know quite why, but I think people were just too demoralized by the betrayals. Now, as a result of a legal action by former Chancellor Helmut Kohl, there are various limits being imposed on access to files, and repeated threats to shut them.'

Although she had read much of George Orwell's non-fiction, Funder did not read *1984* until she finished writing *Stasiland*. She was amazed by it, saying 'It reads like a manual for the East German state'. Orwell's writing was banned in the GDR along with so many books, but Mielke, the Stasi's chief from 1957–89, had insisted that his office bore the number 101, the number Orwell assigned to his room of terror. As Funder notes, both Honecker and Mielke had access to banned material. When visiting the museum at Stasi headquarters she was told by a guide that 'Mielke wanted this number so much that even though his office was on the 2nd floor, he had the entire first floor renamed the Mezzanine so that he could call his room 101.' It seems that truth really is stranger than fiction.

About the author

Anna Funder was born in Melbourne, Australia in 1966. Fluent in both German and French, she has worked as an international lawyer and a radio and television producer. In 1997 she was writer-in-residence at the Australia Centre in Potsdam and lived in Berlin both before and after the Wall came down. The highly acclaimed *Stasiland*, her first book, was short-listed for the 2003 Guardian First Book Award and went on to win the BBC Four Samuel Johnson Prize in 2004. Anna Funder now lives in Sydney.

For discussion

✪ 'Miriam explains, gently, that in the GDR it was inconceivable that a person would ask a stranger, a total stranger whether they lived near the border.' Why would such a question have been 'inconceivable'? What gave Miriam the courage to make her break when she was only sixteen? How have her experiences shaped her as an adult?

○ 'It took twenty years after the war, he said, for the Nazi regime even to be discussed in Germany, and that process is repeating itself now. "Will it be 2010 or 2020 before what happened there is remembered?" he wrote. And, "Why are some things easier to remember the more time has passed since they occurred?"' What do you think Funder's correspondent meant by the second question? Why is it so important for what happened to be remembered and debated openly? What does *Stasiland* contribute to that debate?

○ '"I just sit there in the car and I feel ... *triumph*!" Miriam makes a gesture which starts as a wave and becomes a guillotine. "You lot are gone."' Despite Miriam's triumph, to what extent do the Stasi continue to exert an influence in Germany despite being disbanded?

○ 'After the Wall fell the German media called East Germany "the most perfected surveillance state of all time".' Why do you think Mielke and Honecker feel the need for such blanket surveillance? What purpose did it serve?

○ 'Does telling your story mean you are free of it? Or that you go, fettered, into your future?' Which of these does it seem to be for Miriam, and for Julia?

○ 'It was a condition of sanity both to accept "GDR-logic" and to ignore it.' How did people find ways to cope with living under an ever-watchful dictatorship?

○ 'If there was never going to be an end to your country, and you could never leave, why wouldn't you opt for a peaceful life and a satisfying career? What interests me is the process of dealing with the decision now that it is all over.' How do the likes of Winz, Christian and Koch deal with their decision to be part of the Stasi?

○ 'This, I think, is his victory. This is what stops him being bound to the past and carrying it around like a wound. If there was "internal emigration" in the GDR, then this was also, perhaps, internal victory.' What is it that helps Klaus cope so well with what has happened to him and his fellow band members in comparison with Miriam, Julia, Frau Paul and even Hagen Koch?

○ 'It was a close call, but Germany was the only Eastern bloc country in the end that so bravely, so conscientiously, opened its files on its own people to its own people.' What do you think of Germany's decision? What were the possible repercussions of opening the files?

○ How does the 'new' east Germany compare with the GDR? To what extent was the revolution welcomed by ordinary people living there? What are the dangers of *Ostalgie* and how prevalent does it seem to be?

○ What seems to you to be the worst aspect of the Stasi's work?

○ Ann Funder becomes closely involved with several of the people who tell her their stories. To what extent does her emotional involvement enhance or detract from the impact of *Stasiland*?

🖳 Resources

http://books.guardian.co.uk/firstbook2003/story/0,,1031819,00.html – review by
the writer Giles MacDonogh published in *The Guardian*

www.worldpress.org/Europe/1199.cfm – interview by Sarah Coleman published at
the Worldpress.org website

http://news.bbc.co.uk/onthisday/hi/dates/stories/november/9/newsid_2515000
/2515869.stm – BBC webpage on the fall of the Berlin Wall

http://en.wikipedia.org/wiki/Berlin_Wall – Wikipedia entry on the Berlin Wall

http://en.wikipedia.org/wiki/GDR – Wikipedia entry on the German Democratic
Republic

http://www.economist.com/cities/printStory.cfm?obj_id=2534113&city_id=BER –
piece on *Ostalgie* published in *The Economist*

📚 Suggested further reading

FICTION

1984 by George Orwell (1949); *Flights of Love* by Bernhard Schlink (translated by
Carol Brown Janeway) (2001); *Field Study* by Rachel Seiffert (2004)

NON-FICTION

The File by Tim Garton Ash (1997); *Café Europa* by Slavanka Drakuli (1996); *Lone
Patriot* by Jane Kramer (2002); *The Berlin Wall* by Frederick Taylor (2006)

LOST IN TRANSLATION: A LIFE IN A NEW LANGUAGE (1989)

Eva Hoffman

📖 About the book

At the age of thirteen, when most of us are beginning to forge an identity for
ourselves, Eva Hoffman was uprooted from her beloved Poland to emigrate with
her family to Canada. Born in 1945, her early years had been spent in Cracow,
surrounded by friends, thoroughly immersed in a way of life she knew and loved.
When she arrived in Vancouver, she had not only to learn a new language but also
a completely different set of cultural references, a long, slow process which set her
at a distance from other young people. When she won a scholarship to a university
in the United States, she began to find ways of belonging in her new world without
rejecting the old. *Lost in Translation* is an eloquent account of Hoffman's
experience of the dislocation of being caught between two cultures.

Background

Lost in Translation is divided into three parts. In 'Paradise' Hoffman writes of her childhood in Cracow, weaving bright memories of friends and family through descriptions of life in post-war Poland. 'Exile' tells of the family's arrival in Vancouver and the difficulty of fitting in to a new and very different culture. 'The New World' is about Hoffman's arrival in the United States where she finally finds a way to be at ease with herself. Her writing gives us a glimpse of how it feels to be an exile trying to navigate a path through a new and foreign world without a map.

Eva Hoffman is the eldest daughter of Polish Jews who spent the Second World War in hiding. Both parents lost many members of their families in the Holocaust and were all too well aware of the anti-Semitism in Poland that followed the War and the need to make public an allegiance to communism. She emigrated in 1956, the year in which the ban on Jewish emigration was lifted, but as she has pointed out, it was not her decision to leave. Hers was a happy childhood in which she fitted neatly into an extended family, and so leaving her homeland gave her a 'great sense of rupture'. In Vancouver, chosen by her parents convinced that Canada was the land of opportunity, she experienced a very great culture shock that reverberated through her life for decades. Hoffman had a strong sense of both her Polish and her Jewish identities, the latter instilled in her by her parents which she describes as 'one of the gifts my parents gave me'. Her parents came from a shtetl a Jewish enclave in a small town in the Ukraine which had been Polish before the war but which was subsumed into soviet Russia (Hoffman traces the history of one such settlement in her book *Shtetl*). Such a strong sense of national and ethnic identity made moving to an entirely different continent difficult. The loss of her language imparted to Hoffman her 'sense of [its] enormous importance'. To be without language she says is to live in 'a very dim world, a very dim exterior world and a very dim interior world'. One of the ways that Hoffman found an escape from her cultural confusion was to find a voice through writing, keeping a diary in English because she 'wanted to make English the language of interiority'. In 1977, twenty years after leaving the country where she was born, Hoffman returned to Cracow. She saw her old friends, walked the streets engraved on her memory and, on her return to America, dreamt in English for the first time. English had, without doubt, become the language of her 'interiority'.

In the early 1980s, a wave of Polish immigrants arrived in New York where Hoffman then lived. She found herself acting as a cultural interpreter, trying to ease them through the difficulties of transition from one culture to another. Finally, it seems that the gap between her Polish and American selves had been bridged.

About the author

Eva Hoffman was born in the city of Cracow in Poland in 1945. She and her family emigrated to Canada in 1959. She was educated at Rice University, Houston, Texas, and went on to take her doctorate in literature at Harvard. She worked for some time as an editor of the *New York Times Book Review*. *Lost in Translation*, her first book, was published in 1989.

For discussion

○ Near the beginning, after recounting several of her parents' wartime experiences in hiding, Hoffman writes that she acknowledges that 'the pain of this is where I come from, and that it's useless to try and get away'. What does she mean by this? How do her parents' experiences affect her life and the way she approaches it? How have they been affected?

○ What difficulties do Hoffman's parents face in post-war Poland? How do they deal with these difficulties? How do things change between the end of the war and their departure for Canada? Why do they decide to leave?

○ How does Hoffman feel about learning English? Why is language so important to her? What is the most painful thing about the loss of her first language? Hoffman's writing is both elegant and eloquent. How important do you think this is to her?

○ Hoffman writes: 'Linguistic dispossession is a sufficient motive for violence, for it is close to dispossession of one's self.' How persuasive is this argument? Can you think of illustrations in the book or in recent history?

○ How is Hoffman expected to change her behaviour when she gets to Vancouver? Why is this particularly difficult and painful for her?

○ Hoffman begins to come into herself at university in Houston. Why do think this happens at this point?

○ Hoffman writes about the quarrels she begins to have with her 'American friends' once she arrives at Harvard. Why do you think this happens? How would you describe the American point of view? How would you describe Hoffman's position? Where would you put your own views?

○ Does the visit to Cracow help Hoffman to resolve anything and, if so, what? How much has Hoffman's view of her own cultural identity changed by 1981 when there is a surge in Polish emigration to New York?

○ Has *Lost in Translation* helped you to understand how it feels to be an immigrant and, if so, how? If you are an immigrant yourself, how does Hoffman's experience compare with your own?

○ Hoffman uses both past and present tenses in her descriptions of past events throughout the book. What effect does this have?

🖳 Resources

http://globetrotter.berkeley.edu/people/Hoffman/hoffman-cono.html – interview with Henry Kreisler at the Institute for International Studies Berkely, University of California

🖢 Suggested further reading

FICTION

By the Sea by Abdulrazak Gurnah (2001); *Fruit of the Lemon* by Andrea Levy (1999); *Accordion Crimes* by Annie Proulx (1996); *The Joy Luck Club* by Amy Tan (1989)

NON-FICTION

The File by Timothy Garton Ash (1998); *Café Europa* by Slavanka Drakuli (1996); *Anne Frank: The Diary of a Young Girl* by Anne Frank (1947); *The Man Who Lost His Language* by Sheila Hale (2002); *Roots Schmoots* by Howard Jacobson (1995); *Konin: A Quest* by Theo Richmond (1995)

OTHER BOOKS BY EVA HOFFMAN

Fiction: *The Secret* (2001)

Non-fiction: *Exit into History: A Journey Through the New Eastern Europe* (1994); *Shtetl: The History of a Small Town and an Extinguished World* (1997); *After Such Knowledge: Memory, History and the Legacy of Holocaust* (2004)

AN UNQUIET MIND: A MEMOIR OF MOODS AND MADNESS (1996)

Kay Redfield Jamison

📖 About the book

An Unquiet Mind is Kay Redfield Jamison's courageous account of her experience of manic depression, an illness which afflicted her as a young student and has continued to do so for most of her adult life. She recalls the many and varied passions that overtook her as a child, echoing the manic enthusiasms that seized her father and eventually led to him losing his job. Drawn to medicine, Jamison became interested in psychology and eventually qualified as a psychiatrist. After years of struggling with vivid but destructive manic episodes followed by paralyzing depressions, Jamison faced up to the truth of her illness and sought treatment. With the help of friends, family and lovers she came to accept the fading of her vibrant moods into a steadier life. Her insight into manic-depressive illness has led her to become one of the foremost American practitioners in its treatment.

Background

As a psychiatrist, Kay Redfield Jamison kept her illness under wraps for many years, afraid that she would lose her licence to practise. In *An Unquiet Mind* she lays bare what it is to be subject to episodes of extraordinary vividness followed by suicidal depressions. Her experience of manic-depression (or bipolar illness as it is now more commonly known), both personal and professional, enabled her to provide a singular insight into an illness that is rarely discussed openly by its sufferers.

Jamison was born into an American Air Force family. Her mother took care to provide a stable home as a counterbalance to a peripatetic life and to the unpredictable enthusiasms which seized her husband. Looking back, Jamison remembers her own mercurial nature, comparing it with the steadiness of her brother who became the emotional lynchpin in her life.

When she was in high school, her father took a civilian job in California which he lost when his own manic-depressive illness became more pronounced. It was in California that Jamison struggled with her first manic episode, filled with restlessness, insomnia and marvellous insights followed by a terrible lethargic depression. Brought up not to complain, she kept her feelings to herself.

Jamison became an undergraduate at the University of Los Angeles. Subject to extreme mood swings, she recognized her symptoms in a lecture on depression and tried to seek help but backed out at the last minute. A year's break in Scotland provided a respite and on her return to UCLA she became a research assistant to a psychology professor, eventually completing a doctoral thesis in psychology. She had enjoyed a remission throughout most of her doctoral study but within three months of her appointment as an assistant professor she was seized by a severe manic attack. During this episode she experienced an hallucination so terrifying that she called a colleague for help. Recognizing her symptoms, he insisted that she see a psychiatrist.

Finally diagnosed as suffering from manic-depressive illness, Jamison began the programme of lithium and psychotherapy that eventually led her to a more stable life. She fought her reluctance to take her medication, whose side-effects affected her vision so that she was unable to read and left her nauseous. Her mood swings were now under control, but she mourned the loss of their vividness. Lapses in medication resulted in manic episodes, one of which led to a suicide attempt.

Throughout this period, Jamison succeeded in concealing her illness from the university authorities. When she set up an Affective Disorders Clinic at UCLA to treat manic-depressive illness she constructed a safety net to ensure that she would not put her patients at risk.

After a love affair that ended tragically, she took a sabbatical in Britain, dividing her time between Oxford and London. Although her grief was terrible, unlike her illness, she was able to control it. Some years later, she married and returned to Washington where she had spent much of her childhood. Finding work as a professor at Johns Hopkins University, she steeled herself to reveal her illness only to find that it had long been an open secret.

An Unquiet Mind has been included on many reading lists of recommended books for those diagnosed as bipolar. Its success gave Jamison a more popular platform from which to address the public about a disorder from which many suffer but few understand. In interviews since the book's publication she has said that there are elements of her illness that she values explaining that 'intensity has its costs, of course – in pain, in hastily and poorly reckoned plans, in impetuousness – but it has its advantages as well'. She tries to persuade less experienced practitioners 'that tumultuousness, if coupled to discipline and a cool mind, is not such a bad sort of thing'. Her courage in dealing creatively with her illness and her openness in discussing it is to be saluted.

About the author

Kay Redfield Jamison was born in 1946. As Professor of Psychiatry at the Johns Hopkins University School of Medicine in Washington DC she has won many scientific awards and was a member of the first National Advisory Council for Human Genome Research. She has also served as the clinical director for the Dana Consortium on the Genetic Basis of Manic-Depressive Illness. Her first book aimed at a general readership was *Touched with Fire: Manic-Depressive Illness and the Artistic Temperament*, published in 1993. It provided the basis of three television programmes in the United States – one on manic-depressive composers, another on Vincent van Gogh and a third on Lord Byron.

For discussion

❍ Jamison writes: 'The long and important years of childhood and early adolescence ... were to be an extremely powerful amulet, a potent and positive countervailing force against future unhappiness.' What aspects of her early life and upbringing helped her in her battle against her illness?

❍ Jamison describes manic depressive illness as 'unique in conferring advantage and pleasure, yet one that brings in its wake almost unendurable suffering'. What 'advantage and pleasure' does she find in her illness?

❍ For many years Jamison told only a few close friends and colleagues about her illness. What had made her conceal it for so long? Why did she decide to lay it bare so publicly?

✪ Given her study of psychology, why does it take Jamison so long to recognize and accept her illness?

✪ How is Jamison's life affected by lithium? The advantages of taking it are obvious; what are the disadvantages? Despite the risks involved in reducing her dosage, why does she decide to do so? How does psychotherapy complement lithium in the treatment of her illness?

✪ When Jamison uses the word madness in the title of a lecture, she is castigated by a member of the public. Where do you stand in the ensuing debate on the use of language in describing mental illness? What difference does it make?

✪ Jamison comes, almost reluctantly, to recognize the importance of emotional stability but she acknowledges that 'somewhere in my heart, however, I continued to believe that intense and lasting love was possible only in a climate of somewhat tumultuous passions'. Do you think that this idea is unusual or do many of us feel that love must be accompanied by passion to be 'real'? How important are love and friendship to Jamison? How is this illustrated in the book?

✪ When Jamison discloses her illness to the colleague and erstwhile friend she calls Mouseheart, he asks her if she really thinks that someone who is suffering from mental illness should be allowed to treat patients. How would you answer this? What light does Jamison's account of her professional experience shed on the question?

✪ When discussing the work of the Human Genome Project with which she was associated, Jamison asks whether 'we risk making the world a blander, more homogenised place if we get rid of the genes for manic-depressive illness'. What would your answer to this question be and why?

✪ How successful is Jamison in conveying how it feels to suffer from manic-depressive illness? How does she set about this?

✪ How well do we deal with mental illness in modern society? Has reading *An Unquiet Mind* changed any ideas you might have had about mental illness and the people who suffer from it? If so, how have your views changed and why?

🖳 Resources

www.npr.org/templates/story/story.php?storyId=4675356 – transcript of The Benefits of Restlessness and Jagged Edges, a broadcast by Kay Redfield Jamison on her book *Exuberance*

📚 Suggested further reading

FICTION

Mouthing the Words by Camilla Gibb (1999); *Sights Unseen* by Kaye Gibbons (1996); *One Flew Over the Cuckoo's Nest* by Ken Kesey (1962); *Last Things* by Jenny Offill (1999); *The Bell Jar* by Sylvia Plath (1963)

NON-FICTION

Virginia Woolf: The Marriage of Heaven and Hell by Peter Dally (1998); **Skating to Antarctica by Jenny Diski** (1997); *Girl, Interrupted* by Susanna Kaysen (1993); *Genome: The Autobiography of a Species in 23 Chapters* by Matt Ridley (1999); *Darkness Visible* by William Styron (1992); *Prozac Generation* by Elizabeth Wurtzel (1995)

OTHER BOOKS BY KAY REDFIELD JAMISON

Touched with Fire: Manic-Depressive Illness and the Artistic Temperament (1993); *Night Falls Fast: Understanding Suicide* (2000); *Exuberance: The Passion for Life* (2004)

THE DROWNED AND THE SAVED (1986)

Primo Levi

📖 About the book

In *The Drowned and the Saved* Primo Levi attempts to understand the rationale behind the systematic atrocities committed by the Nazis at concentration camps such as Auschwitz and Treblinka. Drawing on his experiences in Auschwitz, where he was held for a year from January 1944 until the liberation of the camp by the Russians, Levi explores the painful issues of collaboration between prisoners and their guards, the shame felt by survivors and explains his premise that those who survived were not the true witnesses. Clearly, lucidly and without resorting to stereotypes, Levi discusses the ways in which prisoners were treated by their SS guards in an attempt to understand how such horrors could be perpetrated. *The Drowned and the Saved* was Primo Levi's final book before his death in 1987.

Background

Unlike Primo Levi's best-known book, *If This is a Man*, *The Drowned and the Saved* is not a straightforward autobiographical account of his experiences in Auschwitz. It is more an attempt to understand how such atrocities came to be committed and to convey the repercussions of survival as well as a necessary continuation of bearing witness. This is a slim but profound and sometimes harrowing book that requires time and a good deal of reflection.

Levi begins by explaining the difficulties of remembering for both sides. Stressing the importance of bearing witness to the horrors of the camps, he reminds us that memories become distorted by distance, that they are also subjective and may be shrouded in self-justification and shame.

The 'grey zone', as Levi calls the issue of collaboration, is particularly painful and difficult to remember. Those prisoners who expected to find comfort from their fellows on arrival at the camps were shocked when they were first beaten or betrayed by their own kind. Levi explains that there were many who collaborated either in a small way or, perhaps most shockingly, as members of the Special Squads who were in charge of the crematoria. He is careful to make it clear that he does not judge collaborators and that we, who have never endured such horrors, are not qualified to do so. Even those who survived but did not collaborate experienced a sense of shame rather than joy at their liberation. They had been stripped of their humanity and were ashamed of their own survival and the small acts of selfishness or failure to help others it had required.

There were many ways in which the Nazis systematically destroyed the dignity of the prisoners, from the frequent public nakedness to the branding of their skin with an identification number. Even the language used to communicate with prisoners was a bastardized form of German. Those who did not understand stood little chance of survival unless they were able to find someone who could speak their own language. Attempts at escape were futile. Even if a prisoner was strong enough, after months of malnourishment, and succeeded in penetrating the stringent security of the camps, who would have helped him on the outside?

Levi explains that the hierarchy of the outside world was turned upon its head in the camps. The educated, with their inability to cope with manual work, were at the bottom of the pile. He compares his ideas on the advantages and disadvantages of being an intellectual with those of his friend, the philosopher Jean Améry, who later committed suicide.

In his final chapter, Levi discusses the letters that he was sent by Germans in response to the publication of *If This is a Man* in Germany in 1961.

About the author

Primo Levi was born in Turin in 1919. He graduated with honours in chemistry shortly before laws were passed which prohibited Jews from taking academic degrees. In 1943 he joined a Partisan group in northern Italy. He was arrested and taken to Auschwitz where his knowledge as a chemist helped him to survive. When the Russians liberated Auschwitz in 1945, Levi and his fellow Italian inmates were sent to White Russia. On his return to Italy he found work as a chemist from which he retired in 1975. Levi's first and best-known book, *If This is a Man*, is an account of his experiences at Auschwitz and is published in a single volume together with *The Truce*, in which he tells of his long and arduous journey home to Italy. On April 11th, 1987, Levi is believed to have committed suicide by throwing himself down the stairwell of the apartment building where he had been born and where he had lived for much of his life. *The Drowned and the Saved* was his last book.

For discussion

❍ What is the significance of the quotation from Coleridge's *The Rime of the Ancient Mariner* which prefaces the book?

❍ At the end of his introduction, Paul Bailey applies to Primo Levi's work Geoffrey Grigson's comment that W.H. Auden's poetry contained 'explicit recipes for being human'. What are Levi's 'explicit recipes'?

❍ In his preface, Levi says that he wants to try to answer the questions: 'How much of the concentration camp world is dead and will not return … How much is back or coming back? What can each of us do, so that in this world pregnant with threats, at least this threat will be nullified?' These are difficult questions. To what extent do you think Levi answers them? What are his answers? How would you answer them?

❍ How does Levi explain the collaboration which took place between some of the prisoners and the Nazis? How important were the collaborators to the Nazis? Who were most likely to become Kapos and why? Why does Levi call the creation of the Special Squads who tended the crematoria, the Nazis' 'most demonic crime'? How difficult do you find it to follow Levi's example in not passing judgement on these people? What does Levi mean when he states after the story of Chaim Rumkowski that 'we are all mirrored in Rumkowski'?

❍ In his introduction, Bailey states that many have interpreted the chapter in which Levi discusses the shame suffered by survivors at being alive when others are dead as evidence of Levi's intent to kill himself. Bailey disagrees with this. What are his arguments on this point? Have you formed an opinion on this since finishing the book? How does Levi explain his feelings of shame when he is released from Auschwitz?

❍ When Levi's religious friend says that Levi was chosen to survive in order to bear witness, Levi is troubled by this idea because he 'cannot see any proportion between the privilege and its outcome'. How important do you think Levi's testimony and the testimony of other camp survivors is? Do you think it can make a difference and, if so, how?

✪ Levi speculates about the possibility of a future genocide, mentioning Cambodia in passing. In more recent times there has been slaughter on an appalling scale in Rwanda. Can what happened in the camps be compared with what happened in Rwanda? What are your reasons for your answer?

✪ How does Levi define the 'useless violence' which he describes in chapter 5? Might the stripping of prisoners of their dignity have been useful to the Nazis and, if so, how?

✪ What advantages does Levi's philosopher friend, Jean Améry, see in being an intellectual in the camps? What disadvantages does he cite? To what extent does Levi agree or disagree with Améry?

✪ Levi says that he has often been faced with the questions 'Why did you not escape? Why did you not rebel? Why did you not avoid capture beforehand?' How does he proceed to answer these questions?

✪ When Levi's account of his incarceration in Auschwitz, *If This is a Man*, was published in Germany, his introduction stated that he could not understand the Germans and that he hoped the book would have an 'echo' in Germany. What kind of echo did it have? Do any of the letters that Levi received help you to understand what happened or do they simply throw up more questions?

✪ Paul Bailey begins his introduction with a quotation from *The Drowned and the Saved* – 'We, the survivors, are not the true witnesses'. He goes on to say that this 'deeply held conviction informs virtually everything Primo Levi wrote'. How do you interpret this quotation and how does it inform the book?

🖳 Resources

http://books.guardian.co.uk/reviews/politicsphilosophyandsociety/0,,99025,00. html – review by Peter Porter published in *The Guardian*

http://query.nytimes.com/gst/fullpage.html?res=940DEFD61338F933A25752C0A9 6E948260 – review by the writer and editor Irving Howe, published in *The New York Times*

http://books.guardian.co.uk/departments/biography/story/0,,664298,00.html – article on Levi by his biographer, Carole Angier, published in *The Guardian*

http://books.guardian.co.uk/departments/classics/story/0,,370034,00.html – article on Levi by his biographer, Ian Thomson, published in *The Guardian*

http://www.nytimes.com/learning/general/onthisday/bday/0731.html – obituary by John Tagliabue published in *The New York Times*
www.wiesenthal.com/site/pp.asp?c=fwLYKnN8LzH&b=242023 – website for the Simon Wiesenthal Centre

🕮 Suggested further reading

FICTION

The Archivist by Martha Cooley (1998); *The Tin Drum* by Günter Grass (1959); **Stones From the River by Ursula Hegi** (1994); *Schindler's Ark* by Thomas Keneally (1985); *The Time of Light* by Gunnar Kopperud (1998); **Fugitive Pieces by Anne Michaels** (1997); **The Reader by Bernhard Schlink** (1997); *The Dark Room* by Rachel Seiffert (2001); *Music for the Third Ear* by Susan Schwartz Senstad (1999); *One Day in the Life of Ivan Denisovitch* by Aleksandr Solzhenitsyn (1963); *A Model Childhood* by Christa Wolf (1988)

AUTOBIOGRAPHY

The Past is Myself by Christabel Bielenberg (1970); *All But My Life* by Gerda Weissmann Klein (1997); *Speak You Also* by Paul Steinberg (2001); *Night* by Elie Weisel (1981)

HISTORY

Bad Faith by Carmen Callil (2006); *Hitler's Willing Executioners* by Daniel Jonah Goldhagen (1996); *Konin: A Quest* by Theo Richmond (1995)

BIOGRAPHIES OF LEVI

The Double Bond: Primo Levi, a Biography by Carole Angier (2002); *Primo Levi: A Biography* by Ian Thomson (2002)

OTHER BOOKS BY PRIMO LEVI

If This is a Man (1958)/*The Truce* (1963) published in one volume; *The Periodic Table* (1975); *The Wrench* (1979); *Moments of Reprieve* (1981); *If Not Now, When?* (1982)

PUBLISHED POSTHUMOUSLY

Survival in Auschwitz: The Nazi Assault on Humanity (1993); *The Search for Roots* (2001)

GIVING UP THE GHOST (2003)

Hilary Mantel

📖 About the book

Born in Derbyshire in 1952, Hilary Mantel spent much of her childhood in and out of her grandparents' house and playing at being a priest with her great-aunt Annie next door. A spirited yet sickly child, she was often at home, escaping the straitjacket of unfathomable school rules. When she was seven Jack (later Mantel's stepfather) moved in to the family home, an unorthodox arrangement that continued until her mother, Jack and the children moved to Cheshire, assuring Mantel of a place at the local convent school. A bright student, she read law at the London School of Economics until, tired of smuggling her boyfriend into her room, she transferred to Sheffield to be with him. As she grew into adulthood, Mantel's health worsened. Her doctors were both mystified and dismissive of her, until, finally, aged twenty-seven, she was diagnosed with endometriosis and faced both the loss of her fertility and her ballooning weight, a side effect of the drugs prescribed. Writing with an acerbic humour, a characteristically sharp eye for the quirky and a searing honesty, Hilary Mantel paints vivid word pictures of a life quietly haunted by what might have been.

Background

Hilary Mantel has published several critically acclaimed novels most notably *A Place of Greater Safety*, the novel set during the French Revolution to which she refers in *Giving Up the Ghost*. Often stamped by her interest in the eccentric, and by her concern with the societal injustice, Mantel's novels are all very different, ranging from *The Giant O'Brien*, the tale of an eighteenth-century Irish giant's travels to London to make his fortune in a freak show, to *Eight Months on Ghazzah Street*, which exposes the repression of women in Saudi Arabia and draws on her experience of living in that country. Her writing is characterized by a sly, often biting, wit and a depth of imagination which can be clearly seen in the young Hilary of *Giving Up the Ghost*, so absorbed in her world of camel training and knights errant.

Giving Up the Ghost is Mantel's first work of non-fiction. It was followed by her ninth novel, *Beyond Black*, which echoed the preoccupation with ghosts which runs through her memoir. In *Beyond Black* Alison Hart, a medium, carries trivial messages from the dead around the country, accompanied by her manager Colette, and haunted by her own demons. Reviewers often linked the two books when discussing the novel and Mantel has said that she 'clearly rooted [her] own experience in Alison'.

In her memoir Mantel's father, Henry, swiftly disappears from her life when her mother and Jack move the family to Cheshire. She has since found that Henry married a widow, a mother of six. One of his step-daughters made contact with Mantel after she read *Giving Up the Ghost*, and restored to her the travelling chess set that had meant so much to her as a child. He died in 1997.

Mantel's health continues to be poor and she continues to struggle with the side effects of drugs. She describes herself has 'a creature of pharmaceuticals', the only consolation being that she doesn't think she would have been a writer if she hadn't been ill: 'Illness forces you to the wall, so the stance of the writer is forced on you. Writing keeps you still and as long as your brain is working it doesn't matter if your body isn't.'

About the author

Hilary Mantel was born in Glossop in Derbyshire in 1952. She studied law at the London School of Economics, completing her degree at Sheffield University. She was briefly employed as a social worker in a geriatric hospital, then taught in Botswana for five years, followed by four years in Saudi Arabia, returning to the United Kingdom in 1986. She began writing full time in 1985. In 1987 she was awarded the Shiva Naipaul Memorial Prize for travel writing, and became the film critic of the *Spectator*. She was awarded the Winifred Holtby Memorial Prize for her fourth novel, *Fludd*, and the Hawthornden Prize for her seventh, *An Experiment in Love*. *Giving Up the Ghost* is her first work of non-fiction. She suffered for many years with undiagnosed endometriosis and is patron of the SHE Trust which offers support to women in similar circumstances. Hilary Mantel lives in Berkshire with her husband.

For discussion

✪ Hilary Mantel's memoir does not follow a strictly linear narrative but flicks back and forth across her life, vividly evoking her childhood but referring only obliquely to some periods in her life. How successful did you find this? What effect does it achieve? How would you describe the tone and style of her narrative? Why do you think she chose to write about her own life?

✪ Ghosts are mentioned throughout the book: Mantel sees Jack's ghost on the stairs, she writes of the lives she might have had, the children she might have borne, describing them as ghosts or ghostly. How apt did you find this description? Which ghost do you think Mantel meant when she chose her title?

✪ How important is Mantel's Catholicism to her?

○ Mantel's descriptions of her childhood are extraordinarily vivid. What kind of a child was she? What kind of childhood did she have? Who were the most important people in her childhood and why?

○ 'Sometimes you come to a thing you can't write ... It wrapped a strangling hand around my life, and I don't know how, or what it was.' How did you interpret what happens to Mantel in her 'secret garden'? What effect does it have on her life?

○ 'I complained I had a pain in my legs, and I went to the doctor: and that was my big mistake.' What do you think of Mantel's treatment by the medical profession? Would such treatment have been different had she been a man suffering from an undiagnosed illness?

○ How does Mantel cope when she no longer has the option to have a child? What do you make of her ambivalence about having children? How does society react to childless women, whether they are childless by choice or by circumstance?

○ Why do you think that Mantel and her husband find it so hard to settle when they return from Saudi Arabia? What do you make of Mantel's image of herself in the final chapter, picking her way across the rutted fields that she can see from her balcony?

○ 'Once you have learned the habits of secrecy, they aren't so easy to give up. That is why this chapter is shorter than it might be.' Mantel is unusually frank about withholding secrets, whether willingly or unwillingly, from her readers. Do you expect to learn the whole truth in an autobiography?

○ If you have read Hilary Mantel's fiction did *Giving Up the Ghost* shed any light on it for you? What relevance do you think knowledge of a writer's life is to their work?

▄ Resources

www.newstatesman.com/200305190041 – review by Carmen Callil published in the *New Statesman*

http://books.guardian.co.uk/review/story/0,12084,952391,00.html – review by the writer Kathryn Hughes published in *The Guardian*

www.theage.com.au/articles/2004/05/07/1083881471653.html?from=storyrhs – review by the writer Brenda Niall published in *The Age*

www.nybooks.com/articles/18251 – review of *Beyond Black* by the novelist John Banville, which makes lengthy references to *Giving up the Ghost*, published in *The New York Review of Books*

www.contemporarywriters.com/authors/?p=auth67 – profile of Hilary Mantel at the British Council website including a critical essay by Garan Holcombe

http://books.guardian.co.uk/departments/generalfiction/story/0,6000,1468815,00.
html – interview by Rachel Cooke, published in *The Guardian*
www.shetrust.org.uk – SHE trust website

📚 Suggested further reading

Flickerbook by Leila Berg (1997); *Hidden Lives: A Family Memoir* **by Margaret
Forster** (1995); *Borrowed Finery* by Paula Fox (2001); *And When Did You Last See
Your Father* **by Blake Morrison** (1993); *Bad Blood* **by Lorna Sage** (2000); *Toast*
by Nigel Slater (2003); *The Child the Books Built* by Francis Spufford (2002)
OTHER BOOKS BY HILARY MANTEL
Novels: *Every Day is Mother's Day* (1985); *Vacant Possession* (1986); *Eight
Months on Ghazzah Street* (1988); *Fludd* (1989); *A Place of Greater Safety* (1992);
A Change of Climate (1994); *An Experiment in Love* (1995); *The Giant O'Brien*
(1998); *Beyond Black* (2005)
Short stories: *Learning to Talk* (2003); Non-fiction: *The Woman Who Died of
Robespierre* (2006)

AND WHEN DID YOU LAST SEE YOUR FATHER?
(1993)

Blake Morrison

📖 About the book

Blake Morrison's moving and candid memoir of his father covers the few short
weeks between his diagnosis with terminal cancer and his death. Morrison travelled
to Yorkshire to stay with his mother in the village where he grew up, visiting his father
at the hospital where he had spent so much time with his own patients as a GP. As
his father's condition worsens Morrison contemplates their shared experiences, the
intimacies and the irritations of their relationship. After his father's death Morrison
questions the nature of the bond between them, articulately expressing the
contradictions, frustrations, love and loss bound into the complicated relationships
which many of us have with our parents when we become adults.

Background

Perhaps best known as a poet before the publication of *And When Did You Last See
Your Father?*, Blake Morrison has pursued a literary career distinguished by its

diversity. He has been literary editor for both *The Observer* and *The Independent on Sunday* and his writing encompasses poetry, fiction, drama, libretti and children's literature. With its raw, unflinching honesty *And When Did You Last See Your Father?* seemed to hit a chord with the book-buying public, remaining in the bestseller charts for many months after it was published. Morrison has said of his writing that it 'nurtures a secret desire to affect and move people', declaring that without 'the wish to make something happen, or make someone (if only myself) feel better – I doubt I'd feel the urge to write at all'. His aspiration for his memoir of his father was that it would 'demystify death and give voice to emotions which many of us (especially men) prefer to repress'. It is also in keeping with what he describes as the 'perennial' themes of his writing: 'love, childhood, memory and loss'.

A decade after his book was published Morrison reflected on the process of writing it and the reactions it had provoked amongst his family and friends, noting that sometimes those reactions were not quite what they seemed or what had been expected. While she had given her approval, asking for just a few changes, Morrison's mother had confessed her unhappiness to his sister just before the book's publication. Sandra who had been given a pseudonym to avoid possible embarrassment at the inclusion of her sexual relationship with the 14-year-old Morrison complained that her real name had not been used while Auntie Beaty, tacitly accepted by the family as Arthur's mistress, was horrified at the thought of exposure and greatly relieved to be assured of her anonymity. This renewed contact had the pleasing, although perhaps surprising, result of a close relationship with both Morrison and his mother.

After his mother's death, Morrison discovered a cache of letters between his parents which revealed not only their passion for each other but that his mother had completely reinvented herself. The daughter of a desperately poor Irish Catholic family, Kim had been born Agnes O'Shea. She had fought her way out of poverty and into the respectable English middle classes, carefully hiding her origins even from her children. In *Things My Mother Never Told Me* Morrison tells her story through his parents' correspondence, exercising the same combination of honesty, delicacy and tenderness that make *And When Did You Last See Your Father?* such a moving testament of love from a son to his often very difficult father.

About the author

Blake Morrison was born in Yorkshire in 1950. He has taught at both London University and the Open University. He is a prominent critic of both poetry and fiction and has contributed reviews to *The Observer*, *The Times Literary Supplement*, *The Literary Review* and *The Independent* as well as publishing his own poetry. *And When Did You Last See Your Father?* was published to great acclaim in 1993 when it won the *Esquire*/Volvo/Waterstone's prize for non-fiction. It was made into a film in 2007 starring Jim Broadbent and Colin Firth. His first novel, *The Justification of Johan Gutenberg*, was published in 2000. *Things My Mother Never Told Me*, a companion volume to *And When Did You Last See Your Father?* was published in 2002.

For discussion

✪ How would you describe Arthur Morrison's character? What are the traits that his son has most difficulty in accepting? What is it that he loves about his father? Are there any traits that they share? How would you describe their relationship?

✪ What impression did you gain of Arthur's relationship with his wife? They are both doctors. To what extent do you think he treats her as an equal?

✪ Morrison is very careful in his choice of words. How does he use language to convey the intimacy of his relationship with his father? How would you describe his tone?

✪ The book is unflinching, sometimes painful, in its honesty. Why do you think Morrison refuses to spare us the details of his father's illness and death, no matter how intimate? How do we cope with death and illness in society today?

✪ At several points before his father's death, Morrison describes himself as 'scared' and 'frightened'. What is it that frightens him about his father's death?

✪ At one point, when Morrison presses his father about his relationship with Beaty, Arthur says he was obsessed. Morrison also seems to be obsessed with the relationship. Why do you think this is so? To what extent is the matter resolved at the conclusion of the book?

✪ Why do you think Morrison decided to write the book? Why do you think he chose the title?

▉ Resources

www.contemporarywriters.com/authors/?p=auth75 – page for Blake Morrison at the British Council website which includes a statement by the author.

http://observer.guardian.co.uk/review/story/0,6903,1318259,00.html – Blake Morrison's reactions to his book, taken from *The Observer* website and originally published in *Granta* literary magazine

⮱ Suggested further reading
FICTION
One True Thing by Anna Quindlan (1994)

NON-FICTION

Paula **by Isabel Allende** (1995); *Iris and Her Friends* by John Bayley (1999); *Hidden Lives* **by Margaret Forster** (1995); *The Shadow Man* by Mary Gordon (1996); *Father and Son* by Edmund Gosse (1907); *Remind Me Who I Am, Again* by Linda Grant (1998); *Seeking Rapture* by Kathryn Harrison (2003); *My Ear at His Heart* by Hanif Kureishi (2004); *Family Romance* by John Lanchester (2007); *The Undertaking: Life Studies from the Dismal Trade* by Thomas Lynch (1997); *On the Death of a Parent* edited by Jane McLaughlin (1994); *A Voyage Around My Father* by John Mortimer (1971); *In the Blood* by Andrew Motion (2006)

OTHER BOOKS BY BLAKE MORRISON

Fiction:

The Justification of Johan Gutenberg (2000); *South of the River* (2007); *The Yellow House* (children's) (1987)

Non-fiction: *The Cracked Pot* (1996); *Pendle Witches*, with Paula Rego (1996); *As If* (1997); *Too True* (1998)

Poetry: *The Penguin Book of Contemporary Poetry* (1982), co-edited with Andrew Motion; *Dark Glasses* (1984); *The Ballad of the Yorkshire Ripper* (1987); *Selected Poems* (1999)

Autobiography: *Things My Mother Never Told Me* (2002)

BAD BLOOD (2000)

Lorna Sage

📖 About the book

Born in Hanmer, Flintshire in 1943, Lorna Sage spent her first years with her mother and grandparents in the village vicarage. Locked in constant combat, Thomas and Hilda were an ill-matched pair: she, constantly hankering after the sweet delights of the Rhonnda where she was born, while he drowned his sorrows in communion wine and philandered. When Lorna's father returned from the army, the family moved to a council house. Lorna was a lonely child, forever on the fringes, seeking refuge in books. At Whitchurch High School for Girls she and her new-found friend Gail formed a fiercely intense 'girl gang'. Sexually alluring yet desperately naïve she became pregnant at sixteen by Vic Sage, a fellow misfit. The two married and, doggedly determined to continue with her studies, Lorna took her A-levels shortly after giving birth to her daughter She won a scholarship to Durham University where both she and Vic gained Firsts. Both witty and emotionally wrenching, this wonderfully eloquent memoir captures a very particular life at a very particular time in British history.

Background

Lorna Sage's memoir begins with a vivid image of her and her grandfather: 'Grandfather's skirts would flap in the wind along the churchyard path and I would hang on.'Theirs was a relationship that, despite his self-absorption, his drunkenness and his womanizing, would be the most formative influence in Sage's life. Shortly before she died she wrote of him as 'my great familiar and mentor, the making of me'. It was her grandfather who named her after R.D. Blackmore's heroine Lorna Doone, and it was her grandfather who taught his precocious three-year-old granddaughter how to read, sparking a relationship with literature that would last a life time.

The time and place of Sage's upbringing were also potent forces in forming her character. Hanmer in the 1940s and 1950s was a claustrophobic place where all were supposedly born into their station in the world and expected to remain there, especially women. Sage's memoir is infused with a wry remembrance of 1950s attitudes to women, a remembrance that is tinged with fury when she recounts her experience as a sixteen-year-old determined to continue her education after the birth of her daughter. Despite her frequent references to her timidity Sage proves herself to be marvellously courageous, insisting in the face of outraged and affronted nursing staff that she should be discharged from hospital so that she can take her A-Levels, a courage that is quietly supported by her unmarried female teachers. Sage's feminism continued to inform her work as an academic, leading her to specialise in the work of women writers.

Her death met with great sadness, not simply the grief of family and friends mourning the passing of a woman with tremendous wit and *joie de vivre*, but also for what might have been. As she wrote in her *Guardian* obituary of her close friend, Angela Carter, who died of lung cancer aged fifty-one 'it's no use pretending that she wouldn't have produced new work just as wonderful given the chance'.

About the author

Lorna Sage was born in 1943 at Hanmer in North Wales. Despite becoming pregnant at sixteen with her daughter Sharon, she won a scholarship to read English at Durham University, where she and her husband, Victor Sage, both gained first-class honours degrees. She went on to take an MA from Birmingham University and taught English Literature at the University of East Anglia where she specialized in women writers, becoming a professor in 1994. Sage regularly reviewed for *The London Review of Books*, *The Times Literary Supplement* and *The New York Times Book Review* and published several respected academic works but *Bad Blood* was her first popular book. It won the 2001 Whitbread Prize for Biography. Lorna Sage died on January 11 2001, having suffered from emphysema for many years.

For discussion

○ 'In fact, he got so impatient with my favourite books (which both he and I knew by heart) that one momentous day, before I was four, he taught me to read in self-defence.' Why is this such a 'momentous day' for Sage? How important is reading to both Lorna Sage and to her grandfather?

○ How important is her relationship with her grandfather to Sage? How would you describe that relationship? How does Sage view her grandfather during her childhood? What changes her view of him?

○ What kind of place is Hanmer? How does it change throughout the time that Sage lives there? How does she fit into the class structure of the village? What difficulties does her position present her with? How does the predominant idea of each person being born into his or her own place fit with the national mood of the 1950s?

○ 'The children of violent unhappy marriages, like my mother, are often hamstrung for life, but the children of happier marriages have problems too – all the worse, perhaps, because they don't have virtue on their side.' How has Thomas and Hilda's example influenced Valma and Eric's marriage? How, in turn, does Valma and Eric's happiness effect Sage? What is Sage and Vic's 'mutant version of marriage', as she describes it, and how does it compare with the two previous generations' marriages?

○ Sage and Gail's relationship is both passionate and intense despite its inauspicious beginnings. What is it that they find in each other?

○ Sage offers her readers an extraordinarily intimate view of her young self in her memoir. How would you describe her?

○ How potent a force is the treatment of women in the 1950s and 1960s in shaping Sage's life? How has that treatment changed?

○ How would you describe the tone and style of Sage's prose? What is the effect of the family photographs that are scattered throughout the book? Why do you think she chose to write a memoir? How does she view her past?

○ What is the significance of the book's title? Whose blood is bad and why?

📖 Resources

http://books.guardian.co.uk/reviews/biography/0,6121,366020,00.html – review by Frances Wilson in *The Guardian*

http://books.guardian.co.uk/whitbread2000/story/0,6194,421322,00.html – article in *The Guardian* written by Sage on the writing of *Bad Blood* shortly before her death

www.nybooks.com/articles/15480 – an appreciation in *The New York Review of Books* by the writer James Fenton

http://books.guardian.co.uk/extracts/story/0,6761,545023,00.html – an abridged version of Marina Warner's introduction to Lorna Sage's last book, *Moments of Truth*, which includes an appreciation of her work

http://news.bbc.co.uk/1/hi/entertainment/1113931.stm – tribute to Lorna Sage at BBC News website

📚 Suggested further reading

Once in a House on Fire by Andrea Ashworth (1998); **Hidden Lives: A Family Memoir by Margaret Forster** (1995); *Borrowed Finery* by Paula Fox (2001); **Giving Up the Ghost by Hilary Mantel** (2003); **And When Did You Last See Your Father by Blake Morrison** (1993); *The Child the Books Built* by Francis Spufford (2002); *The Boy Who Loved Books* by John Sutherland (2007)

OTHER BOOKS BY LORNA SAGE

Flesh and the Mirror: Essays on the Art of Angela Carter (1994); *Women in the House of Fiction: Post-War Women Novelists* (1992); *Moments of Truth: Twelve Twentieth Century Women Authors* (2001); *Good as Her Word: Selected Journalism* (2003)

Edited: *The Cambridge Guide to Women's Writing in English* (1999)

THE HACIENDA: MY VENEZUELAN YEARS (1997)
Lisa St Aubin de Terán

📖 About the book

Married at the age of seventeen to a Venezuelan aristocrat turned bank robber who pursued her mercilessly, Lisa St Aubin de Terán spent the next two years travelling around Europe with her husband and his two compadres. When the Venezuelan government pardoned Don Jaime, St Aubin de Terán returned with him to his beloved but dilapidated *hacienda* where she was left to fend for herself with only two beagles, a vulture and a servant girl for company. As her husband became increasingly withdrawn, hardly ever present and often violent when he was, St Aubin de Terán began to doubt his sanity. With the help and support of the farm workers, she succeeded in taking control of the estate, getting it back on its feet and providing a home for her baby daughter. She remained in Venezuela for seven years until it became apparent that the lives of both her daughter and herself were in great danger as Jaime Terán lost his tenuous grip on his sanity.

Background

The bare bones of *The Hacienda* read like the synopsis of a florid romantic novel – beautiful, ethereal schoolgirl is pursued by South American aristocrat, marries him and travels around Europe until she returns with him to his Venezuelan estate. But the reality was far from romantic. Virtually abandoned by her unstable husband and snubbed by his contemptuous relatives, Lisa St Aubin de Terán was left to make her own way in a culture where her every action was closely monitored for social acceptability. Her courage in the face of her strange and taxing new life would be extraordinarily impressive in a more mature woman but from a desperately naïve teenager it is astonishing. Written with wit and an engagingly wry view of her youthful self, St Aubin de Terán's vivid account of the transformation of that teenager into a woman determined to do what is best both for her household and her child is moving and uplifting.

In her first novel *Keepers of the House*, which won the Somerset Maugham Award, St Aubin de Terán poured her Venezuelan experiences into her fiction. Seventeen-year-old, Lydia Sinclair, finds herself marooned at her new husband's family home, the crumbling Hacienda La Bebella. Left to herself by the erratic Don Diego Beltran, Lydia sets about unearthing his family history, listening to tales of baroque splendor told by Benito, the loyal family retainer. The novel won her a good deal of acclaim and marked the beginning of a literary career which has encompassed fiction, autobiography and travel writing. Over a decade later, St Aubin de Terán brings a lightness of touch to her experiences in *The Hacienda*, expressing incredulity that she endured both the privations of Jaime Terán's decaying estate and his terrifying unpredictability.

In 2004, in a continuation of her desire to help others less fortunate than herself first awakened when she established a dispensary for the *hacienda* workers, St Aubin de Terán set up The Teran Foundation a charitable organization that works to establish schools and farm projects in the north of Mozambique,

About the author

Lisa St Aubin de Terán was born in 1953. Her first novel, *Keepers of the House*, won the Somerset Maugham Award in 1982 and was followed by *The Slow Train to Milan*, which won the John Llewelyn Rhys Prize in 1983. She currently lives in Amsterdam.

For discussion

✪ What effect does the dictum '*Qué dirán* – what will people say', which seems to rule all sections of Venezuelan society, have on St Aubin de Terán's life?

✪ 'When I first arrived on the *hacienda*, I felt ashamed.' Why does St Aubin de Terán feel this way? To what extent do you think her shame is justified? How do you think you would have felt in her circumstances?

✪ Venezuelan society seems to be very rigidly structured. What factors make it difficult for St Aubin de Terán to find a niche for herself? What are the differences between English and Venezuelan culture that make life most difficult for her and how does she overcome them?

✪ How does St Aubin de Terán's narrative differ from her letters to her mother? What might account for these differences? What do you learn of her character from the letters?

✪ What are the problems faced by *la gente*? How does St Aubin de Terán try to help? How successful is she?

✪ When St Aubin de Terán is told to get the priest for Capino's burial she writes: 'I was timid, shy and absurdly passive'. To what extent do you agree with her opinion of herself. How does she change during her time at the *hacienda* and what brings about these changes?

✪ Are there particular ways in which St Aubin de Terán finds comfort? If so, what are they and how do they help?

✪ Jaime is an absence rather than a presence for the most part. His violence is rarely referred to although veiled references such as the one to '"the accident" caused by a monumental blow to the top of my head' make it clear that it must have been very frightening. Why do you think she stays for seven years at the *hacienda*? What makes her finally decide to leave and how difficult is this decision?

🖥 Resources

www.nytimes.com/books/98/04/12/reviews/980412.12upchurt.html?_r=1&oref=slogin – review by the writer Michael Upchurch published in *The New York Times*
www.teranfoundation.org – Teran Foundation website

Suggested further reading

Paula **by Isabel Allende** (1995); *Not a Hazardous Sport* by Nigel Barley (1989); *Lost in Translation* **by Eva Hoffman** (1989)

OTHER BOOKS BY LISA ST AUBIN DE TERÁN

Novels: *Keepers of the House* (1982); *The Slow Train to Milan* (1983); *The Tiger* (1984); *The Bay of Silence* (1986); *Black Idol* (1987); *Joanna* (1990); *Nocturne* (1992); *The Palace* (1997); *Otto* (2005); *Swallowing Stones* (2006)

Short stories: *The Marble Mountain and Other Stories* (1989); *Southpaw* (1999); *Sapa's Blessing and Other Stories* (2005)

Travel: *Off the Rails* (1989); *Venice: The Four Seasons* (Mike Lindberg, 1992); *A Valley in Italy* (1994); *Elements of Italy* (2001)

Autobiography: *Memory Maps* ((2002)

Edited: *The Virago Book of Wanderlust and Dreams* (2000)

GIRLITUDE: A MEMOIR OF THE 50S AND 60S
(1999)

Emma Tennant

About the book

Girlitude covers the early years of Emma Tennant's life from 1955 when she became a debutante, to the birth of her second child in 1969. Taking the traditional route for both her generation and her class by entering the 'marriage market', Tennant departed from the straight and narrow with a turbulent and dangerous love affair, briefly getting back on track with her marriage to the novelist Henry Green's son, Sebastian Yorke, with whom she had a son. When that marriage ended, Tennant took up a semi-nomadic life, spending time in Paris, Rome, Greece and New York, frequently attracted to unsuitable men. A second hasty marriage to the satirist Christopher Booker ended in divorce. By this time the 1960s were in full swing and Tennant, now attached to the literary and artistic avant-garde, joined the 'revolution'. The book ends with a third marriage and the birth of her second child, a daughter.

Background

Girlitude follows on from *Strangers*, Emma Tennant's fictional memoir of her family, and recounts her experiences in the 1950s and 1960s as she finds her way from her wealthy establishment background into the literary, artistic and political circles that were in the vanguard of the 'Sixties Revolution'. Hers was a world of privilege, a world in which she was expected to remain in a state of 'girlitude', her word for the financial dependence deemed suitable for women in her position at that time. It is her awareness of her seeming inability to pass from a state of 'girlitude' to woman-hood which is central to her book.

Tennant's family was not only wealthy but also very well connected in the literary and artistic world. Her mother counted both Cyril Connolly and Stephen Spender amongst her friends. Tennant, herself, was to marry Sebastian Yorke, the son of Henry Green, her literary idol, and to include amongst her circle Bruce Chatwin, Gore Vidal and Norman Mailer. She became well known as an aristocratic rebel who 'put the Che in Cheyne Walk' and in 1962 wrote her first novel, *The Colour of Rain*. Published under the pseudonym Catherine Aydy, the novel satirized the 'young marrieds of Kensington', some of whom were sufficiently recognizable for lawyers to be consulted.

In the decade after the years covered by *Girlitude* Tennant immersed herself in the literary world, setting up the magazine *Bananas* which gained a reputation for showcasing fantastical writing by writers such as Michael Moorcock, J.G. Ballard and Angela Carter. More controversially it was through the magazine that she met Ted Hughes at a *Bananas* party in 1976, with whom she had an affair in the late seventies. The publication in 1999 of *Burnt Diaries* in which she wrote about their relationship caused something of a stir in the literary world. Tennant had resolved not to publish her book until after Hughes' death but found herself criticized for it nonetheless.

It is not for her undoubtedly colourful life or for the men with which she has been associated that Tennant would wish to be remembered however. As she has declared 'my life has really been about writing, though some think it's all about once having been in a ball dress and having an odd life and marrying all the time. But it's the writing that's always been the point.'

About the author

Emma Tennant was born in London in 1938. She spent much of her childhood in Scotland and was educated at St Paul's Girls' School in London. Her first novel, *The Colour of Rain*, was published in 1964. In the 1970s she founded and edited the literary review *Banana*. In 1998 she published *Strangers*, a fictionalized memoir of her family. The first part of her autobiography, *Girlitude*, appeared in 1999 swiftly followed by *Burnt Diaries*.

For discussion

⊙ How does Tennant feel about her family and her background? How does she seem to fit in to the world of debutantes? What seems to be the role of women of Tennant's class background in the 1950s and early 1960s? How do you think their lives differed from other women's?

⊙ What does Tennant mean by 'girlitude'? Is it a term that could be applied to young women today? The final sentence of the book reads: 'If I have given birth to a woman, I ponder afterwards, can I at last give up being a girl?' Do you think she can?

⊙ How would you describe the young Tennant's character? What factors have contributed to shaping her? What impression do you form of the way Tennant feels about her younger self? She says, 'Yet again I am so unsure of who I am that I don't even know who I'm trying to look like.' Do you think she has a better idea of who she is by the end of the book and, if so, why?

⊙ Tennant suggests that the novelist Henry Green, her first husband's father, is rather contemptuous of her own family. How do the two families differ in the way that they live?

⊙ Tennant says: 'I shall leave "Mr Booker" – but I don't know yet for whom.' What do you think of this remark? Why is it so difficult for Tennant to contemplate life without a man? What do you make of Tennant's attitude towards men and marriage? Why do you think she is attracted to so many men who are unlikely to return her interest?

⊙ How different is the young woman in the photograph Tennant describes at the beginning of the book from the thirty-one-year-old at the end? What are the most important factors in bringing about that change?

⊙ Tennant's novels have been described as being written in powerful poetic prose. How would you describe her style in *Girlitude*?

⊙ Tennant has described her book *Strangers: A Family Romance* as a fictional memoir of her family, while *Girlitude* is classified as autobiography. Can autobiography be considered to be completely factual?

🖥 Resources

www.findarticles.com/p/articles/mi_qn4158/is_19990502/ai_n14234182 – review by Mark Bostridge published in *The Independent*
www.findarticles.com/p/articles/mi_qn4158/is_19990417/ai_n14223292/pg_1 – interview published in *The Independent*

🕮 Suggested further reading

The Ossie Clark Diaries by Ossie Clark, edited by Lady Henrietta Rous (1998); *All Dressed Up* by Jonathon Green (1999); *Hons and Rebels* by Jessica Mitford (1960); *Hippie Hippie Shake* by Richard Neville (1995); *Promise of a Dream: Remembering the Sixties* by Sheila Rowbotham (2000)

OTHER BOOKS BY EMMA TENNANT

Fiction: *The Colour of Rain* (1964); *Hotel De Dream* (1976); *The Bad Sister* (1978); *Wild Nights* (1979); *Alice Fell* (1980); *Woman Beware Woman* (1983); *The House of Hospitalities* (1987); *A Wedding of Curiosity* (1988); *Sisters and Strangers: A Moral Tale* (1990); *Faustine* (1992); *Tess* (1993); *Strangers: A Family Romance* (1998); *The Ballad of Sylvia and Ted* (2001); *Felony* (2002); *Heathcliff's Tale* (2005); *The Harp Lesson* (2005); *The French Dancer's Bastard: The Story of Adele from Jane Eyre* (2006); *The Amazing Marriage* (2006); Emma Tennant has written 'sequels' to Jane Austen's *Pride and Prejudice* and *Emma: Pemberley* (1993), *An Unequal Marriage* (1994), *Emma in Love* (1999)

Autobiography:

Burnt Diaries (1999); *A House in Corfu* (2001); *Corfu Banquet: A Seasonal Memoir with Recipes* (2003)

NO PLACE LIKE HOME (1999)

Gary Younge

📖 About the book

Born and brought up in the sixties in the quiet Hertfordshire New Town of Stevenage, Gary Younge was used to looking elsewhere for his sense of racial identity. His mother made her own idiosyncratic contribution by declaring their house an outpost of Barbados but Younge found himself looking to the American South, his imagination caught by the brave dignity of the civil rights movement, and in particular the Freedom Riders who rode the Greyhounds from Washington DC to New Orleans in 1961, challenging racial segregation. Boarding a Greyhound in DC Younge retraces the steps of the heroes of his youth to see how things have changed. Along the way he frequently faces incomprehension at the combination of his English accent and black skin, and meets several members of the Civil Rights movement, sometimes finding long-cherished ideas overturned. Part memoir, part travelogue, part searching examination of what it is to be both black and American or British, *No Place Like Home* combines thought-provoking analysis with witty anecdotal style.

Background

In the late 1940s, its economy in tatters after the Second World War, Britain embarked on a programme of encouraging Caribbean and Asian immigration to fill its many job vacancies and help put the country back on its feet. Often intelligent, well educated and instilled with a confidence that they would be welcomed in what they had been brought up to think of as the 'mother country' many immigrants were unpleasantly surprised by their reception. They were often treated with disdain or intrusive curiosity, assumed to be ignorant and stupid, and expected to understand that although they had British passports, their neighbours were unlikely to consider them to be so. Although, by the 1970s Gary Younge did not find himself subjected to such overt racism he encountered a more subtle form which often manifested itself in an inability to accept the idea that black person could also be British.

As an adolescent Younge looked to America to construct an identity for himself, his attention caught by the spirit and bravery of the Freedom Riders and their valiant challenge to the segregation of the American South. Black American identity had a much stronger foundation than black British identity, despite the fact that black people have lived in Britain since the twelfth century, swelling in numbers in the seventeenth and eighteenth centuries. The expansion of the black population of the American South had been fuelled by the importation of Africans and West Indians forced into a slavery upon which the South's considerable wealth had been built, a trade which had begun in the seventeenth century and lasted until Emancipation in 1863 brought about by the American Civil War. Emancipation, however, was a very long way from equality, and it was out of that desire for equality and justice that the Civil Rights movement, which so inspired Younge, was born. For the British reader familiar with such celebrated names as Martin Luther King and Rosa Parks, *No Place Like Home* throws a welcome light on lesser known but equally courageous figures such as Claudette Colvin, Edward Brown and Gwen Patton, while reminding those of us who are white that racism, subtle and not so subtle, is still alive and a discomfiting reality for our black compatriots

About the author

Gary Younge was born in Stevenage in 1968. He studied languages at Heriot-Watt University in Edinburgh. He has worked as a journalist for *The Guardian* since 1994 and became their New York correspondent in 2002. *No Place Like Home* was shortlisted for *The Guardian* First Book Award in 1999.

For discussion

⚙ 'Mrs Stilling embodied one of three types of reactions a black family could expect in a place like Stevenage. There were those who, like her, welcomed us. There were those who tolerated us. And there were those who positively despised us.' To what extent do you think reactions to black people have changed in the UK? What do you think of Gary Younge's mother's solution? How important were her efforts to establish a black identity for her sons? What made Younge look to the American South for affirmation?

⚙ 'Race in America is everywhere. From the pulpit to the turntable, from the newstand to the mailman, you cannot get away from it. For a black Briton this is both a relief and a burden.' What do you think Younge means by this? How do British attitudes to race differ from those he encounters in America? Why do you think this might be?

⚙ 'There are lots of ways to define the South,' Susan Glisson tells Younge. After reading *No Place Like Home* how would you define it? How does the 'New South' differ from the traditional idea of the South?

⚙ 'When segregation went we lost the very foundation of our community' declares Ernest Brown head of the local NAACP in Rock Hill. Are you persuaded by either Brown's argument, or by Younge's ensuing analysis?

⚙ Younge mentions South Africa several times in the book. How would you compare the segregation once practised in America with the apartheid regime in South Africa?

⚙ 'But in Britain you are born into a class. And regardless of how much you earn or what you have achieved, your die has already been cast' states Younge in his assertion that Britain will never have the black middle class that exists in America. How accurate do you think this is, for black or white people?

⚙ 'Standing at the plaque, at the foot of Edmund Pettus Bridge, I began to see how it is possible for African-Americans to join the army, salute the flag and sing the anthem, and why I could never do the same in Britain' thinks Younge in Selma. What do you think of his ensuing argument?

⚙ 'If it is staggering to think that a lynching could take place in 1981, it is no less shocking that a government can retaliate with an execution in 1997.' What do you think of his statement? If you share his ambivalence towards capital punishment did the Hays case change your view as it did his? What are your reasons for your answer?

⚙ After reading Younge's book have your own attitudes towards race changed at all, and if so why?

⚙ Why do you think Younge chose the title *No Place Like Home*?

▨ Resources

www.spartacus.schoolnet.co.uk/USAfreedomR.htm – webpage on the Freedom Rides published at Spartacus.schoolnet.co.uk which includes testimony from some of the Freedom Riders

www.stanford.edu/group/King/about_king/encyclopedia/freedom_rides.htm – webpage on the Freedom Rides published as part of the King Encyclopedia at Stanford University's website

www.bbc.co.uk/legacies/immig_emig/england/berkshire/article_1.shtml – web-pages at the BBC's website on the experiences of Barbadian immigrants to the UK

▨ Suggested further reading

FICTION

Invisible Man by Ralph Ellison (1952); *To Kill a Mocking Bird* by Harper Lee (1960); *Small Island* by Andrea Levy (2004)

NON FICTION

Almost Heaven by Martin Fletcher (1998); *The Autobiography of Martin Luther King Jr.* by Martin Luther King (1998); *The Great American Bus Ride* by Irma Kurtz (1993); *Walking with the Wind by* John Lewis and Michael D'Orso(1998)

OTHER BOOKS BY GARY YOUNGE

Stranger in a Strange Land: Encounters in the Disunited States (2006)

RESOURCES

The resources listed below include books, magazines and websites aimed at helping you choose new books and seek out background information such as author profiles, book reviews or historical background, for your discussions. You'll also find several online reading groups listed in the Internet section, together with a directory of more online groups should you want to explore that option further.

Books

The Reading Groups Book by Jenny Hartley (Oxford University Press, 2002). The result of a survey of 350 groups in the UK, Jenny Hartley's book offers an insight into the history of reading groups as well as examining their current popularity. Packed with information on the way groups work, the book includes lots of anecdotes and members' comments plus lists of favourite books.

1001 Books You Must Read Before You Die by Peter Boxall (Cassell Illustrated, 2006).

The Rough Guide to Cult Fiction by Paul Simpson, Michaela Bushell and Helen Rodiss (Rough Guides, 2005)

Good Reading Guide edited by Nick Rennison (A.&C. Black, 2006).

Opening the Book (1996) by Rachel van Riel and Olive Fowler with a foreword by Alan Bennett, obtainable from Opening the Book, 181 Carleton Road, Pontefract, West Yorks WF8 3NH, tel: 01977 602188, fax: 01977 690621, e-mail info@ opening thebook.com.

The Good Fiction Guide edited by Jane Rogers (Oxford University Press, 2005)

The latter three books are packed with recommendations along the 'if you like that, you'll like this' basis, with the emphasis on modern fiction. A.&C. Black also publishes a series of guides to particular genres such as Nick Rennison's *100 Must-read Classic Novels* (A.&C. Black, 2006) and *100 Must-read Science Fiction Novels* by Nick Rennison and Steven Andrews (A.&C. Black, 2006, and plan to publish more.

How to Read a Novel: A User's Guide by John Sutherland (Profile, 2006) – advice on how to approach reading fiction a little more thoughtfully.

The Writers' and Artists' Yearbook (published annually by A.&C. Black) lists contact details for UK and Irish publishers. You should be able to find a copy in your local library.

HarperCollins has introduced additional content into their Harper Perennial paperback imprint which includes books such as Alex Masters' biography *Stuart: A Life Backwards* and Tash Aw's *The Harmony Silk Factory*, some of which can be very useful in promoting discussion. Printed in the PS section at the back of the book, content varies but may include an interview with the author, a critical perspective and suggested further reading.

Magazines

The Mail on Sunday's You Magazine hosts an immensely successful reading group. Information can also be found at the *You* Reading Group website (www.you-reading-group.co.uk) which has details of past choices.

newbooks is aimed at all readers, with a particular emphasis on reading groups, and includes book extracts, interviews and lots of recommendations and reviews contributed by reading group members. The magazine is available in bookshops and libraries or from 4 Froxfield Close, Winchester, SO22 6JW, tel: 01962 620320, and its website can be found at www.newbooksmag.com/index.html

Waterstone's Books Quarterly includes a wide selection of articles together with reviews of over 100 new books per quarter and is available at all branches of Waterstone's.

Radio and television

Radio 4 is an excellent source of information on books, from *Start the Week* to the early evening arts review *Front Row*, which includes coverage of events in the book world. Three programmes are likely to be of particular interest for reading group members.

The Radio 4 Bookclub, hosted by Jim Naughtie, is broadcast monthly and, where possible, features the author of the current book choice in conversation with reading group members from around the country. Details of both the current choice and previous choices can be found on the internet at www.bbc.co.uk/radio4/arts/bookclub/.

A Good Read is a series in which the presenter plus two guests each nominate a favourite book to discuss. Choices are often a little outside the mainstream and the resulting discussions are lively, enthusiastic and often inspiring.

Open Book is a weekly programme featuring author interviews, discussions and a round-up of new fiction and non-fiction paperbacks. Its website can be found at www.bbc.co.uk/radio4/arts/openbook

Radio 5 Live has a weekly book panel spot as part of *The Daily Mayo* which covers titles as diverse as Harlan Coben's *Promise Me*, Jane Harris's *The Observations* and Yasmin Crowther's *The Saffron Kitchen*.

Begun in 2004, Channel 4's *Richard and Judy Book Club* and *Summer Read* selections are, without doubt, one of the single greatest influences on the reading public. Their format of choosing a set of books, discussing each one with a household name then inviting the public to vote for their favourite is a very engaging one. Details of the current selection up for discussion together with past selections, reading notes, a chance to write a review plus a chat room can be found at www.richardandjudybookclub.co.uk

The internet

The internet has always been an excellent place to research background information to bring to discussions, book reviews and articles about books and since the first edition of this book was written such sites have proliferated. There is a multitude of reading groups based throughout the world online; if you want to chat with someone in New York about the latest Philip Roth or to someone in Sydney about Kate Grenville's *The Secret River* opportunities abound. Below is a small selection of websites that may appeal and, of course, as is the way with the web, many are linked to others likely to be of interest.

Online reading groups

Many daily newspapers now offer the chance to engage in a little online book discussion, most of them with lively exchanges and interesting book choices. These can be reached via the URLs listed under the heading 'Literary magazines and newspapers' in this section. The addresses listed below offer something a little different and include a directory to many more

www.nytimes.com/ref/readersopinions/reading-group-picks.html
   The New York Times' reading group offers a chance to join a transatlantic discussion on books ranging from Mrs Dalloway to Joan Didion's moving memoir, *The Year of Magical Thinking*.

www.oprah.com/obc/obc_landing.jhtml
   Oprah Winfrey can claim some credit for the phenomenal rise of reading groups in the US and her monthly book choices have all become instant bestsellers. To join in the discussion you'll have to register as a member although information about past choices, ranging from Toni Morrison's *Song of Solomon* to Joyce Carol Oates's *We Were the Mulvaneys* is available without registering.

www.bookgrouponline.com/forum

Lively, informal book discussion site run by Bill Matthews (creator of the BBC's *They Think It's All Over*) and journalist Luise Finan

www.reader2reader.net

Part of the Museum, Libraries and Archives Council's People's Network, this site hosts a reading group with a different book under discussion each month. There are also lots of book recommendations and the chance to contribute your own.

www.encompassculture.com

The British Council's global book group. The site also includes lots of resources such as a reading group toolkit, booklists and information on reading group projects and initiatives.

www.bookcrossing.com/home

A book club with a twist: release your favourite book into the wild, track it to see who discovers it and what they have to say about it.

www.bookgroup.info

Not so much an online group as the website of an enthusiastic book group eager to exchange recommendations and advice with a forum attached.

http://dir.groups.yahoo.com/dir/Entertainment___Arts/Humanities/Books_and_ Writing/Reading_Groups Yahoo's well-organized directory of online reading groups.

General reading group resources

www.cllc.org.uk/graphix/pdfs/TAF_SharingTheBuzz_2005.pdf

For those wanting very detailed advice on setting up and running a group the Welsh Books Council has written an excellent and very thoroughly researched guide called *Sharing the Buzz*, available to download as a PDF file.

http://bcs.bedfordstmartins.com/litlinks/Pages/Main.aspx

This is a useful site for readers seeking advice on developing a more critical approach to reading.

www.twbooks.co.uk

The Tangled Web is a specialist crime fiction site hailed as 'a tremendous resource' by Ian Rankin.

www.whichbook.net/index.jsp

Whichbook.net offers a novel way to choose your next book. Its starting point is your mood, taste or particular interest rather than titles and authors.

www.storycode.co.uk

The Story Code site enables you to share book recommendations with other readers and look for suggested reading along the 'If you like this you'll like ...' lines.

http://library.christchurch.org.nz/Guides/IfYouLike

Part of New Zealand's Christchurch City Libraries' website, this is an excellent site for recommendations along the 'If you like this you'll like ...' lines.

www.contemporarywriters.com

This section of the extensive British Council Arts website has entries for many authors from the UK and the Commonwealth, complete with an author biography, bibliography and, in many cases, a critical essay. An excellent resource for research.

www.readinggroupguides.com

Frequently updated American website containing a wide range of readers' guides, interviews with reading group members, links to other reading group sites and, to round it all off, a monthly recipe.

Publishers' sites offering reading group resources

Many publishers have set up websites offering extracts, author interviews and quizzes to readers but the following have devoted specific areas of their sites to reading groups. You'll find much more in the away of reading guides on offer at American publishers' websites

www.bloomsbury.com

Bloomsbury features a book of the month and offer a wide selection of detailed reading guides.

www.faber.co.uk

Faber's website includes a selection of detailed reading guides and features a book of the month

www.harpercollins.co.uk

HarperCollins include a selection of reading guides plus competitions for free books in the reading group section of their site.

www.orionbooks.co.uk

Orion's site includes a small selection of detailed reading group guides.

www.penguin.co.uk

As well as articles, book extracts and author profiles, Penguin's website also has a lively readers' group section which includes a notice board plus a reading group directory to help groups get in touch with each other.

www.penguinclassics.co.uk

Not a huge amount for reading groups at the Penguin Classics site but it does have a few very detailed reading guides in the Resources section.

www.randomhouse.co.uk/readersgroup/index.html

Random House hosts a lively magazine-style section for readers' groups at its website. It features competitions, a Q&A page where readers can put questions to a featured author, recipes contributed by reading group members and a special feature which might cover anything from author recommendations to articles about particular genres.

Literary magazines and newspapers

Listed below is a tiny selection of the literary magazines available on the web together with a portal which will lead you to many more, plus British newspaper sites which offer interesting book coverage.

http://books.guardian.co.uk

The books pages of *The Guardian*'s website offer an excellent source of information for readers and reading groups. Alongside the usual articles and reviews the site has a database of information on a wide range of authors, from Peter Ackroyd to Emile Zola, plus a growing selection of first chapters and book extracts to dip into.

http://entertainment.timesonline.co.uk/tol/arts_and_entertainment/books/books_group/

The Books section of *The Times*' website has adopted a magazine format which includes features, podcasts, blogs, quizzes and *The Times*' Book Group

http://arts.independent.co.uk/books/features/article2962164.ece

The books pages of *The Independent* website which includes a diary feature, reviews and other book news articles.

www.telegraph.co.uk/arts/main.jhtml?menuId=570&menuItemId=-1&view=SUMMARY&grid=P16&targetRule=1

The books page of *The Telegraph*'s website includes reviews and features as well as hosting a family book club. The book club features a monthly choice for parents and older children to discuss backed up with reading notes and a competition.

www.richmondreview.co.uk

This site offers interviews, features, short stories and strong review coverage.

www.salon.com/books

The influential American online magazine's website which has excellent book pages.

www.spikemagazine.com/index.php

The idiosyncratic *Spike Magazine*'s site offers an archive packed with author interviews, book reviews and comment.

www.crimetime.co.uk/index.php

The specialist magazine *Crime Time*'s website offers features, author profiles and reviews

www.aldaily.com

The Arts and Letters Daily portal leads to a wealth of information and links to a multitude of international book review, magazine and news paper sites.

Literary festivals

www.britishcouncil.org/arts-literature-literary-festivals.htm

The British Council has set up a handy database of literature festivals through-out the UK, complete with dates and contact details.

www.bathlitfest.org.uk

Bath Literature Festival

www.cheltenhamfestivals.co.uk

Cheltenham Festivals

www.edbookfest.co.uk

Edinburgh Literary Festival

www.hayfestival.com

The Hay-on-Wye Festival

www.sundaytimes-oxfordliteraryfestival.co.uk

Oxford Literary Festival

www.wayswithwords.co.uk

Ways with Words festivals in Dartington, Southwold, Cumbria and holidays/ workshops in Italy

Literary prizes

www.themanbookerprize.com

The Man Booker prize

www.orangeprize.co.uk

The Orange Broadband Prize

www.costabookawards.com

The Costa Book Awards (formerly the Whitbread Book Awards)

www.impacdublinaward.ie

The International IMPAC Dublin Literary Award

www.commonwealthwriters.com

The Commonwealth Writers' Prize

http://nobelprize.org

The Nobel Prize

www.pulitzer.org//index.html

The Pulitzer Prize

Miscellaneous

http://dspace.dial.pipex.com/town/square/ac940/weblibs.html

Useful directory of public libraries in the UK.

www.booktrust.org.uk

Founded in 1926, Booktrust is a charity set up to promote reading and literacy in the UK. Its website offers a wide range of information on the book world, from the latest publications to announcements of literary prize winners. Booktrust can also be contacted at Book House, 45 East Hill, London SW18 2QZ, tel: 020 8516 2977, fax: 020 8516 2978.

www.bbc.co.uk/arts/bigread

The website for the Big Read, the BBC's search for the nation's favourite novel. Set up in 2003 the site remains a useful source of information with its list of the UK's top 100 books.

www.poetrysociety.org.uk

The Poetry Society's website.

www.pmpoetry.com/index.shtml

Poetry portal with links to wide range of forums.

www.bl.uk

The British Library's website, handy for planning a reading group trip.

SUGGESTEDFURTHER READING

If you've enjoyed the seventy-five books featured in this guide, the following seventy-five (in addition to the other books suggested for further reading in the readers' guides) also come highly recommended both as 'good reads' and as material for lively group discussions.

Fiction

The Yacoubian Building by Ala Al Aswany (translated by Humphrey Davis) (2007)
Maps for Lost Lovers by Nadeem Aslam (2004)
The Hero's Walk by Anita Rau Badami (2001)
The Kindness of Women by J.G. Ballard (1991)
The Girls' Guide to Hunting and Fishing by Melissa Bank (1999)
Five Miles from Outer Hope by Nicola Barker (2000)
K-Pax by Gene Brewer (1995)
The Swimmer by Bill Broady (2000)
The Year of Wonders by Geraldine Brooks (2001)
Audrey Hepburn's Neck by Alan Brown (1996)
The Amazing Adventures of Kavalier and Klay by Michael Chabon (2000)
River Theives by Michael Crummey (2003)
Becoming Strangers by Louise Dean (2004)
Buddha Da by Anne Donovan (2003)
Flying to Nowhere by John Fuller (1983)
The Provinces of Night by William Gay (2000)
Sweetness in the Belly by Camilla Gibb (2006)
Virtual Light by William Gibson (1993)
The Pirate's Daughter by Robert Girardi (1997)
Dogs Days, Glen Miller Nights by Laurie Graham (2000)
The Cast Iron Shore by Linda Grant (1996)
Cassandra's Disk by Angela Green (2002)
White Ghost Girls by Alice Greenway (2006)
Satisfaction by Gillian Greenwood (2006)
The Confessions of Max Tivoli by Andrew Sean Greer (2004)
Plainsong by Kent Haruf (1999)

The Fall of a Sparrow by Robert Hellenga (1998)
Underground by Tobias Hill (1999)
Amaryllis Night and Day by Russell Hoban (2001)
What I Loved by Siri Hustvedt (2003)
The Prince of West End Avenue by Alan Isler (1994)
The Underground Man by Mick Jackson (1997)
The Mighty Walzer by Howard Jacobson (1999)
Mr Pip by Lloyd Jones (2006)
Everything You Need by A. L. Kennedy (1999)
Boxy an Star by Daren King (1999)
The Namesake by Jhumpa Lahiri (2003)
Mr Phillips by John Lanchester (2000)
The Funnies by J. Robert Lennon (1999)
Homestead by Rosina Lippi (1998)
Dancer by Colum McCann (2003)
Amongst Women by John McGahern (1990)
If Nobody Speaks of Remarkable Things by Jon McGregor (2002)
The People's Act of Love by James Meek (2005)
Grand Ambition by Lisa Michaels (2001)
Ghostwritten by David Mitchell (1999)
Astonishing Splashes of Colour by Clare Morrall (2003)
Kafka on the Shore by Haruki Murakami (2004)
Something Might Happen by Julie Myerson (2003)
Twelve Bar Blues by Patrick Neate (2001)
The Puttermesser Papers by Cynthia Ozick (1997)
The Book of Lights by Chaim Potok (1981)
Snow is Silent by Benjamin Prado (2000)
Day of Atonement by Jay Rayner (1998)
The Thirteenth Tale by Diane Selterfield (2006)
The Accidental by Ali Smith (2005)
The Book of Revelation by Rupert Thomson (1999)
A Map of Glass by Jane Urquart (2005)
Bless the Thief by Alan Wall (1997)
Almost Heaven by Marianne Wiggins (1998)

Non-fiction

Stet by Diana Athill (2000)
Boychiks in the Hood by Robert Eisenberg (1995)
Almost Heaven by Martin Fletcher (1998)
Bury Me Standing by Isabel Fonseca (1995)
The Devil That Danced on the Water by Aminatta Forna (2003)
Younghusband by Patrick French (1994)
Rodinsky's Room by Rachel Lichenstein and Iain Sinclair (1999)
Stuart: A Life Backwards by Alexander Masters (2005)
The Snow Leopard by Peter Matthiessen (1979)
Our Lady of the Sewers by Paul Richardson (1998)
Midnight in Sicily by Peter Robb (1996)
Touching the Void by Joe Simpson (1988)
Hearing Birds Fly by Louisa Waugh (2003)
Bloody Foreigners by Robert Winder (2004)
An Intimate History of Humanity by Theodore Zeldin (1994)

INDEX

Bold page numbers indicate main references

Abbey, Edward 107
Abraham, Pearl 8, 13, 19, **21–23**, 187
Ackroyd, Peter 32, 196
Addison, C.C. 35
Al Aswany, Ala 184, 259
Alderman, Naomi 23
Alexie, Sherman 107
Ali, Monica 113
Alias Grace 12, 16, 19, **29–32**
Allende, Isabel 9, 61, 97, 190, **202–205**, 238, 244
And When Did You Last See Your Father? 9, **235–238**
Anderson, Sherwood 155
Andrews, Steven 251
Angier, Carole 231
Animal Dreams 13, 18, **104–107**
Anita and Me 7, 9, 10, 13, 18, **184–187**
An Unquiet Mind 16
Arendt, Hannah 168
Arnott, Jake 15, 16, **23–26**
Aslam, Nadeem 113, 259
Ash, Timothy Garton 220, 223
Ashworth, Andrea 241
Athill, Diana 214, 261
Atkinson, Kate 7, 9, 11, 15, 18, **27–29**, 58, 67, 70, 104, 127, 144
Atwood, Margaret 12, 16, 19, **29–32**, 79, 127, 187, 201
Auster, Paul 35, 140, 152

Bad Blood 8, 9, **238–241**
Badami, Anita Rau 259
Bail, Murray 17, **33–35**, 201
Bainbridge, Beryl 55
Baker, Kevin 97
Ballard, J.G. 259
Balzac and the Little Chinese Seamstress 10, 13, 15, **178–180**
Balzac, Honore de 180

Bank, Melissa 259
Banks, Iain 8, 9, 10, 11, 13, 16, 18, **35–38**, 49, 58, 89
Banks, Russell 15, **38–41**, 146, 161
Barker, Nicola 259
Barker, Pat 73
Barley, Nigel 244
Barrett, Andrea 10, 12, 18, 19, **41–44**, 91, 144, 164
Bayley, John 61, 238
Behind the Scenes at the Museum 7, 9, 11, 15, 18, **27–29**
Being Dead 9, 10, 18, **58–61**
Bennett, Ronan 41
Berendt, John 16, 17, **205–208**
Berg, Leila 235
Berne, Suzanne 89, 134
Bernières, Louis de 47, 70, 73, 138, 205
Bielenberg, Christabel 94, 231
Bigsby, Christopher 94
Billingham, Mark 26
Binding, Tim 14, 16, **44–47**, 73, 155, 196
Binebine, Mahi 82
Birdsong 10, 14, **70–73**
Black and Blue 16, **158–161**
Blackburn, Julia 12, 16, **47–49**, 110, 196
Blixen, Karen 177
Bloom, Amy 64, 152
Bloomsbury 2
Blunden, Edmund 73
books, resources 251–252
bookshops 1, 4
Boswell, Robert 89
Bowen, Elizabeth 193
Bowering, Marilyn 9, 10, 11, **50–52**
Boxall, Peter 251
Boy in the Moon, The 9, 11, **144–147**
Boyd, William 26

Boyle, T. Coraghessan 44, 58, 97, 107, 164
Bradbury, Ray 180
Brewer, Gene 259
Brightness Falls 10, 11, 15, **122–125**
Briscoe, Joanna 67
Brittain, Vera 73
Broady, Bill 259
Broks, Paul 104
Brooks, Geraldine 76, 259
Brown, Alan 259
Bruhns, Wibke 94, 168
Buddha of Suburbia, The 8, 9, 15, **110–113**
Bulgakov, Mikhail 116
Bushell, Michaela 251
Bunting, Madeline 47
Byatt, A.S. 67, 201
By the Sea 13, 15, **80–82**

Cadwalladr, Carole 29
Callil, Carmen 231
Camus, Albert 124
Canin, Ethan 97, 122, 134
Capote, Truman 208
Carey, Peter 23, 164
Carr, Caleb 32, 196
Carter, Angela 8, 11, 17, 18, 29, 35, **53–55**, 140
Carver, Raymond 155
Chablis, Lady 208
Chabon, Michael 259
Chalfour, Michelle 158
Chamberlain, Lesley 127
Chandler, Raymond 198
Chapman, Gary 55
Chandra, Vikram 184
Chang, Jung 180
Charming Billy 10, 11, **120–122**
Chatwin, Bruce 130, 164
Chaucer, Geoffrey 35, 49
Cherry-Garrard, Apsley 210
childhood, themes 7

choosing books 4
Clark, Alan 73
Clark, Ossie 247
Clarke, Lindsay 79
Claudel, Philippe 73
Coe, Jonathan 11, 16, 18, 29, 38, **56–58**, 104, 113, 155
Cold Mountain 12, 14, 19, **74–77**
Collins, Warwick 110, 140
Collishaw, Stephan 100
colonialism, themes 12
Connelly, Michael 161
Conrad, Joseph 41, 44
Cooley, Martha 94, 138, 168, 231
Crace, Jim 9, 10, 18, **58–61**, 110
Crane, Stephen 76
crime, themes 16
Crow Road, The 8, 9, 10, 11, 13, 16, 18, **35–38**
Cruickshank, Charles 47
Crummey, Michael 44, 164, 259
cultural differences, themes 13
Cunningham, Michael 9, 10, **62–64**, 70, 152, 155
Cutting Room, The **196–199**

Dally, Peter 227
Darling, Julia 29
Darling, The 13, 15, 29, **38–41**
Dasgupta, Rana 35
Davis, Martin 201
Dawson, Jill 29
Dean, Louise 259
Death and the Penguin 13, 15, 17, 18, **114–116**
death, themes 9
Death of Vishnu, The 13, **181–184**
Dickens, Charles 29, 55, 201
Didiou, Joan 61
different cultures, themes 13
discussion points 5–6
discussions, leading 5
Diski, Jenny 7, 16, 18, 79, **208–211**, 227
Disobedience 8, 9, 10, 11, **86–89**
Donovan, Anne 113, 259
D'Orso, Michael 250
Dostoevsky, Fyodor 168

Drakuli, Slavanka 220, 223
Drewe, Robert 208
Drowned and the Saved, The 14, **227–231**
Dubus III, Andre 124
Dudman Clare 32, 44
Duncker, Patricia 70
Dunmore, Helen 7, 10, 11. **64–67**, 79, 146
Dunn, Suzannah 187

eccentricity, themes 17
Eco, Umberto 201
Edelman, Gwen 168
Edric, Robert 55
Eisenberg, Robert 23, 261
Eliot, George 94, 155
Ellison, Ralph 250
Empress of the Splendid Season 8, 13, **95–97**
Erdal, Jennie 17, **211–214**
Erdrich, Louise 107
Eucalyptus 17, **33–35**
Eugenides, Jeffery 9, 16, 17, **67–70**
Evans, Diane 149
exploration, themes 12

family life, themes 9
Faulkner, William 61
Faulks, Sebastian 10, 14, 47, **70–73**, 76
Fielding, Helen 171
Fine, Anne 67, 119, 122
Fitch, Janet 104
Fitzgerald, F. Scott 124
Flanagan, Richard 130, 164
Fleming, Anne Taylor 119
Fleming, Fergus 44
Fletcher, Martin 250, 261
Fletcher, Susan 127
Foer, Jonathan Safran 94, 138, 168
Fonseca, Isabel 261
Ford, Maddox Ford 193
Forna, Aminatta 261
Forster, E.M. 130
Forster, Margaret 9, 11, 19, 29, 61, 119, 122, 146, **214–216**, 235, 238
Forty, G. 47
Fowler, Olive 251
Fowles, John 32, 91, 196

Fox, Paula 235, 241
Francis, Richard 86
Frank, Anne 94, 138, 223
Frazier, Charles 12, 14, 19, **74–77**, 89
French, Patrick 261
Freud, Esther 127
friendship, themes 10
Fugitive Pieces 14, **134–138**
Funder, Anna 15, **217–220**
Fuller, John 49, 259

Gaiman, Neil 171
Gale, Patrick 155
Garner, Alan 164
Gates, David 174
Gay, William 259
Ghosting 17, **211–214**
Gibb, Camilla 104, 227, 259
Gibbons, Kaye 76, 144, 227
Gibson, William 259
Gilbert, Martin 73
Gilman, Charlotte Perkins 149
Girardi, Robert 208, 259
Girlitude 8, 19, **244–247**
Giving up the Ghost 19, **232–235**
Glaister, Lesley 10, 17, 67, **77–79**
Glendinning, Victoria 32
Gold, Glen David 55
Goldhagen, Daniel Jonah 231
Golding, William 44, 130
Gordon, Mary 61, 216, 238
Gosse, Edmund 61, 238
Gould, Glen David 152
Graham, Laurie 29, 127, 259
Grant, Linda 61, 238, 259
Grass, Günter 94, 168, 231
Graves, Robert 73, 171
Gray, Alistair 198
Green, Angela 259
Green, Jonathon 247
Greene, Graham 85
Greenway, Alice 259
Greenwood, Gillian 259
Greer, Andrew Sean 259
Greig, Jane 76
Grenville, Kate 130, 152
growing older, themes 8
growing up, themes 8
The Guardian, website 2
Gurganus, Alan 76

Gurnah, Abdulrazak 13, 15, **80–82**, 100, 223
Guterson, David 16, 17, 18, **83–86**, 130

Hacienda, The 8, 13, 16, **241–244**
Haddon, Mark 104
Haig, Jennifer 174
Hale, Sheila 223
Hamilton, Jane 8, 9, 10, 11, 64, **86–89**, 140, 158
Hampson, Norman 140
Hansen, Ron 85
Happe, Peter 196
Hardy, Jules 147
Harrison, Kathryn 17, 18, 61, **89–91**, 164, 190, 210, 238
Hart, Josephine 177
Hartley, Jenny 251
Haruf, Kent 259
Harvey, Jack (Ian Rankin) 161
Hegi, Ursula 7, 14, 47, **92–95**, 138, 168, 231
Hellenga, Robert 260
Heller, Joseph 52
Hensher, Philip 100
Hicks, Robert 76
Hidden Lives 9, 11, 19, **214–216**
Hijuelos, Oscar 8, 13, 70, **95–97**, 122, 174
Hill, Justin 180
Hill, Tobias 260
historical themes 12
Hoban, Russell 260
Hoffman, Eva 8, 13, 23, **220–223**, 244
Holocaust, themes 14
Home at the End of the World, A 9, **62–64**
Homer 70, 74, 76
Hosseini, Khaled 7, 10, 13, 82, **97–101**, 127, 134, 138
Hough, Robert 55
House of Sleep, The 11, 16, 18, **56–58**
Hughes, Robert 164
humour, themes 18
Hundred Secret Senses, The 9, 11, 13, 17, **187–190**
Hustvedt, Siri 147, 260
Huxley, Aldous 86

Icarus Girl, The 7, 16, 17, **147–149**
In a Land of Plenty 8, 9, 15, **152–155**
infidelity, themes 10
Ingenious Pain 12, 17, **138–141**
internet 2, 4, 253–254
Irving, John 52, 64, 94, 155, 174
Isherwood, Christopher 124
Ishiguro, Kashuo 193
Island Madness 14, 16, **44–47**
Isler, Alan 260

Jackson, Mick 127, 260
Jacobson, Howard 223, 260
Jamison, Kay Redfield 16, 210, **223–227**
Japrisot, Sebastien 73
Jensen, Liz 16, 29, **101–104**
Jian, Ma 180
Jiles, Paulette 76
Johnston, Wayne 158
Jones, Lloyd 260
Judy and Richard Book Club v, 253

Kafka, Franz 116, 171
Kaplan, James 125
Kaysen, Susanna 227
Kellerman, Jonathan 161
Kendal, Felicity 55
Keneally, Thomas 94, 138, 168, 231
Kennedy, A.L. 38, 260
Kesey, Ken 227
Khadra, Yasmina 100
King, Daren 260
King, Martin Luther 250
Kingsolver, Barbara 13, 18, 41, **104–107**, 140, 158
Kite Runner, The 7, 10, 13, **97–101**
Klein, Gerda Weissmann 231
Kneale, Matthew 164
Knox, Elizabeth 10, 11, 12, 17, 49, 86, **107–110**, 140, 171
Kolitz, Zvi 138
Kopperud, Gunnar 94, 138, 168, 231
Kramer, Jane 220
Kureishi, Hanif 8, 9, 15, 38, 61, **110–113**, 238

Kurkov, Audrey 13, 15, 17, 18, **114–116**
Kurtz, Irma 250
Kurzweil, Allen 110, 198

Lahiri, Jhumpa 113, 174, 260
Lamb, Wally 149
Lambrianou, Tony 26
Lanchester, John 238, 260
Larry's Party 8, 11, **171–174**
Last Time They Met, The 8, 11, **175–177**
leading meetings 3
Leavitt, David 64
Lee, Laurie 127, 250
Lennon, J. Robert 38, 134, 260
Leper's Companions, The 12, 16, **47–49**
Lessing, Doris 41, 149
Lethern, Joanathan 100
Levi, Primo 14, 35, 94, 138, 168, **227–231**
Levy, Andrea 187, 190, 223, 250
Lewis, John 250
Lewis, Ted 26
Lewycka, Marina 116
Lichenstein, Rachel 261
Lippi, Rosina 260
Literary festivals 257
Literary magazines, resources 256–257
Literary prizes 257–258
Lively, Penelope 10, 11, **116–119**, 122, 171
Long Firm, The 15, 16, **23–26**
Loo, Tessa de 94, 168
Lopez, Barry 44
Lost in Translation 8, 13, **220–223**
love, themes 10–11
Luard, Elizabeth 205, 216
Lynch, Thomas 61, 238

McCann, Colum 97, 260
McCourt, Frank 216
McCracken, Elizabeth 55, 152
McDermott, Alice 10, 11, 119, **120–122**, 144, 193
MacDonald, Ann-Marie 158
Macdonald, Lyn 73
McEwan, Ian 79, 91, 147
McGahern, John 147, 193, 260
McGregor, Jon 184, 260

McInerney, Jay 10, 11, 15, **122–125**, 155
Mackay, Shena 7, 10, 79, 100, **125–128**, 134, 187
McLaughlin, Jane 61, 238
MacLaverty, Bernard 122
McMurty, Larry 55
McNeal, Tom 107, 158
McVicar, John 26
magazines, resources 252
Magician's Assistant, The 9, 11, 17, **150–152**
Malouf, David 12, 13, 32, 44, **128–131**, 164
Mankell, Henning 161
Mann, Klaus 47
Mantel, Hilary 19, 216, **231–235**, 241
Marai, Sandor 82
Marciano, Francesca 177
marriage, themes 10
Marwick, Arthur 216
Masters, Alexander 261
Matar, Hisham 82, 100
Matthiessen, Peter 261
Maxwell, William 8, 10, 101, 122, 127, **131–134**
Meek, James 260
meetings, planning 2–4
Melville, Herman 44
Menaker, Daniel 55
mental disturbances, themes 16
Messud, Claire 125
Michaels, Anne 14, 52, 94, 101, **134–138**, 168, 231
Michaels, Lisa 260
Middlesex 9, 16, 17, **67–70**
Midnight in the Garden of Good and Evil 16, 17, **205–208**
Miller, Andrew 12, 17, 49, 110, **138–141**, 171
Miller, Sue 8, 9, 11, 19, **141–144**
Millhauser, Steven 125
Milton, John 110
Min, Anchee 180
Minot, Susan 177
Minotaur Takes a Cigarette Break, The 17, **168–171**
Mirvis, Tova 23
Mistry, Rohinton 184
Mitchell, David 260

Mitchell, Margaret 76
Mitford, Jessica 216, 247
Modern times, themes 15
Moody, Rick 38, 64, 89
Morality Play 12, **193–196**
Möring, Marcel 35
Morrall, Clare 260
Morrison, Blake 9, 61, 205, **235–238**, 241
Mortimer, John 61, 238
Motion, Andrew 238
Murakami, Haruki 260
Myerson, Julie 67, 147, 149, 177, 260

Nadolny, Sten 44
Naipaul, V.S. 41, 184
Narayan, R.K. 184
natural world, themes 18
Naughtie, Jim v, 251
Neate, Patrick 260
Neville, Richard 247
newspapers, resources 256–257
Ng, Mei 190
Ninth Life of Louis Drax, The 16, **101–104**
No Place Like Home 15, **247–250**
Norfolk, Lawrence 110, 140
Norman, Howard 158
Novick, Peter 168
Nuland, Sherwin 61

Oates, Joyce Carol 155
O'Farrell, Maggie 38, 67
Offill, Jenny 104, 227
Ondaatje, Michael 138
Orange Prize for Fiction 1
Orchard on Fire, The 7, **125–128**
O'Riordan, Kate 9, 11, **144–147**, 177, 193
Orwell, George 220
Our Lady of the Forest 16, 17, 18, **83–86**
Oyeyemi, Helen 7, 16, 17, **147–149**
Ozick, Cynthia 149, 260

Patchett, Ann 9, 11, 17, 64, **150–152**
Paula 9, **202–205**

Pears, Tim 8, 9, 15, 125, **152–155**
Pelevin, Victor 116
Penguin 2
Perec, Georges 35, 184
Perez-Reverte, Arturo 201
Piercy, Marge 41
Pierre, D.B.C. 104
Pietrzyk, Leslie 190
Photograph, The 10, 11, **116–119**
planning meetings 2–4
Plath, Sylvia 227
politics 15
Porter, Roy 140
Potok, Chaim 21–22, 23, 52, 260
Power, Susan 107
Prado, Benjamin 260
Promised Lands 12, 13, **161–164**
Proulx, Annie 11, 97, **155–158**, 223
publishers' websites 255–256
Pullinger, Kate 19, 164, 190

Quindlan, Anna 61, 237

Radio 4 v, 4, 252
Rankin, Ian 16, **158–161**
Rayner, Jay 260
Reader, The 14, **165–168**
readers' guides 20
reading groups
  choosing books 4
  discussion points 5–6
  general resources 254–255
  leading discussion 5
  planning meetings 2–4
  refreshments 4
  setting up and running 1
  size 2
Remarque, Erich Maria 73
Remembering Babylon 12, 13, **128–131**
Rennison, Nick 251
resources 251–258
Richardson, Paul 261
Richmond, Theo 223, 231
Ridley, Matt 70, 227
Riel, Rachel van 251
Rivas, Manuel 201
Robb, Peter 261

Rodiss, Helen 251
Rogers, Jane 12, 13, 44, 86, 91, 130, **161–164**, 251
Romance Reader, The 8, 13, 19, **21–23**
Rosten, Leo 23
Rowbotham, Sheila 247
Roy, Arundhati 184, 187
Rushdie, Salman 70, 107, 184
Russo, Richard 86
Ryman, Geoff 55

Sacks, Oliver 104
Sage, Lorna 8, 9, 214, 216, 235, **238–241**
St Aubin de Terán, Lisa 8, 13, 16, 205, **241–244**
Salinger, J.D. 38
Salzman, Mark 86
Sandbrook, Dominic 26
Schlink, Bernhard 14, 94, 138, **165–168**, 180, 220, 231
Schwarz, Christina 29
Scott, Paul 187
Seal Wife, The 17, **89–91**
Sebold, Alice 104, 147
secrets, themes 11
Seiestad, Asne 99
Seiffert, Rachel 94, 138, 220, 231
Selterfield, Diane 260
Sen, K.M. 184
Senstad, Susan Schwartz 138, 168, 231
Seth, Vikram 184
setting up a group 1–6
Shackleton, Ernest 210
Shadow of the Wind, The 15, **199–201**
Sheer Blue Bliss 8, 10, 17, **77–79**
Shelley, Mary 171
Sherrill, Steven 17, **168–171**
Shields, Carol 8, 11, 144, **171–174**
Shields, Jody 73
Shipping News, The 11, **155–158**
Shreve, Anita 8, 11, 32, 144, 147, **175–177**

Sijie, Dai 10, 13, 15, **178–180**, 201
Simpson, Joe 261
Simpson, Mona 64
Simpson, Paul 251
Sinclair, Iain 261
Skating to Antarctica 7, 16, 18, **208–211**
Slater, Nigel 235
Smiley, Jane 76, 89
Smith, Ali 260
Smith, Zadie 113, 155, 187
So Long, See You Tomorrow 8, 10, **131–134**
Solzhenitsyn, Aleksandr 231
Spufford, Francis 235, 241
Stace, Wesley 70
Stasiland 15, **217–220**
Steinberg, Paul 231
Sterne, Laurence 29, 70
Stones From the River 7, 14, **92–95**
Story of Lucy Gault, The 7, 9, 12, **190–193**
Styron, William 94, 168, 227
Suri, Manil 13, 61, **181–184**
Süskind, Patrick 49, 110, 140
Sutherland, John 241, 251
Swift, Graham 122
Syal, Meera 7, 9, 10, 13, 18, 23, 29, 113, 127, **184–187**

Talking to the Dead 7, 10, 11, **64–67**
Tan, Amy 9, 11, 13, 17, 97, 180, **187–190**, 223
Tartt, Donna 38, 127, 147
Taylor, Frederick 220
Taylor, Laurie 26
Television, resources 251
Tennant, Emma 8, 19, **244–247**
themes 7–19
Thompson, Kate 147
Thomson, Ian 231
Thomson, Rupert 260
Tóbn, Colm 61
Toews, Miriam 23
Tolstoy, Leo 73, 89, 177
Trapido, Barbara 55
Trevor, William 7, 9, 12, 134, **190–193**

Tuchman, Barbara 196
Tyler, Anne 174

Udall, Brady 104
universities 1
Unsworth, Barry 12, 16, 32, 49, **193–196**
Urquart, Jane 260

Vallgren, Carl-Johan 140
Vintner's Luck, The 10, 11, 12, 17, **107–110**
Visible Worlds 9, 10, 11, **50–52**
Voyage of the Narwhal, The 10, 12, 18, 19, **41–44**

Wall, Alan 140, 198, 260
war, themes 14
Warner, Alan 187
Watkins, Paul 52
Waugh, Evelyn 47
Waugh, Louisa 261
websites 2, 253–258
Weisel, Elie 168, 231
Welsh, Louise 16, 23, **196–199**
Wharton, Edith 125
Wheeler, Sara 205, 210
White, Antonia 210
Wiggins, Marianne 260
Winder, Robert 261
Winfrey, Oprah v, 253
Winterson, Jeanette 23, 35
Wise Children 8, 11, 17, 18, **53–55**
Wolf, Christa 94, 168, 231
Wolfe, Tom 125
Wolitzer, Meg 119
women's role, themes 19
World Below, The 8, 9, 11, 19, **141–144**
Wurtzel, Elizabeth 227

Younge, Gary 15, **247–250**

Zafón, Carlos Ruiz 15, 16, **199–201**
Zeldin, Theodore 261